COOPERATIVE ORGANIZATION AND ADMINISTRATION

By

Dr. M. Karthikeyan
Assistant Professor
Department of Cooperatives
Faculty of Business & Economics
Hawassa University
Hawassa
Email: mkeya2003@gmail.com
mkeya2003@yahoo.com

&

Prof. S.Nakkiran
Professor
Department of Cooperatives
Institute of Cooperatives & Development Studies
Ambo University College
Ambo, Ethiopia
Email: doctorsnakkiran@gmail.com

DPH

DISCOVERY PUBLISHING HOUSE PVT. LTD.
NEW DELHI-110 002

Published by:

Tilak Wasan

DISCOVERY PUBLISHING HOUSE PVT. LTD.

4383/4A, Ansari Road, Darya Ganj

New Delhi-110 002 (India)

Phone : +91-11-23279245, 43596064-65

Fax : +91-11-23253475

E-mail : parul.wasan@gmail.com

discoverypublishinghouse@gmail.com

web : www.discoverypublishinggroup.com

***First Edition:* 2012**

ISBN: 978-93-5056-044-0

Cooperative Organization and Administration

Printed at:

Shree Balaji Art Press

Delhi

Preface

Dear Learners! It is my pleasure to introduce the course *Cooperative Organization and Administration* to you. This book is designed in three parts in a detailed manner so as to help you to understand the application of various concepts and themes on cooperative organization and administration. You may have been studying related courses on cooperative management, management of agricultural and non-agricultural cooperatives, and the like. But the course cooperative organization and administration is somewhat different from the above said courses. This book covers the organizational features of cooperatives in terms of their initial organization, steps in organizing new cooperatives, the role of the leaders and members of the cooperative, the role of the external agencies like the government, government bureaus, NGOs, international bodies like ICA and ILO.

This work is based on our experience as teachers, trainers and researchers in the field of cooperatives. The present work is based on Under Graduate programme and outcome of our teaching and research experience, articles published in reputed journals, and discussions with cooperative officials. This book will be very much useful to the student of under graduate, and also to professionals involved in promotion of cooperatives, and the trainers who are working in various training establishments. We have drawn the inputs from various materials; papers, journals, books and we have consulted several of our friends, colleagues and field experts. We are ever grateful and thankful to them for their immense support and healthy criticism. We hope that the readers of this book will get knowledge on Cooperative Organization and Administration. Any useful comments, suggestions to improve the present version are welcome and solicited from the readers. We are thankful and grateful to Parul Wasan, Discovery Publishing House Pvt. Ltd., New Delhi for publishing book neatly under his renowned label for the cooperative knowledge community.

M. KARTHIKEYAN
S.NAKKIRAN

Contents

Part—III
Scope for Organizing Cooperatives

Part—I

Organizational Characteristics of Cooperatives

1 Need to Organize Cooperatives

Why Cooperatives were Organized?

Cooperatives are one of the important economic organizations, which came late after capitalism and public sector organizations. It was the result of efforts undertaken by dedicated leaders and masses who suffered during the times of Industrial Revolution. Cooperatives have not been organized successfully at one stroke. During the formative days, it met with failure. It was Robert Owen who initiated the organization of cooperatives and ultimately became the 'Father of Cooperation'. But his experiments in cooperatives failed. Later people like Dr. William King and host of British leaders took steps to organize cooperatives—all became failure. Only during 1844 the first successful cooperative society, namely 'Rochdale Equitable Society' was formed by the famous Pioneers of England. Thereafter, efforts were taken to organize cooperatives in Denmark, Germany, Italy, Russia and other European countries. The 20th century saw the organization of cooperatives in colonial countries at the initiative of European colonial countries like England, France, Belgium, Spain and Portugal.

With the first successful cooperative organized in England in 1844, the movement started its roots in other European countries also. The original successful cooperative was started in Consumer area, but the idea of cooperation was taken and cooperatives were started to suit problems like agriculture (Denmark), agricultural credit (Germany), labour problems (Italy), etc. Based on the above experiences of countries, we can see the factors that led to the organization of cooperatives in Europe.

1. *Evils of Industrial Revolution:* Industrial Revolution took its birth in England during 18th century and the result was introduction of new machineries and the change in the production pattern from small-scale production to large-scale production. Machines have replaced men in many areas. At the same time it led to poverty, unemployment and

exploitation of labour, women and children in England. Labours were exploited with over-work and with poor salary. There were shortage of foodgrains, increase in price of daily goods and non-interference of government. All these led to make labour leaders to think of organizing cooperatives.

2. *Exploitation by moneylenders and middlemen:* In countries like Germany and Italy farmers were exploited by the Jewish moneylenders, which led to the sufferings of farmers. The farmers paid very high rate of interest to their loans and ultimately they were forced to sell their lands or completely under the mercy the moneylenders. People like Raiffeisen saw the misery of the farmers and organized agricultural credit cooperatives.

3. *Strong leadership:* The early cooperatives were provided with dedicated, selfless and strong leadership by cooperators like Robert Own, Dr. William King, Rochdale Poineers, Neale, Grundtvig, etc. These leaders came from the background of trade unions and they saw the misery of farmers, workers and the consumers. Their selfless attitude and service mindedness made them to organize cooperatives to avert the sufferings of people.

4. *It is a form of self-help:* Cooperatives became the major form of self-help for the people who suffered from exploitation, shortage of goods, increase in price, etc. During those periods, there were no voluntary organizations available to people like that of the cooperatives. Cooperatives, which have the basic principle of self help and mutual help made people to solve their basic social and economic problems.

5. *Laissez -faire policy of governments:* During 18th century the governments did not follow the policy of welfare to people. The governments, which were procapitalistic did not hear the problems of ordinary citizens. This led to the exploitation of poor by the rich and educated over the uneducated. Such things necessitated the organization of cooperatives.

6. *To tackle poverty and famine:* During 18th century and onwards, the world witnessed occurrences of famine and poverty. Poverty and famine became a regular feature in Asian and African countries, which were ruled by colonial European countries. In these countries, the colonists started a mercy measure of helping the people by organizing cooperatives especially the agricultural cooperatives.

Need to Organize Cooperatives in Ethiopia

Ethiopia is one of the ancient and civilized nations in Africa. Its culture and tradition are age-old and dates back to 3,000 years. It is the third biggest populated country in Africa and agriculture is the important occupation of the people. More than 80 per cent of the population is still depending on agriculture and exportable goods are formed by agricultural commodities like, coffee and cattle hides. Ethiopia has not seen the colonial occupation by a European country, like other African countries. Naturally, this led to the formation of cooperatives very late in Ethiopia. The cooperatives in countries like Nigeria, Kenya, Tanzania, Ghana, etc were organized by the British rulers a century ago. On the other hand, the first formal cooperatives were started in Ethiopia during 1960s and during the Derg period (1974-1991) efforts were taken to organize cooperatives compulsorily, which met with failure. With the democratic process revived, cooperatives are started since 1998 after the passing of the Cooperative Proclamation. With this background, let us see the need to organize new cooperatives and reviving previous cooperatives in Ethiopia.

1. *To revive failed cooperatives and to strengthen existing cooperatives:* As noted above, cooperatives started during 1960s and later period met with failure due to the non involvement of the members. Cooperatives were thrusted on the farmers during Derg period. Compulsion made the people not to take interest in the affairs of the cooperatives, which led to failure. So at present there is a need to revive the old cooperatives and to strengthen existing cooperatives.

2. *Speed up agricultural development:* The population of Ethiopia is growing fast. The population of Ethiopia was 72 million in 2004, which may increase to 170 million during 2050. Being the third populated country in Africa, agriculture needs to be developed fast in Ethiopia. During the past years there were deficiencies in food production, which warrants the need to increase agricultural production. Cooperatives are the best agencies to promote agriculture through providing credit, marketing and other services.

3. *To provide input and service and service to the farmers:* Farmers are in need of agricultural inputs like credit, seeds, fertilizers and pesticides. They are also in need on agricultural services like marketing, storage, transport, etc. Such services can be provided cheaply by the cooperatives and cooperatives can relieve the farmers from the exploitation of moneylenders and middlemen.

4. *Employment opportunities:* Cooperatives can provide employment opportunities to the farmers, weavers, artisans and educated youth. By means of organizing various cooperatives employment opportunities can be increased to the population.

5. *Price control:* Cooperatives have proved that they can control price level by means of doing selfless service to the community. Consumer

cooperatives and marketing cooperatives in various countries have proved that they can control the general price level and relieve the population from the exploitation of middlemen.

6. *Women empowerment:* Cooperatives can improve the social and economic conditions of women by means of providing them opportunities to become members and leaders of cooperatives. Women can use cooperatives to improve their social and economic conditions and employment opportunities.
7. *Third sector of the economy:* In almost all developing countries cooperatives have become the third sector of the economy, the others being the private and public sectors. In Ethiopia, opportunities are wider to organize new cooperatives and make it a third sector of the economy.
8. *To improve the bargaining power:* Cooperatives can improve the bargaining powers of the farmers, weavers, workers and women by means of providing good prices to the produce of the farmers, weavers, artisans and women. They avoid the role of middlemen and exploiters in the society.
9. *Reduce the cost:* Cooperatives can reduce the cost of goods by means of economy in their operations. The cost of service provided by the cooperatives is very low, which can end reducing the final price of goods and services.
10. *Improve the market access:* Cooperatives can provide very good market with an attractive price to the farmers and artisans. Cooperative marketing can make the farmers come nearer to their services.
11. *Improve the service and product quality:* Cooperatives are dedicated to provide efficient service to the members and public. By means of providing attractive customer service they improve the quality of products also.
12. *Increasing the income:* Cooperatives strive to increase the income of various segments of the community like farmers, workers, artisans and women. By averting middlemen they provide good price and income to the farmers and others. They encourage increase in production and quality in production, which ultimately result in increased income.
13. *To rectify social imbalances:* Cooperatives work for the reduction of imbalances between the poor and rich. Cooperatives avoid the concentration of wealth and income in few hands and pave the way for a balanced society.
14. *To promote cooperation among cooperatives:* Cooperatives in Ethiopia at present are isolated from the world cooperatives. They do not have

affiliation with other countries cooperatives. Further, cooperation among the cooperatives of Ethiopia is also very poor. To improve this cooperatives are to be strengthened in Ethiopia.

Self-learning Activity

Try to answer the following questions on your own.

1. What are the needs of organizing cooperatives?

Summary

- Cooperatives have been introduced during industrial revolution and cooperatives were the outcome of exploitation.
- The first successful cooperative was organised in England during 1844 in the field of consumer cooperatives and the idea of cooperation was applied to dairy farming in Denmark, agricultural credit in Germany, etc.
- There is need to organize and expand various types of cooperatives in Ethiopia to improve agricultural production and food security, to increase employment opportunity, to improve the conditions of the farmers, to empower women and to increase the bargaining power and income of the members.

2 Conditions and Motives Favour the Organization of Cooperatives

Conditions that Favour Starting Cooperatives

Certain conditions are need for starting cooperatives successfully. Such conditions are as follows:

(*a*) The cooperative that is to be started must be *socially viable*. Those who are starting such cooperatives must be willing to provide all needed cooperation. "The persons forming local organization have to be prepared to cooperate—there has to be a minimum of sociability" —*Munkner*.

(*b*) The members who are entrusted in starting a cooperative must commit themselves to mobilize *needed resources*. This should be on a voluntary basis and not for a pressure from outside.

(*c*) There should be the *community of interest* between the proposed members. That means, the proposed members should have a common problem to be solved among themselves. "The persons forming the local organization have to have at least one economic interest in common, a broader base of interest is favourable" —Munkner.

(*d*) The cooperative must be *economically viable* and provide at short notice tangible advantages for the members individually or as a group, otherwise, the interest in the cooperative will rapidly decline.

(*e*) There must be the questions to be raised among the members as to why the cooperative must be formed and the uses of *group action*.

(*f*) The proposed cooperatives must be given the chance to develop on their own. Any stimulation from outside is desirable but should not lead to artificial growth. This is the bane of state-sponsored cooperatives in certain developing countries.

(*g*) The proposed cooperatives must be given the opportunity of evolving their own rules, regulation and patterns of organization.

(h) Certain external forces like the governments, taxation policy, land policy, and political developments are to be considered while starting new cooperatives.

Economic and Social Motives to Organize Cooperatives

Economic Motives

The motives for joining the cooperatives are those which have a direct effect on the economic life of members. The members join cooperatives because it promises to be the most effective instrument towards gaining increased income. The joining of cooperative is an attempt to reap relatively higher economic advantage. This can come about by the way of cooperative providing goods and services which are regarded as important or either not available or available but beyond the reach of the member or the members enjoy them but at very high cost.

The cooperation can thus help satisfy this motive of increased income either in the form of:

(*a*) Reducing the cost of members business;

(*b*) Increased revenue.

Sociological (Emotional) Motives

The urge to join may result from and individual feelings of:

(*a*) ***Isolation and loneliness:*** This is an individual feeling which is regarded as a weak point for change, to be safe they assume that joining the cooperative can thus be an attempt to regain the missing emotional way of life.

(*b*) ***The search for security*** may also be a motive for joining cooperative. This is normally motivated by a sort of general or individual crisis. The time and magnitude of the occurrence of each crisis cannot be known in advance. It can happen without our knowledge. This magnitude can also be beyond the means of the individual. Individual strength often provides insufficient. This enables the cooperatives that offer relatively more security/insurance through pooled efforts.

(*c*) ***The search for protection*** can also be motive for joining cooperative because, when the member is integrated into an existing cooperative the group is able to protect itself against physical or spiritual threats from outside. They may feel exploited by other more powerful persons, groups or force against whom they are individually powerless.

In most societies in the developing countries, wisdom, knowledge and status have been considered the function of age. The aged thus tend to dominate and try to maintain the status quo. Without such a protection from modern groups like the cooperatives, the already slow technological development adoption of the new technology would be slower. Thus motive of the individual cooperative member to shift responsibility for modern/progressive decisions and action which they could otherwise not dare to take because, they may be regarded as running counter to old traditions. So the capacity of the cooperative to jointly accept this responsibility and protect the individual member is very important for introducing and accepting change in the social structure of developing regions.

(*d*) Some people may also join the cooperative simply because *they want to be seen*. This is often the cause when membership in a cooperative is correctly or incorrectly looked upon and viewed as one outward sign of superiority over another. As a desire to catch up, individuals decide to join the cooperative.

(*e*) The motive to *avoid being out*. This is often the cause when people discover that virtually everybody around them has joined the local cooperative. They have feelings of having been left out and not being normal. Their membership in the cooperative may then result as a response to this.

(*f*) Some persons also join the cooperative with the motive of not missing out on any unspecified, possible advantage which such an institution may offer. Such people do not join the cooperative because they are sure of the advantages or because they are convinced that they need the cooperative. They do so mainly because if many people join, they believe that so many people can not all be wrong that *one or the other advantage must exist*, and if so, they would not want to miss out.

(*g*) The urge to join the cooperative may also result from *a desire to adhere to customs or tradition*. This is usually the case in relatively old, often rural cooperative in which a number of families have always lived a face to face life inside the cooperative and one generation seen to bequeath the cooperative as part of the inheritance to the next generation.

(h) Another motive which may give rise to membership in a cooperative is the possibility of using cooperatives *as spiting board to some higher social or political position in the community*.

External Pressure

A motive for some people joining the cooperative may also be that of satisfying some external power under whose pressure they have come. This is the case when revolutionary government which claims to be socialist in nature, regarded cooperative as a socialistic organization which can serve their aims.

They enact legislation which makes membership mandatory for farmers who seek private use of his plot. Failure to join the cooperative would mean having to give up the only profession and means of livelihood. They have no option but to join the cooperative. A slightly milder variation often comes in the form that access to specific services such as supply of essential consumer goods, subsidizing of input credit are made conditional upon membership in the cooperative.

Self-learning Activity

Try to answer the following questions on your own.

1. Explain about economic motives in organizing cooperatives?
2. Discuss conditions favouring organization of cooperatives.

Summary

- To organize cooperatives the social and economic conditions must be favourable. There must be a felt need and realization among the people to organize cooperatives.
- There are various economic motives to organize cooperatives like improving the living standard, reducing the cost of operations and increasing the income of the members. The social motives to organize cooperatives are: search for security, search for protection, get integrated with others, avoiding isolation, and to get a social status.

3 Managerial and Organizational Characteristics of Cooperatives

Managerial and Organizational Characteristics of Cooperatives

The managerial characteristics of cooperatives are as follows:

1. ***Cooperatives are associations of human beings:*** Cooperatives are formed by members to solve their economic problems. In that process they have to mobilize capital. It is subordinated to human interests. Capital is not allowed to dominate in cooperatives over human beings.
2. ***Democracy in cooperatives:*** Cooperative management strictly follows the principles of democracy. All are equal here and 'one man one vote' principle is followed. No single individual is allowed to dominate, by virtue of large number of shares held by him.
3. ***Service motive:*** Service is the motive and not profit in cooperatives. In doing such service, efficiency is emphasized in cooperative management. P.R. Dubhashi, has viewed that "the principle of efficiency is vital in cooperative management. But in so far as the market mechanism of private enterprise, turns the principle of maximum efficiency into maximum profit, it becomes in compatible with the cooperative management and needs modification".
4. ***Equality:*** Equality is practiced in cooperative management. All members are given equal opportunity to enjoy the benefits of cooperative and they can exercise equal control without any narrow rise to the level of the president of a National Federation through his leadership.
5. ***Application of principles of cooperation:*** Cooperatives have to first follow the principles of cooperation laid down by ICA, then they have to go for applying the management process. It has to keep a balance between these two. Weeraman states that "the proper application of cooperative principle is necessary for the success of the movement, for cooperative principles are those which are essential, that is absolutely indispensable to the achievement of cooperatives movements role".

6. ***Different aims system:*** Cooperatives have to satisfy the aims of different people composed under its management. They are members, office bearers, personnel and government, so it has to harmonize the interest of these complex aims system and to maintain a balance.

7. ***The Control Process:*** In cooperatives, the members are users and owners. Varied interests of members must be met with utmost efficiency. In that process cooperatives should not loose their control over factors of production. Prof. Laidlaw, stresses that, "it is a business organization in which the components of ownership — use — control are integrated by being all vested in one body of people, the members".

8. ***Cooperative management is governed by cooperative legislation:*** The cooperative societies Act of respective states directly and indirectly control the management of cooperatives. The Registrar of Cooperative Societies is assigned with enormous powers to interfere in the management of cooperative institutions.

9. ***Integrating government policies:*** In countries like India cooperative movement had its origin with initiative of government. In the Planning process, specific roles have been assigned to the cooperatives. Here the cooperatives have to sacrifice some of their autonomy and freedom.

10. State (government) interference is quite common in the management of cooperatives in countries like India. Boards are very often dissolved to suit the political convenience of ruling parties.

11. ***Cooperatives strive to introduce professional management in their administration:*** In that process they have to face so many hurdles and interferences. Without minding that large sized cooperatives and processing cooperatives go ahead with professional management.

12. ***Tools and techniques of management applied by cooperatives vary from society-to society:*** Primary cooperative societies, with smaller area of operation and smaller area of transactions offered to use only elementary tools whereas bigger cooperatives use latest and sophisticated techniques of management.

13. ***It is an art as well a science:*** It is an art as it effects changes or accomplishes goals by deliberate efforts. It is a science as cooperative management strives to acquire body of knowledge through observation, speculation and forecasts, which are capable of verification.

14. ***Practice of cooperative management is based on knowledge and responsibility:*** Entire gamets of management technique are applied under various situations to get things done, at lesser cost and at the cost of giving enough training and experience to the people concerned.

15. ***Cooperative management involves group effect at all levels:*** It combines the efforts of all individuals and bodies (Board, general body, etc.) at every stage of activity. At the culmination, the Board and executive sit together to discharge responsibilities.

16. ***Economic liberalization:*** Last decade saw the liberalization of the economy world over. The implication was that, private sector has been given a free hand. Till recently, cooperatives have been enjoying lot of privileges from government and they have to loose such privileges in during course. Cooperatives have to adjust themselves to the changing economic climate.

17. ***Competition:*** Cooperatives are given thorough competition by private and public sector organizations. They have to improve their operational efficiency by means of using modern management techniques. Otherwise they cannot survive in the competition.

Organizational Characteristics of Cooperatives

1. ***Business organization:*** Cooperatives are one of the business organizations like the sole enterprise, partnership firms, joint stock companies and public sector organizations. But their motive is service, and not profit like the private organizations.

2. ***Homogeneous group:*** Cooperatives are organized by homogeneous groups consisting of like minded individuals. People who are having common problems like credit, marketing, housing, etc., joint together and organize cooperatives to solve their problems.

3. ***Corporate status:*** In developing countries, cooperatives are registered under separate cooperative societies acts/proclamations promulgated by respective governments. A registered cooperative society has legal status and protection from government.

4. ***Democracy:*** One of the salient organizational features of cooperatives is their democratic character. All members are given equal opportunities and the principle of 'one man one vote' is strictly followed.

5. ***Cost effective service:*** Cooperatives work under competitive situations and they have to provide cost effective service to the members. Almost all types of cooperatives are providing services for a lower cost than the market cost.

6. ***Exploitation by middlemen:*** Cooperatives, since their beginning have challenged the exploitive forces like money lenders, middlemen, traders and contractors. The combined effort of members have kept these forces at a distance.

7. ***Application of modern management tools:*** Cooperatives have applied modern management tools and techniques to improve their operational

efficiency and customer services. Technology up-gradation takes place in processing and industrial cooperatives.

8. *Team work:* One of the basic organizational characteristics of cooperatives is the effective teamwork at all levels. In majority of the cooperatives cordial employer-employee relationship exists, which favours the effective functioning of the cooperatives.

Cooperative Governance

"Governance is one of the characteristics of any institution that is concerned with governance or management of governance. Governance is the reflection of the quality of management".

The four key components of governance are: accountability, transparency, predictability, and participation. Cooperatives are having good governance. A contributory factor for bad governance is corruption, which is avoided in cooperatives.

(*a*) ***Accountability:*** Accountability is the capacity to call officials to account for their action. Effective accountability has two components viz., answerability and consequences. Answerability is the requirement to respond periodically to questions concerning one's official action. There is also a need for predictable and meaningful consequences without which accountability is only a formality. Cooperative activities discharged by officials and leaders have accountability.

(*b*) ***Transparency:*** Transparency denotes low cost access to informations. Reliable and timely economic and financial informations are a must for the cooperatives. Cooperatives never keep secrecy and every member has a right to the information.

(*c*) ***Predictability:*** Predictability results from rules and regulations, that are clear, known in advance. Lack of predictability makes it difficult for officials to plan for the provision of services. Cooperative laws are clear and things can be predicted.

(*d*) ***Participation:*** participation is needed to obtain reliable information and to serve as a check and watch dog for the organisation's actions. In a cooperative members and leaders participate in various democratic forums like the board and general assembly meetings.

Some of the possible indicators of good governance in cooperatives are as follows:

1. How much of awareness the leaders and members have about the principles of cooperation and the basic value of cooperative philosophy?
2. How clearly they understand the ethical and moral elements which are the essential components of the cooperative philosophy?

3. How different is the cooperative enterprise from a private enterprise or a state enterprise?
4. How conscious are the board members about their rights and responsibilities? To what extent the board members realize that they accountable and answerable to the members who have reposed their confidence in them?
5. How much operational powers are delegated to the chief executive?
6. How smooth are the communication channels between the board and chief executive?
7. How much is the level of transparency in dealing with the employees?
8. How smooth is the channel of communication between the cooperative and its stakeholders and business partners?
9. Whether there is any discipline outlined on the use of assets of the organization?
10. How often the meetings are held?
11. To what extent the cooperative institution obeys the directives of the state at the cost of its autonomy and freedom of action?

Self-learning Activity

Try to answer the following questions on your own.

1. List out organizational characteristics of cooperatives?
2. Describe the pillars of cooperative governance.

Summary

- Cooperatives are having certain managerial characteristics like the application of the management principles, professionalizing the management, etc. They have the organizational characteristics like the business organization, homogeneous group, corporate status, democracy, and cost effective service.

4 Formalities and Types of Cooperatives to be Organized

Formalities to be followed by Government

In developing countries like Ethiopia, the government has greater responsibility in encouraging and promoting cooperatives. Government has to show a very favourable attitude and set a climate conducive for the growth and development of cooperatives. The tasks, which properly belong to government, can be summarized as follows:

(*a*) To *create a favourable climate* for the development of cooperatives. By this is meant the removal of obstacles, resistance to unfair competition and to the efforts of private dealers and moneylenders to bind the cooperative members through permanent indebtedness.

(*b*) To provide *adequate and clear legislation* on cooperation, regulating the rights and duties of cooperatives and their members, their liability, legal personality and the like. This legislation has where necessary to be supplemented by regulations for its implementation and model bylaws for the cooperatives. These need to cover, among other things, members' contributions to capital, the distribution of surpluses, reserves and similar matters.

(*c*) To establish an *information and inspection* service for cooperatives, the job of the service being to encourage, to advise and to supervise the cooperatives.

(*d*) To provide for the *coordination of cooperative* activities with those of the agricultural advisory service, agricultural credit institutions, marketing boards and other relevant government services.

(*e*) To assist with *education and training* for those on the management committee and the people actually running the business, for the benefit of the cooperatives; and to help in establishing educational schemes for the membership and to promote the spread of cooperative information.

(*f*) To provide *financial assistance* to cooperatives in the form of grants and loans, as a means of providing working capital or capital for necessary investment in buildings, machinery and so on. Such help should, however, be supplementary only, in order to ensure that cooperatives attempt to provide as far as possible for their own financing needs – from members' share capital, reserves built up from undistributed trading surpluses, voluntary deposits by members and possible loans obtained from or via agricultural credit banks or other credit institutions.

(*g*) To encourage and assist the *establishment of federations and national cooperative unions*. These, belonging as they do to the cooperative movement of which they form part, need to be put together and managed democratically; and they also need to be able at the appropriate time to take over the advisory and supervisory functions of government from the authorities, together with responsibility for education, inspection and so on.

An international symposium on the dynamic of the relationships between government and cooperatives was held in Tel Aviv in 1964 and came to the following conclusions:

(*a*) Relations between government bodies and cooperatives should not be a one-way traffic from above, with the cooperatives being used by the authorities as an instrument for the imposition and implementation of government planning. Many countries try too hard to realize political ends through cooperatives. Instead, there has to be "an exchange of capacities and functions of opposed interests and advantages" between government and cooperatives. "These functional relationships need to be realized in a form such that, in the interests of the common good, just balance can be achieved with regard to both functions and powers."

(*b*) The maintenance of an adequate measure of autonomy by the cooperatives is of great and positive value. An excess of control and interference, or even of support, is harmful to the sound development of cooperation.

(*c*) In those cases in which cooperatives have come into being autonomously from below, a strengthening of the ties with government may be desirable to ensure greater correspondence between private and public interests.

Types of Cooperatives to be Organised

What Type of Cooperatives Can Be Organized?

The type of cooperative to be organized depends on the social, economic, political, and educational climate of a country. The early cooperatives organized in European countries are more than 150 years old. By that time, the European countries were under the evil effect of Industrial Revolution. Later, when cooperatives were started in Asian and African countries, a century ago, these countries were under the colonial rule of European countries. Cooperatives were started in these countries officially by the colonial governments. The initiative did not come from the users of cooperatives. On the other hand it was thrusted from above. This made the cooperatives to have slow growth in many developing countries. In Ethiopia the conditions were different when the cooperative movement was started during 1960s. The foregoing analysis will show what type of cooperatives can be started.

A. According to the economic status of the members of the cooperative

(i) Producers:

- Farmers, fishermen (compare the Raiffeisen) cooperatives;
- Dealers and traders;
- Craftsmen (compare Rochdale)

(ii) Consumers

(iii) Employees.

B. According to the sector of the economy in which the cooperatives are active

(i) Agriculture

(ii) Fishing

(iii) Forestry

(iv) Industry and manufacture

(v) Retail and wholesale trade

(vi) The provision of services (credit and banking, transport, insurance and so on).

C. According to the cooperative's economic functions

(i) Purchasing/supply cooperatives, for the purchase of business essentials and for consumption.

(ii) Marketing cooperatives

(iii) Processing cooperatives

(iv) Cooperatives providing services (credit, insurance, irrigation, transport, tractor services and such like, artificial insemination)

(v) Production cooperatives

D. According to the member-businesses' degree of integration

(i) Complementary activities undertaken by the cooperative in the service of its members — 'auxiliary societies', cooperatives providing services (in general terms, categories *Ci* to *Civ* inclusive).

(ii) Partial integration of the member-businesses in cooperative activities: the member-businesses have not only hived off some of their functions to the cooperatives but have also tied themselves to the cooperative's planning of various activities. These are what is meant by 'integrated cooperatives'.

(iii) Complete integration, in which the member-businesses are completely subsumed in the cooperative, examples are cooperative farming, joint farming, collective farming and the kolkhoz.

(iv) Production cooperatives. Here the members are nothing more than workers in the common enterprise.

E. According to the organizational structure (the categorization suggested in Dulfer (11) (pages 56-57).

(i) Traditional cooperatives = executive-operated cooperatives. The cooperative in this scheme is but the executive body for the member-firms (compare *Di*). The member-businesses determine the cooperative's activities.

(ii) Market-linkage cooperatives. These are commonly found in the developed world. The cooperative enterprise is completely autonomous in this case and does no hove close ties with the constituent businesses. The manger of the cooperative implements his own policy, directed towards competition in an open-market economy.

(iii) Integrated cooperatives. This form is of particular interest in the context of regional development programmes and those connected with irrigation, land reform and settlement projects. The member-businesses, though legally independent, are tied to the cooperative in such a way that its management can take decisions about the activities to be carried out on the individual businesses' premises and the way in which their interests shall be safeguarded. The members do, certainly, keep their autonomy and a certain degree of control over matters relating to production, but they have in doing so to align themselves with a common strategy and a common production plan, drawn up by and under the supervision of the cooperative's top management. Schiller (28) terms this the "cooperative promotion of agricultural production".

F. According to cooperatives' geographical areas of activity

(i) Urban cooperatives. This category includes urban consumer cooperatives, house building cooperatives, savings and credit cooperatives for urban salary earners and so on.

(ii) Rural cooperatives, particularly in agriculture and fishing.

(iii) Craft and manufacturing cooperatives. These can be either urban or rural.

G. According to the level of organization (apex systems)

(i) Primary cooperatives—mostly at local level.

(ii) Secondary cooperatives—mostly at a regional level.

(iii) Tertiary cooperatives or federations of cooperatives – mostly at a national level.

H. According to the cooperatives' legal status

(i) Unregistered, therefore not enjoying legal personality.

(ii) Registered (equalling 'recognized') cooperatives, possessing legal personality:

- With the liability of the members excluded;
- With the members having limited liability, their liability being restricted to one or more times the amount of their share;
- With the members' liability being unlimited. In this case the members are wholly responsible, to the extent of all they possess for the debts of the cooperative.

I. According to the number of tasks assumed by the cooperative

(i) Single purpose cooperatives

(ii) Single commodity cooperatives

(iii) Multipurpose cooperatives

(iv) All purpose (= integrated) cooperatives

Self-learning Activity

Try to answer the following questions on your own.

1. Write about the formalities of the government in organizing cooperatives?
2. What are the classifications of cooperatives?

Summary

- In organizing cooperatives, in developing countries, the government has to create favourable climate by means of providing clear legislation, financial assistance, education and training, and by encouraging the organization of national level cooperatives.
- Various types of cooperatives can be organized according to the economic status of the members, according to the sector of economy, according to the economic functions, according to the organizational structure, according to the number of tasks assumed by the cooperative, etc.

5 ILO's Policy on Cooperatives and Potential Surveys

ILO's Policy on Cooperative Organization

The International Labour Organization, which is taking good efforts in promoting cooperatives, has given the following guidelines for cooperatives in its Recommendation Number 127 dated 1st June 1966.

Objectives of Policy Concerning Co-operatives

1. The establishment and growth of co-operatives should be regarded as one of the important instruments for economic, social and cultural development as well as human advancement in developing countries.
2. In particular, co-operatives should be established and developed as a means of:
   - (*a*) improving the economic, social and cultural situations of persons of limited resources and opportunities as well as encouraging their spirit of initiative;
   - (*b*) increasing personal and national capital resources by the encouragement of thrift, by eliminating usury and by the sound use of credit;
   - (*c*) Contributing to the economy an increased measure of democratic control of economic activity and of equitable distribution of surplus;
   - (*d*) Increasing national income, export revenues and employment by a fuller utilization of resources, for instance in the implementation of system of agrarian reform and of land settlement aimed at bringing fresh areas into productive use and in the development of modern industries, preferably scattered, processing local raw materials;
   - (*e*) Improving social conditions, and supplementing social services in such fields as housing and, where appropriate, health, education and communications;

(*f*) Helping to raise the level of general and technical knowledge of their members.

3. Governments of developing countries should formulate and carry out a policy under which co-operatives receive aid and encouragement, of an economic, financial, technical, legislative or other character, without effect on their independence.

4. (1) in elaborating such a policy, regard should be had to economic and social conditions, to available resources and to the role which co-operatives can play in the development of the country concerned.

(2) The policy should be integrated in development plans in so far as this is consistent with the essential features of co-operatives.

5. The policy should be kept under review and adapted to changes in social and economic needs and to technological progress.

6. Existing co-operatives should be associated with the formulation and, where possible, application of the policy.

7. The co-operative movement should be encouraged to seek the collaboration in the formulation and, where appropriate, application of the policy, of organizations with common objectives.

8. (1) The governments concerned should associate co-operatives on the same basis as other undertakings with the formulation of national economic plans and other general economic measures, at least whenever such plans and measures are liable to affect their activities. Co-operatives should also be associated with the application of such plans and measures in so far as this is consistent with their essential characteristics.

(2) For the purposes provided for in Paragraph 7 and Paragraph 9, subparagraph (1), of this Recommendation, federations of co-operatives should be empowered to represent their member societies at the local, regional and national levels.

Methods of Implementation of Policy Concerning Cooperatives

A. Legislation

9. All appropriate measures, including the consultation and existing co-operatives, should be taken:

(*a*) to detect and eliminate provisions contained in laws and regulations which may have the effect of unduly restricting the development of co-operatives through discrimination, for instance in regard to taxation or the allocation of licenses and quotas, or through failure to take account of the special character of co-operatives or of the particular rules of operation of co-operatives;

(b) to avoid the inclusion of such provisions in future laws and regulations;

(c) to adapt fiscal laws and regulations to the special conditions of cooperatives.

10. There should be laws or regulations specifically concerned with the establishment and functioning of co-operatives, and with the protection of their right to operate on not less than equal terms with other forms of enterprise. These laws or regulations should preferably be applicable to all categories of co-operatives.

11. (1) Such laws and regulation should in any case include provisions on the following matters:

(a) a definition or description of a co-operative bringing out its essential characteristics, namely that it is an association of persons who have voluntarily joined together to achieve a common end through the formation of a democratically controlled organization, making equitable contributions to the capital required and accepting a fair share of the risks and benefits of the undertaking in which the members actively participate;

(b) a description of the objects of a co-operative, and procedures for its establishment and registration, the amendment of its statutes, and its dissolution;

(c) the conditions of membership, such as the maximum amount of each share and, where appropriate, the proportion of the share due at the moment of subscription and the time allowed for full payment, as well as the rights and duties of members, which would be laid down in greater detail in the by-laws of co-operatives;

(d) methods of administration, management and internal audit, and procedures for the establishment and functioning of competent organs;

(e) the protection of the name 'co-operative';

(f) machinery for the external audit and guidance of co-operatives and for the enforcement of the laws and regulations.

(2) The procedures provided for in such laws or regulations, in particular the procedures for registration, should be as simple and particular as possible, so as not to hinder the creation and development of co-operatives.

12. Laws and regulations concerning co-operatives should authorize co-operatives to federate.

Potential Surveys

A potential survey is a systematic appraisal of the economic and possibly social effects, which the realization of a certain project will have, and a survey of the technical problems involved. Co-operatives can be confronted with the need for such an analysis, for example, if a new society or a new branch is to be established, if new activities are to be undertaken, etc. In a wider sense a similar study, though perhaps not so elaborate, should precede any decision which could decisively alter the course of a society.

In smaller matters this analysis can be prepared and assessed by the society's staff or, in the case of societies to be formed, by a pre-co-operative study group of prospective members, but in most cases a qualified economist or engineer, or both, have to be consulted. Within the co-operative sector this type of extension service can usually be contacted through central business organizations, auditing associations or government departments. In some instances surveys are also carried out by international organizations involved in co-operative extension work or by private consulting firms.

Contents of a Potential Survey

1. Background

The background information to be collected is as follows:

(*a*) General aspects which may affect the project, such as the relevant legislation, the structure of local administration, income statistics, etc., and a general description of the area where the project will be carried out, its geographical factors, climate, communication system, people and customs. In the individual case it may also include specialized information, in rural projects, for example, about soil qualities, rainfall, land tenure and utilization, average farm size, methods of farming, etc.

(*b*) The scope for development or the need for new facilities, at present as well as in the future, by showing the faults and disadvantages of the present set-up or situation, or by proving, by way of market analysis, the room for expansion.

(*c*) The suggested target for expansion or the proposed capacity of any new facilities.

(*d*) The possible approach or method to be used and, if necessary, a comparison of several methods, and the planned location of any facilities.

(*e*) The time schedule for the realization of the project considering the recruitment and training period for any new staff, the delivery period for any new machinery and the construction time for any new buildings required as well as the most favourable time to start the project with regard to the market.

(*f*) The size of membership related to the set targets and the possibility of attracting new members.

(*g*) The expected response from present or prospective members, especially whether they realize the necessity of the project and are willing to co-operate, or what steps can be taken to enlist their collaboration.

2. Market issues

The key questions that should be answered in the Market issues are presented below:

(*a*) What is the current or projected demand for your proposed products or services? In other words, how many units can you reasonably expect to sell each month?

(*b*) What are the target markets for this product or service? What demographic characteristics do these potential customers have in common? How many of them are there?

(*c*) What is the projected supply in your area of the products or services needed for your project?

(*d*) What competition exists in this market? Can you establish a market niche, which will enable you to compete effectively with other providing this product or service?

(*e*) Is the location of your proposed business or project likely to affect is success? If so, is the identified site the most appropriate one available?

The market issues should be conducted first because it is critical to the success of the business. If it cannot substantiate through research that adequate demand for the product or service exists, or if it cannot obtain sufficient quality to meet expected demand, then the project is not feasible.

3. Organizational Issues

(*a*) What organizational structure is the right one?

(*b*) Who will serve on the board of directors?

(*c*) What qualifications are needed to manage this business?

(*d*) Who will manage the business (if possible)?

(*e*) What other staffing needs does the co-op have? How do the staffing needs to change over the next 2-3 years?

4. Technical requirements

(a) The feasibility of using the existing facilities and the present staff for the new task and the possible changes to be made for their adaptation.

(b) Any new facilities and manpower needed and their availability.

   (i) land and buildings, their size design, outlay and equipment.
   (ii) machinery, type, make, capacity.
   (iii) transport, type, capacity.
   (iv) manpower, required skill and experience, recruitment plan.

Key Questions to answer include:

(a) What are the technology needs for the proposed business?

(b) What other equipment does your proposed business need?

(c) Where will you obtain this technology and equipment?

(d) When can you get the necessary equipment?

(e) How much will the equipment and technology cost?

5. Capital outlay and finance

(a) The total cost of the project assessed according to a detailed list of the costs of any building, machinery or vehicles needed and, if possible, accompanied by tenders of the relevant suppliers.

(b) The required rate of finance calculated on the basis of the expected average lifetime of the invested assets.

(c) The source of finance available for the purpose of the project.

The following financial aspects are to be considered.

(a) ***Start-up Costs:*** These are the costs incurred in starting up a new business, including 'capital goods' such as land, buildings, equipment, etc. The business may have to borrow money from a lending institution to cover these costs.

(b) ***Operating Costs:*** These are the ongoing costs, such as rent, utilities, and wages that are incurred in the everyday operation of a business. The total should include interest and principle payments on any debt for start-up costs.

(c) ***Revenue Projections:*** How will you price your goods or services? Asses what the estimated monthly revenue will be.

(d) ***Sources of Financing:*** If your proposed business will need to borrow money from a bank or other lending institution, you may need to research potential lending sources.

(*e*) ***Profitability Analysis:*** This is the 'bottom line' for the proposed business. Given the costs and revenue analysis above, will your business bring in enough revenue to cover operating expenses? Will it break even, lose money or make a profit? Is there anything you can do to improve the bottom line?

6. **Analysis of operating costs** (Includes salary, taxes, interest, etc.)

   (*a*) The breakdown of the expected operating cost including the proportional overhead expenses calculated for various levels of output or development.

      (*i*) based on estimated costs

      (*ii*) by comparison with a society which has already carried out a similar project taking into account the cost variations caused by differences in size, location, structure of membership and efficiency in management.

   (*b*) The comparison of differing methods with respect to operating costs.

7. **Analysis of expected benefits**

The assessment of added revenue gained from the project or of the expected decrease in cost or improvement in service.

8. **Final assessment**

   (*a*) The comparison of the increased operating cost with the additional revenue expected (break-even graph).

   (*b*) The influence of the new project on the overall profitability of the society.

   (*c*) The reasons which would make the project feasible despite a decrease in profitability, for instance, the long-term effect on the development of the society.

9. **Appendix**

The appendix should include all those documents, statistics, tenders, drawings to which the text of the survey refers.

Self-learning Activity

Try to answer the following questions on your own.

1. Briefly state the objectives of ILO Policy concerning cooperatives?
2. What are the issues related to market survey?

Summary

- ILO is an international body, which is interested in the promotion of cooperatives. It has given certain guidelines to the governments for the promotion of new cooperatives.
- Potential surveys are undertaken before a cooperative is started. Through potential surveys we can come to know the feasibility of the successful organization and running of a cooperative society.
- Potential surveys concentrate on the locational factors, market issues, organizational issues, technical requirements, capital outlay and finance, cost aspects and benefit aspects.

6 Organizational Factors

While organizing a cooperative, certain organizational factors are to be considered. These factors have been drawn from other countries experiences and applied to Ethiopia.

1. Size of a Society

The size of an enterprise is especially important in its economic aspects. One of the problems of every co-operative society is to reach a size, which allows the economic effects of co-operation to gain their full advantage.

(i) a monopolistic situation in their area of operation protecting them from competition.

(ii) A high degree of vertical integration with a central business organization giving them some of the advantages of large-scale enterprise.

(iii) A strong co-operative spirit among members manifested in absolute loyalty and volunteer work in the society.

Where these special conditions do not prevail, the expansion of the enterprise must be an essential part of the business policy of a co-operative society. The increase in size may be achieved by:

- attracting new members within the area of operation;
- increasing the area of operation;
- increasing the turnover with the present members in the existing lines or by taking up new activities;
- amalgamation with other societies;
- buying out competing enterprises.

In practice the lack of capital and of dynamic and imaginative management, the pressure of competition and the parochial attitude of neighbouring societies resisting amalgamation are some of the major obstacles in the way of expansion.

A further problem related to expansion is that in many cases it is only possible to accomplish in fixed stages. The expansion into a higher stage of growth may lead to a temporary decrease in profitability before a further increase in size can fully utilize the new stage.

Problems also exist for those societies that have outgrown their optimum size. Certain cost groups have the tendency to rise disproportionately after a certain stage of development has been reached, for example, the administrative expenses when indirect control replaces direct control or, in the case of supply societies, the distributive costs if the area of operation extends too far. Decentralization through the formation of branches may provide a partial solution to these problems.

Another aspect of size is the sociological effect. Regarding the relationship between the members and the society the optimal size is the small, face-to-face group, where co-operative spirit and loyalty are much more easily instilled than in mass membership. The ideal size in this respect is normally well below the economic optimum. However, in the interests of progress, economic considerations must take priority. The resulting increase in efficiency and of benefits to members makes the question of loyalty less important. In addition, modern methods of public relations can compensate to a certain degree for the loss of direct contact among the members and thus avoid the inner dilution of the society.

2. Location

Location refers to the geographical situation of the society's premises within the area of operation. The selection a suitable location can have considerable influence on the operating costs, the capital requirements, the relationship between members and society, and the contact with market partners.

The factors which have to be considered are:

(i) Geographical factors

- the distance and access to sources of supply, to market outlets and to members;
- the adequacy of the available transport and communication systems to the market and to members;
- the availability and comparative costs of power and water;
- the climate and its effects on working conditions and operating methods,

(ii) Community factors

- the availability, skill and cost of local labour,

- the availability and standard of business services such as banking, insurance, lawyers, accountants, etc.
- the availability of public facilities such as police, fire brigade, etc.
- local laws and taxes.

3. Exploratory Meeting

To determine the level of interest in starting and supporting a cooperative, invite potential members to a general meeting. Announce the meeting date, time, and place by letter, or word or mouth. Invite outside advisers.

The leadership group should develop an agenda and select a presiding officer who can conduct a business meeting. Sometimes, and adviser can act as chair or help answer questions. Primary agenda items should include:

- What is the need;
- Possible solutions;
- Cooperative principles and terminology;
- Cooperative operating practices;
- Advantages and disadvantages of a cooperative;
- General risk capital equity and financial requirements; and
- Various forms of member-user commitment needed.

One approach is to have one member of the leadership group discuss the need and another summarize how the proposed cooperative might solve it. In addition, a representative of a successful cooperative might explain its operations, benefits, and limitations.

Allow plenty of time for discussion. Prospective members should be encouraged to express their views and ask questions. All issues raised should be addressed, although answers may be delayed until later meetings when more information becomes available.

Questions to be Raised

1. What is cooperative and how is it different from other business?
2. Who controls a cooperative?
3. How much is my initial investment?
4. Will my investment (equity) requirement be determined by volume or by number of members?
5. How much money can I lose if the cooperative fails?

6. Can I get out of the cooperative whenever I want?
7. What are marketing or purchasing agreements and why are they needed?
8. What are net margins and net earnings?
9. What are the patronage dividend?
10. Can we restrict cooperative membership?

4. Steering Committee Formation and Duties

If the group wants a more detailed study after discussion is completed, it should select a steering committee. This group should have a keen interest in the cooperative, be well-respected within the community, and have sound business judgment. Committee members often become the initial organizers and members of the cooperative's first board of directors.

The first function is to select officers of the steering committee, usually at the close of the general informational meeting. Next, establish a deadline for completing a business analysis, including a target date for surveying potential members. Periodic progress meetings retain interest of prospective members.

The steering committee, with the help of one or more advisers, determines if a cooperative is feasible. *First*, it judges whether the proposed cooperative is likely to succeed and benefit its members, *Second*, if the proposal passes this test, the committee prepares a specific, detailed business plan for the new cooperative.

Assistance from specialists in law, accounting, finance, economics, engineering, and cooperative business operations is critical during the business analysis phase.

Economic need is fundamental to the formation and successful operation of any cooperative. The committee should examine what products or services the cooperative could provide, those needed from other source, and whether costs would be reduced or quality improved. Intangible functions also should be considered. Will the cooperative provide a needed service, preserve a market, stabilize prices, or encourage more orderly marketing?

Is the projected initial investment within the financial ability of the potential members involved?

The committee should consider alternatives to start a new cooperative. Could similar services be provided by another nearby cooperative, either directly or by establishing a branch? In forming a new cooperative is the best alternative, the group should consider linking with regional cooperatives to obtain additional benefits.

A new cooperative should initially limit services to avoid elaborate or costly facilities above those absolutely needed. If successful, services can later be expanded.

5. Member-user Survey

Formal survey techniques are best for estimating potential membership. The adviser usually drafts the survey questionnaire for the steering committee to review.

The following list gives a general idea of the needed information:

1. Member-user experience and capabilities—years in present location, overall success, demand specific to the cooperative venture, and production and marketing success;
2. Variety of products or services to be offered or needed;
3. Period of need services;
4. Current unit value-cost per unit;
5. Member-user-location of use or need;
6. Familiarity with and use of other cooperatives and willingness to join, finance, and use one.

While the questionnaire is being prepared, the steering committee should develop a list of potentially interested member. When the questionnaire is completed and approved, the committee interviews potential members.

The adviser analyzes the survey, prepares a report, and presents it to the steering committee. The results and implications are then discussed at a meeting of all persons surveyed. Survey results should reveal how potential members identify the economic need and the degree of interest in a cooperative to fulfill that need. The survey should indicate the level of support in terms of business volume and if financial commitment is sufficient to organize and successfully operate the cooperative.

Factors determining the initial situations are:

(i) The economic and social relationships within the social groupings (village, district) where it is sought to bring about the development of co-operative forms of co-operation. An important determinant for these relations is the access to, basic production resources (land, water); e.g. land can be communally owned and/or individually, fairly equitably distributed or otherwise, tilled by its owners, tenants, sharecroppers and/or landless labourers. Where different economic and social groupings co-exist, economic interests also will differ and ask for different forms of co-operative organization. Co-operative organization, so promoters should realize, will reduce or worsen inequalities or stabilize them depending on who the beneficiaries are;

(ii) The Perception by the potential members of the co-operative of their economic and social position and of the possibility of bringing about a change in this through joint action. This is decisive for their readiness to organize themselves co-operatively;

(iii) The potential members' ability to solve their problems independently through co-operation. This ability is determined by the locally available knowledge, skills and other means;

(iv) The functions which are performed by already existing co-operatives and similar enterprises, the measure of autonomy granted to them and the extent to which they need assistance and control;

(v) The existing economic order at supra-local level with its ramifications at local level, in particular the position of private undertakings, state enterprises or official institutions providing services which will not allow, or will oppose, competitive activities by co-operatives in their particular field;

(vi) The existence or otherwise of co-operative legislation and other statutory provisions;

(vii) The physical environment (precipitation, nature of the soil, etc.) which does not allow of the introduction of new forms of economic enterprises or of the expansion of existing forms;

(viii) The available manpower and the requisite funds, to be supplemented by foreign help if necessary, for manning and equipping the 'promoting machinery' (= the organisation or complex of organizations which assist the co-operatives);

(ix) The available financial resources for provision of credit for co-operative enterprises insofar as these are not completely self-financing.

Additional Informations to be Collected

A. Projected Volume of Business

The best source for these projections comes from the potential member survey conducted as a part of the feasibility study. If the business is seasonal, it is important to accurately characterize how production or purchasing and sales occur to determine the appropriate facility and equipment needs.

Market Information

Lenders don't want to finance a proposed business without a market. They want to know who the customers are, if markets have been located, and expected prices and volumes.

Cash Flow

Projected cash flow information may be the most important to the lender. It gives a continuous month-by-month cash income and expense prediction. Key items in the final analysis are the net cash flow for the month and the ending cash balance. Lenders are particular concerned with the net ending cash balance. Does the cooperative have sufficient funds to operate and pay bills? Is additional borrowed capital needed, particularly for operating during heavy seasonal periods? Can control lable expenses be reduced during periods of low income? Are cash reserves adequate to overcome adverse market swings? And, most importantly, can the cooperative repay its loans? Most lenders want three years projections.

Operating Statement

For a new cooperative, the projected operating statement provides and expected picture of operations for one or more years. It contains information on sources of income as well as expenses. The key figure is the 'bottom line' that indicates whether net margins (profits) are anticipated. A monthly operating statement provides information to lenders and assists the board in making major policy and management decisions.

Balance Sheet

For the newly formed cooperative seeking financing from outside sources, the projected balance sheet is extremely important. It projects the future value of the cooperative and indicates it solvency and ability to satisfy creditors' claims when due. In summary, it lists the cooperative's assets, liabilities, and net worth.

Loan Package

A summary of scheduled financing needs and sources saves the lender time in assembling the various pieces of data for analysis. It should show major items for which loans and member capital will be spent. These items are extracted from the projected cash flow data. A brief resume of the designated manager should be included in the documents given to the potential lender.

B. Maintain Good Board-Manager Relations

The differing responsibilities of the board of directors and the manager must be clearly understood and carried out.

Directors represent members and are legally responsible for the performance and conduct of the cooperative. All corporate powers of the cooperative, other than those specifically conferred on members, are vested in its directors and outlined in the bylaws an in the State and Federal legal statutes.

Directors' three major responsibilities are to set policies, employ and evaluate the general manager's ability to carry them out, and provide adequate financing for the cooperative.

The board also has some specific management responsibilities such as functioning as trustees for the members in safeguarding their assets in the cooperative; setting goals, objectives, and general policies; adopting long-term strategic plans; employing a competent manger and evaluating performance; preserving the cooperative character of the organization; establishing an accurate accounting system; adopting an annual operating budget; appointing an outside firm to perform an annual audit; controlling the total operation; and authorizing distribution of cooperative net earnings and redemption of members' equities.

The board, in turn, delegates responsibility for daily operations to a hired general manager or chief executive officer. The general manager hires or discharges employees, including department heads, who with the manager comprise the hired management staff or team.

Responsibilities of hired management include managing or directing daily business activities; carrying out policies set by the board; setting goals and making short-term plans; employing, training, and discharging employees; organizing and coordinating internal activities in compliance with cooperative goals and objectives and board policies; keeping complete accounts and records and developing an annual operating budget; and providing the board with periodic reports.

Questions often arise as to the division of responsibilities between the board and hired management. Sometimes they overlap and an exact division cannot be made. Some factors to consider are: the time period-long-term decisions are the responsibility of the board while management makes short-term decisions; idea decisions are usually introduced by the board and actual decisions implemented by management; decisions involving policy are the responsibility of the board, and cooperative functions are handled by management; board primary control activities usually concern the board, while secondary controls pertaining to short-run operations are the responsibility of management. When it comes to staffing, the board hires the manager who, in turn, selects the staff of the cooperative.

Use of policy and procedure manuals and job descriptions along with frank discussions of questions when they arise can help maintain an understanding of the division of responsibility.

Conduct Business-like Meetings

A cooperative is a business so its meetings should be conducted in a business-like manner.

Policy should be established for determining a reasonable quorum for membership and board meetings. A quorum is the specific or minimum percentage of members required to be present to conduct official business. Quorum requirements are sometimes written into State statutes, but should be discussed in the by-laws. As membership expands, the percentage of quorum increases the actual number needed. Setting the quorum too high increases the risk of not getting enough member participants to deal with business matters needing attention.

Parliamentary procedure is a appropriate for orderly group action. It enables the chair to lead a group smoothly and efficiently in determining the wishes of the majority while protecting the rights of minority.

Good meetings just doesn't happen. It results in carrying out several successive steps: planning ahead involves members, following a published agenda, and following through on meeting actions.

Forge Links with Other Cooperatives

An early exercise to determine whether to start a new cooperative was to investigate the alternative of liking with an existing cooperative that could expand its service territory. Even if starting a new cooperative is the best course of action, the search for beneficial links with other cooperatives should continue.

Alliances with regional cooperatives or other businesses may be valuable sources for supplies, marketing outlets, and related services. Membership in State and national cooperative associations can keep the new cooperative abreast of what others around the country are doing. These associations can be sources of education and training programmes, legislative and public relations support activities, and help identify sources of special expertise.

C. Things to be avoided by new cooperatives

New organizations are most vulnerable in their early formative years. Here are some tips for new cooperatives to avoid potential pitfalls:

1. *Lack of clearly identified mission*—A new cooperative shouldn't be formed just for the sake of forming one. The potential member-user must identify a clear mission statement with definite goals and objectives.
2. *Inadequate Planning*—Detailed plans for reaching defined goals and the mission are important. In-depth surveys of the potential member-user needs coupled with business feasibility studies are necessary. Stop the organizational process if there isn't sufficient interest in the cooperative by potential member-users or if it isn't a sound business venture. The human cost in time and organization expense may be better used elsewhere.

3. *Failure to use experienced advisors and consultants*—Most persons interested in becoming member-users of a new cooperative haven't had cooperative business development experience. Using resources persons experienced in cooperative development can save a lot of wasted motion and expense.
4. *Lack of member leadership*—Calling on the services of experienced resource persons can't replace leadership from the organizing group. Decisions must come from the potential member-user group and its selected leadership. Professional resource persons should never be in decision-making positions.
5. *Lack of member commitment*—To be successful, the new cooperative must have the broad-based support of the potential member-users. The support of lenders, attorneys, accountants, cooperative specialists, and a few leaders won't make the cooperative a business success.
6. *Lack of competent management*—Most cooperative members are busy operating and managing their own businesses and lack experience in cooperative management. The directors hire experienced and qualified management to increases the chances for business success.
7. *Failure to identify and minimize risks*—The risk in starting a new business can be reduced if identified early in the organizational process. Careful study of the competition, Federal, State, and local Government regulations, industry trends, environmental issues, and alternative business practices helps to reduce risk.
8. *Poor assumptions*—Often, potential member-users and cooperative leaders overestimate the volume of business and underestimate the costs of operations. Anticipated business success that ends in failure places the organizers in a 'bad light'. Quality business assumptions tempered with a does of pessimism often proves to be judicious.
9. *Lack of financing*—Regardless of the amount of time spent in financial projection, most new businesses are underfinanced. Inefficiencies in start-up operations, competition, complying with regulations, and delays often are the causes. Often, the first months of business operations and even the first years are not profitable, so adequate financing is important to survive this period.
10. *Inadequate communications*—Keeping the membership, suppliers, and financiers informed is critical during the organization and early life of the cooperative. Lack of or incorrect information can create apathy or suspicion. The directors and management must decide to whom and how communications are to be directed.

Self-learning Activity

Try to answer the following questions on your own.

1. Discuss about factors related to location of organizing a cooperative?
2. What do you understand by member-user survey?

Summary

- Under the organizational aspects, the promoters have to decide the size of a cooperative society. They have to conduct exploratory meetings to consult the members about the future prospects of the cooperative.
- As part of the organizational aspect a member-user survey must be conducted, which can explain the continued supply of goods to the cooperatives and the reactions of the members to the supply of inputs and outputs.
- Additional informations relating to the projected volume of business on various aspects like market information, cash flow, balance sheet and loan package must be collected.
- The feasibility of having cordial board-manager relationship should also be studied and such aspect should be discussed in the business like meetings.
- The new cooperative must also be careful about things to be avoided such as inadequate planning, failure to use experienced advisors, lack of member commitment, lack of finance and inadequate communication.

7 Legal Aspects of Organizing Cooperatives

In Ethiopia, the Co-operative Societies' Manual includes specific guidance on the promotion and organization of a proposed Co-operative Society and the preparation of an Economic Appreciation of the project, etc. (pages 3-15 of the English version of the Manual). The Manual also includes a copy of Ethiopian Co-operative Legislation (i.e., the Proclamation and Regulations made under it) and Model Rules for five major types of Society.

Sections *(a)* and *(b)* of the Economic Appreciation are obviously designed to build up a realistic and relevant 'picture' of the area where the proposed Society will be and of the people living and working there. Much of the information may already be available in various government offices (e.g., Administration, Agriculture, Community Development, etc) and it is essential that the co-operative project should relate to the work of other 'development agencies' in the area so that all efforts reinforce and support each other. In short, there must be team work in the overall attack on poverty and all the handicaps associated with it. A Co-operative Society will usually be the nucleus providing legal, financial and business organization for those aspects of an overall programme which need it.

Sections *(c)* and *(d)* might be called the 'business part' of the Economic Appreciation although it must obviously take into account essential information about the people and the area.

Since Co-operative Societies could be formed in a variety of situations in Ethiopia (e.g., among a group of people not specifically part of some development scheme in Package Area schemes; in Special Scheme area such as WADU, etc) it is appropriate to list certain things they—would or should —have in common:

1. They should have been formed only because their members wanted to form them: it is wrong for anyone to urge people to form co-operatives. If members have formed a society to 'please' anyone but themselves they will not feel that the problems, which will surely arise, belong to

them. Where co-operative have to be formed to carry out special aspects of some development scheme (e.g., a Minimum Package Area scheme) it is all the more necessary to carry out co-operative education amongst members. If all that evolves is a 'trading centre' it will not play a full part in the long-term aims of the scheme.

2. They should relate closely to the lives and needs of their communities, and have sound economic aims and business prospects.
3. They should be registered under Co-operative Law and guided, supervised, and audited under arrangements made by the Government official appointed under that Law.
4. They should follow the universally accepted Principles of Co-operation and feel themselves to be part of the wider Co-operative Movement, in order to bring fullest benefits to their members and communities.
5. They should, in due time, help to set up a national co-operative organization which arranges or co-ordinates the educational, training, trading, advisory and representational services of the Ethiopian Co-operative Movement. The ultimate aim must be a strong, healthy and self-reliant Movement with can play a constructive role in the life of the nation.

Legal Aspects

In Ethiopia, the legal aspects relating to the organization of cooperatives are discussed below:

Proclamation No. 274/2002

A Proclamation to Establish Cooperatives' Commission

Whereas, it has become necessary to enable the rural and urban working people to solve the economic and social problems they face by themselves depending on local resources and become self-reliant by being organized in cooperatives societies different in type and standard;

Now therefore, in accordance with Article 55 (1) of the Constitution of the Federal Democratic Republic of Ethiopia and Article 55 of the Cooperative Societies Proclamation No. 147/1998, it is hereby proclaimed as follows:

1. Short Title

This Proclamation may be cited as the Cooperatives' Commission Establishment Proclamation No. 274/2002.

2. Establishment

1. The Cooperatives' Commission (hereinafter referred to as 'the Commission'), is hereby established as an autonomous Federal Government Organ.

2. The Commission shall be accountable to the Ministry of Rural Development.

3. Head Office

The Head Office of the Commission shall be in Addis Ababa.

4. Objective of the Commission

The objective of the Commission is to enable rural and urban working people to solve the economic and social problem they face by themselves and become self-reliant by being organized in cooperatives different in type and standard depending on the local resources.

5. Power and Duties of the Commission

The Commission shall have the powers and duties to:

1. formulate policies and prepare draft laws suitable for the activities and development of cooperative societies, and submit the same to the government and follow-up their implementation;
2. encourage that the organization of cooperative societies be in accordance with Cooperatives' Proclamation No, 147/98 and in line with the international principles of cooperatives' organization;
3. direct and supervise cooperatives' training institute to be set up at federal level;
4. undertake research and study to promote traditional and local self-help associations to modern cooperative societies, it shall make known and disseminate the results of the study, and follow-up the implementation thereof;
5. make that the values, principles, organization, and benefits of the cooperatives be further known by the society and educational establishments;
6. organize, register, and issue licences of the legal personality to, the cooperative societies to be organized at federal level, and the cooperative societies to be established by:
   (*a*) two or more primary societies found in different regions, and unable to be organized at regional level due to their peculiar nature;
   (*b*) regional cooperative societies found in two or more regions;
   (*c*) the union cooperative societies organized pursuant to (a) and (b) of this Sub Article;
7. audit and inspect the accounts of cooperative societies to be set up at federal level and assign a liquidator, cancel them from its record

when dissolved: and it shall provide uniform standards of accounting and audit for cooperative societies throughout the country;

8. promote the product of the cooperative societies so that they may find market, and facilities conditions in order to bring consumers and producers to direct communication in the home market;
9. provide professional and technical support to process agricultural products of the cooperative societies to industrial products so that they will have better added-value, and to develop artisans products;
10. provide professional assistance to create the organization of cooperatives based on the culture and experiences of pastoralists and which enables them to improve their living conditions;
11. facilitate, in cooperation with regions as may be necessary, means to provide support for societies by studying and preparing projects suitable for the development of cooperative societies;
12. facilitate conditions to enable the cooperative societies in different regions to exchange their products and information about the market, and to share experiences with one another;
13. provide technical and professional assistance for the bureaux and cooperative societies to be set up in the regions;
14. establish relationship with concerned local and international organizations in order to expedite the progress and the activities of the cooperative societies;
15. formulate and distribute model by-laws of societies which may vary according to the type and level of societies;
16. submit reports on its performances to the concerned government organ;
17. own property enter into contracts, sue and be sued in its own name;
18. carry out other duties helpful for the implementation of its objectives.

6. Organization of the Commission

The Commission shall have:

1. A Commissioner and a Deputy Commissioner to be appointed by the government; and
2. The necessary staff.

7. Powers and Duties of the Commissioner

1. The Commissioner is the Chief Executive of the Commission and shall direct and administer the activities of the Commission.

2. Without prejudice to Sub-Article (1) of the Article, the Commissioner shall.

   (*a*) discharge the powers and duties stated in Article 5 herein;

   (*b*) employ and administer the staff of the Commission pursuant to the Federal Civil Service Laws;

   (*c*) draw up work programmes and budget; and implement the same upon approval;

   (*d*) effect expenditures in accordance with approval work programmes and budget of the commission;

   (*e*) represent the Commission in all its dealings with third parties;

   (*f*) present reports on the activities of Commission.

3. The Commissioner may delegate part of his powers and duties to other officials and employees of the Commission to the extent necessary for the efficiency of the Commission.

8. The Deputy Commissioner

1. He shall act on behalf of the Commissioner in his absence.
2. He shall carry out other activities to be entrusted to him by the Commissioner.

9. Budget

The income of the Commission shall be drawn from the following sources:

(*a*) the budget allocated by the Federal Government.

(*b*) aid received from domestic and foreign donors and other resources.

10. Books of Accounts

1. The Commission shall keep complete and accurate books of accounts.
2. The books of accounts and financial documents of the commission shall be audited annually by the Auditor General or by auditors assigned by him.

11. Inapplicable Laws

Any law inconsistent with this Proclamation shall not be applicable to matters provided for herein.

12. Transfer of Rights and Obligations.

All right and obligations relating to the matters provided for by this Proclamation and given to other organs are hereby transferred to the Commission.

13. Effective Date

This Proclamation shall enter into force as of the 14th day May, 2002.

(Since 2004, the cooperative commission has been renamed as Federal Cooperative Agency, and the designation of the commissioner has been renamed as General Director)

Cooperative Proclamation, 147/1998

The Cooperative Proclamation 147/1998 is the existing legal document under which cooperatives in Ethiopia are organized and administered. As per the above Proclamation, the following formalities are to be followed in registering a cooperative in Ethiopia.

1. 'Society' means a cooperative society established and registered in accordance with this Proclamation and it shall in particular include the following:
   (*a*) Agricultural Cooperative Societies;
   (*b*) Housing Cooperative Societies;
   (*c*) Industrial and Artisans Producers' Cooperative Societies;
   (*d*) Consumers Cooperative Societies;
   (*e*) Savings and credit Cooperative societies;
   (*f*) Fishery Cooperative Societies;
2. Objectives of a Society

The society to be established under this proclamation shall have one or more of the following objectives:

1. to solve problems collectively which members can not individually achieve;
2. to achieve a better result by coordinating their knowledge, wealth and labour;
3. to promote self-reliance among members;
4. to collectively protect, withstand and solve economic problems;
5. to improve the living standards of members by reducing production and service costs by providing input or service at a minimum cost or by finding a better price to their products or services;
6. to expand the mechanism by which technical knowledge could be put in to practice;
7. to develop and promote savings and credit services;
8. to minimize and reduce the individual impact of risks and uncertainties;

9. to develop the social and economic culture of the members through education and training.

3. Guiding Principles of Co-operative Societies

1. Co-operative societies are voluntary organizations open to all persons able to use their services and willing to accept the responsibilities of membership without gender, social, racial, political or religious discrimination.

2. Co-operative societies are democratic organizations controlled by their members who actively participate in setting their policies and making decisions. Every member has equal voting rights and according one member shall have one vote.

3. Members shall receive devideneds from profit according to their shares and contribution after deducting and setting aside an amount necessary for reserve and social services.

4. Co-operative societies are autonomous self help organizations controlled by their members. If they enter into agreement with other organizations; including governments or raise capital from external sources, shall do so on terms that ensure democratic control by their members and maintain their autonomy.

5. Co-operative societies provide education and training for their members, elected representatives, mangers and employees so as to enable them toe contribute effectively to the development of their societies. They inform the general public, particularly the youth about the nature and benefit of societies.

6. Co-operative societies serve their members most effectively and strengthen the societies movement by working together through local, national, regional and international structures.

7. Co-operative societies work for the sustainable development of their communities through policies approved by their members.

Formation and Registration of Co-operative Societies

4. Formation of Co-operative Societies

1. Co-operative societies may, according to their nature, be established at different levels from primary up to the federal level.

2. A primary society shall be established by persons who live or work within a given area.

3. The number of members in a primary society to be established shall not be less than ten.

4. Notwithstanding Sub-Article (2) of this Article the appropriate authority may specify in the directive, the minimum number of members that could make a society economically feasible.

5. A society may sell some of its shares to persons outside its area when the society faces shortage of capital.

5. Types of Societies

1. A society may engage in either production or service rendering activities or in both.

2. The field of activities to be engaged in by any society shall be determined by the by-laws of the society.

6. Name of Society

1. Any society shall have its own name.

2. Words 'Cooperative Society and Limited Liability' shall appear in the name of every society.

3. A name or distinguishing mark registered by one society shall not be used by any other society.

4. The name of every society shall be written boldly and be put at every place where the society's activities are performed. It should also be written or sealed on every notices letters, other specifications and documents which are signed on behalf of the society.

7. Registration of a Co-operative Society

1. Any society shall be registered by the appropriate authority.

2. Any society, when established, shall submit an application for registration together with the following particulars to the appropriate authority:

(*a*) minutes of the founders meeting;

(*b*) the by-laws of the society inn three copies;

(*c*) names, address and signature of the members;

(*d*) name, address and signature of the members of the management committee of the society;

(*e*) a detailed description which proves that the registered members of the society have met the requirements for membership in accordance with the provisions of this Proclamation and the by-laws of the society;

(*f*) name, address and signature of members of the societies above primary level;

(*g*) plan of the society;

(*h*) documents showing that the amount of capital of the society and the capital has been collected and deposited in a bank account, if there is no bank in the area, that it has been deposited in a place where the appropriate authority has designated;

(*i*) the description of the land on which the society operates;

(*j*) other particular that may be specified in the regulations or directives issued for the implementation of this Proclamation.

3. The appropriate authority shall register a society and issue a certificate of registration when it is satisfied that the application for registration submitted to it has fulfilled the requirements for registration.

4. When the appropriate authority rejects the application for the registration of a society, it shall give a written explanation to the representatives of the society within 15 days. The representatives may appeal to the high court which has jurisdiction on the decision of the appropriate authority.

5. The certificate of registration issued to a society pursuant to Sub-Article (3) of this Article is in accordance with this Proclamation.

6. Juridical Personality and Responsibility

1. Any society registered in pursuance of Article 9 of this Proclamation shall have juridical personality from the date of its registration.

2. Any society shall not be liable beyond its total asset. It has limited liability.

8. By-laws of Society

1. Every society shall have its own by-laws.

2. The contents of the by-laws shall include the following particulars:

(*a*) name and address of the society;

(*b*) objectives and activities of the society;

(*c*) working place (area) of the society;

(*d*) requirements necessary for membership of the society;

(*e*) the rights and duties of members of the society;

(*f*) the powers, responsibilities, and duties of management bodies;

(*g*) conditions for withdrawal and dismissal from membership;

(*h*) conditions for reflection appointment, term of office and suspension or dismissal of the members of the management committee or other management bodies;

(*i*) conditions for calling of meeting and voting of the society;

(*j*) allocation and distribution of profit;

(*k*) auditing;

(*l*) employment of workings;

(*m*) other particulars not contrary to this Proclamation.

3. By-laws of society may be amended by the special resolution of the general assembly. However, the amendment of the by-laws of the society shall be effective on the date of its submission to and registration by the appropriate authority.
4. Where the Society decides on the amendment of its by-laws three copies of the amendment and the special resolution of the society made in accordance with this Proclamation shall be submitted to the appropriate authority within 30 days from the date of the decisions.
5. The appropriate authority shall register the amendment and give evidence or its registration to the society where it is satisfied that the amendment of the by-laws was made in accordance with this Proclamation.

Self-learning Activity

Try to answer the following questions on your own.

1. List out the functions of Registrar of Cooperatives?
2. What are the contents of a bye-law?

Summary

- In the context of Ethiopia, cooperative societies are organized and governed by the Cooperative Proclamation No. 147/1998. This proclamation has been amended during the year 2004.

8 Stages in Organizing Cooperatives

Because each situation is unique, there is no specific recipe for forming a cooperative. The steps for starting a co-op recommended here should be considered guidelines.

A. Steps to Starting a Cooperative

Like other businesses, every co-op starts with the recognition of a need or an opportunity. One or two people willing to put in some time and energy can spark a group interested in starting a co-op.

Members of such a group have a mutual need that can be addressed through joint action. They could, for example, lack a market for their products or lack necessary supplies or services. Acting together to address that need, they can achieve something which none of them could achieve alone.

Basic Steps in Starting a Cooperative

1. Hold an organizing meeting; establish steering committee
2. Conduct a feasibility study
3. Hold a meeting of potential members to report on the results of the feasibility study
4. Incorporate the co-op by filing articles of incorporation and bylaws
5. Prepare a business plan
6. Secure financing for the co-op.
7. Recruit/Admission of members for the co-op.
8. Hire co-op management and staff
9. Hold the co-op's first membership and board meetings
10. Start Cooperatives

1. Hold an organizing meeting and establish a steering committee

(*a*) A core group of interested individuals should hold an informational meeting of potential co-op members and others in the community. The primary purpose of the meeting is to explain the identified need and how a co-op would address it.

It is important that the group come to general agreement on the nature and importance of the problem and the potential for a cooperative to address it. Such an agreement will become the group's shared vision, so it is worth spending as much time as necessary to achieve it.

(*b*) Provide informational handouts that explain what a co-op is and how it would work. Also provide information about the steps involved in starting a co-op so people have a sense of what they may be getting into. Determine the level of interest in exploring a co-op among meeting participants.

Many organizing groups have found it helpful to invite speakers from other cooperatives in order to highlight their success stories. This often gives meeting participants a more down to earth vision of what a co-op is and how it can work for them.

(*c*) A steering committee should be formed of participants at the meeting which will coordinate activities on behalf of the group. Committee members must be able to provide leadership to the larger group and be willing to put some time and energy into researching the feasibility of the proposed cooperative.

(*d*) Allow plenty of time for questions and discussion. A meeting like this often works best if it is led by an experienced facilitator. In many cases, it is necessary to hold more than one meeting to give all interested parties in the community a chance to participate.

Typical Steering Committee Members

1. President

   Often the 'project champion'. Facilitation skills a big plus.

2. Vice President

   May chair key subcommittee.

3. Treasurer

   Manages funds. May lead business plan phase. Accounting skills a big plus.

4. Secretary

   Coordinates all communications. Computer skills a big plus.

5. Non-officers

Group Dynamics (Adapted from Henehan)

Various issues must be resolved to proceed:

- Potential members must see that the benefits in adopting a cooperative approach are attainable.
- Individuals must emerge who are willing to assume a leadership role and take the agreed-upon vision to the next steps.
- A level of trust and confidence must evolve within the group.
- The creative tension between visionaries and doers must be harnessed effectively. It cannot be allowed to prevent the group from moving forward.
- Participants must be convinced that the initial risks and costs in adopting the proposed approach are outweighted by the potential benefits to be obtained.
- Roles of members, management and board members should be clear to all.
- Everyone involved should have confidence that the proposed organization is the best alternative available.

Typical Sub-committee Areas

- Business plan committee;
- By-laws and policies committee;
- Purchasing and construction committee; and
- Personnel committee.

2. Conduct a Feasibility study

(*a*) The steering committee can either conduct a feasibility study (using the guidelines provided), or hire a consultant to carry out the study. The purpose of a feasibility study is to examine critical opportunities and obstacles that might make or break the proposed cooperative business. The feasibility study should give the group a good idea of whether the co-op is likely to be successful as a business.

The critical issues that a feasibility study analyzes include the number and interest level of potential members; market issues (can the co-op get better prices, better quality or better services than potential members currently get through other means?); operating costs; start-up costs; and availability of financing.

If insurmountable obstacles are discovered in the feasibility study, the development of the cooperative should be abandoned or shelved before too much time and money has been expended.

(*b*) In some cases, local or state governments or foundations may provide financial or technical assistance with the feasibility study. *The quality of the feasibility study is critical because it will influence all future decisions on the development of the co-op.* Don't hesitate to bring in outside expertise when you need it.

Contributions by potential co-op members are often used to help cover the cost of a feasibility study. These members will be the primary beneficiaries of the cooperative, so naturally they should assume some responsibility for the financial costs of assessing its feasibility.

3. Report on the Results of the Feasibility Study

(*a*) The steering committee should hold a follow up meeting with potential co-op members to report on the results of the feasibility study. A summary of the feasibility report should be distributed to participants, and the full report made available to anyone who wishes to see it. Allow plenty of time to discuss the report and ensure that potential members understand the results.

(*b*) Be sure to spend time reviewing the financial section of the report. The preliminary financial projections should tell the group how much equity will be required from each member of the co-op, and whether or not the co-op is projected to return any patronage refunds (shares of the profits) to members during the first few years of operation. These are key pieces of information that will influence each person's decision about whether to join the co-op.

This should be a major decision point. If the feasibility study indicates that the co-op is not a viable business, or if sufficient commitment does not exist among the group, the steering committee should not proceed with forming the co-op.

4. Incorporate the Cooperative and File Articles of Incorporation and Bylaws

(*a*) In most states, a cooperative has to be incorporated under the appropriate state statute in order to conduct business. Most states have statutes specifically governing cooperatives. The articles of incorporation describe the kind and scope of the cooperative's business. Incorporation takes place when a co-op files its articles with the secretary of state. If the steering committee wishes to, it may draft the articles of incorporation and bylaws. Make sure to have a lawyer who is familiar with cooperatives review these documents before they are presented to the membership.

(*b*) The bylaws state how the cooperative will conduct business, and must be approved by the membership. Note that a co-op can start out with very basic bylaws and refine them after the business plan has been developed.

(*c*) As soon as the cooperative is incorporated and thus exists as a legal entity, two members of the steering committee should open a bank account in the co-op's name. This account will be used to deposit equity contributions from new members.

(*d*) *A note about stock:* Articles of Incorporation allow the steering committee to decide whether the co-op will issue stock or not. We recommend that the co-op do so. In recruiting new members, it can be an important symbolic act to hand over a stock certificate to each individual who joins the co-op. Many new members feel more comfortable having something in hand to show for their contribution. Some potential members also find a stock cooperative easier to understand than a non-stock structure.

Blank stock certificates are available at most office supply stores. Just fill in the blanks to indicate the number of shares each member buys and the cost per share.

5. Prepare a Business Plan

(*a*) If the feasibility study results are favourable, the steering committee carries out or hires a consultant firm to develop a detailed business plan. The business plan serves two primary purposes: to provide a blueprint for the development and initial operation of the co-op and to provide supporting documentation for potential members, financial institutions and other investors.

(*b*) A typical outline of a business plan includes a description of the company, a market analysis, research and development related to the co-op's product or service, a marketing and sales plan, a description of the organizational structure and key personnel, and financial data.

(*c*) In most cases, a new co-op will need to borrow capital from a bank or other lending institution in order to get started. The business plan serves a vital function in describing to the bank the co-op's goals and how it plans to accomplish those goals. Most lending institutions will not consider a loan request that is not accompanied by a detailed business plan. In addition, it is a very useful document when recruiting new members to the cooperative.

(*d*) Few steering committees have sufficient skills to develop a thorough business plan. Obtaining technical assistance can make the difference between a business plan that gets a loan and one that does not. Note that many state governments offer grants and loans to assist start-ups with technical assistance and business planning.

A cooperative's business plan should include many of the components of a business plan for any type of firm. However, there are additional considerations for cooperatives which should be addressed in a well thought out plan.

For example, cooperative finance involves a number of unique aspects such as the variety of ways to raise or revolve member equity. Governance structure should be spelled out in the plan to insure that an effective decision making capacity is designed. Will voting be by member, proportional to patronage, or proportional to investment? Member rights and responsibilities in relation to the cooperative should also be presented.

Financial projections should be built on several scenarios reflecting the impact of various member actions, such as a given percentage of members not meeting their patronage or investment obligations. What level of losses or prices might members be willing to tolerate? What happens if a share of members over produce or find more attractive alternatives?

6. Secure Financing

(*a*) Cooperative businesses vary greatly in the amount of capital they need to get up and running. The business plan should include the amount and type of financing needed by the co-op and a strategy for obtaining it. The steering committee and its advisors are responsible for implementing this strategy.

(*b*) Virtually all co-ops require some level of member financing, usually in the form of stock purchases or membership fees. Member financing not only provides equity for the co-op, it also provides a financial base that helps other investors, particularly banks, feel more secure in investing in the co-op. The steering committee should prepare a membership application for new members to fill out and sign. It should identify the member's name, address, and phone number; the number of shares of stock being purchased (or the amount of the membership fee if it is a non-stock co-op); and a stated agreement that the new member agrees to belong to and abide by the bylaws and contracts of the co-op.

Each member's initial financial contribution should be collected at the time the membership application is submitted.

(*c*) In addition to member equity, most co-ops need to borrow money to get started and to maintain their operations. Loans can come from banks and other financial institutions (including several national banks for cooperatives).

7. Recruit/Admission of Members

(*a*) Laying the groundwork for the co-op's membership base needs to begin when the steering committee first meets. During their organizational phase, many co-ops hold meetings for potential members, conduct surveys and mail organizing updates to them, and collect initial down payments on membership fees.

All of these activities provide a good indication of the level of interest in, and commitment to, the co-op. Thus, when the time comes to actually 'ante-up' and join, potential members are more primed to act. Even so, the steering committee may need to recruit new members in addition to those who have attended one or more of the organizational meetings. *This should be a major decision point. If the co-op is unable to obtain the necessary debt financing, or if sufficient commitment does not exist among potential members to provide sufficient equity capital, the steering committee should not proceed with developing the co-op at this time.*

8. Hire Cooperative Management

(*a*) Some new co-ops identify management personnel early in their organizing process, especially if one or more key individuals are already known to members of the steering committee. However, recruiting staff personnel is listed as a later step in the co-op formation process because the co-op is not a definite 'go' until the necessary financing has been secured.

One or more of the key individuals can be hired as consultants at an early stage with the mutual intent that they will work for the co-op once it is formally established. This approach also has the effect of making investors feel more comfortable about financing the co-op because proposed management staff have been identified. For some lenders, competent management is the most important thing they look for in making a loan decision.

9. Hold Co-op's First Membership and Board Meetings

(*a*) After financing has been secured and sufficient members have signed up, the first general membership meeting is convened. There are two major pieces of business that must be conducted at this meeting:

- the members adopt the co-op's bylaws; and
- the members elect a board of directors for the co-op.

This meeting marks the transition from a steering committee and interim leadership group to a formally elected board and legally approved bylaws. Allow enough time for members to look over the bylaws and ensure that they are thoroughly understood before the vote takes place. There may be a few amendments suggested; these and the bylaws are approved by majority vote.

In their capacity as owners, members elect the board of directors to function as their representatives in overseeing the administration of the co-op. *It is this mechanism through which a cooperative is member-controlled.* As the members' representatives, the board's primary responsibilities are to develop policies, conduct long-range planning, hire and supervise the co-op manager, and guide the co-op in pursuing its mission and goals.

(*b*) The new board of directors should hold their first board meeting shortly after the first membership meeting. Among other duties, the board should elect officers, develop job descriptions for management personnel, and initiate the hiring process, if necessary.

10. Start Operations

(*a*) During the initial phase of the co-op's operations, management should concentrate on implementing the business plan. It is vital that frequent communication between staff, board and members be maintained during this period. Some co-ops have lost touch with their members after start-up, and have found that to be a recipe for disaster. Management and board need to make sure the co-op is meeting the needs of the members over time. Do this through regular newsletters and member surveys.

(*b*) Another way to maintain good communication between staff, members and board is to conduct educational seminars for them. Remember that continuous education is one of the cooperative principles. It enables members to participate in the co-op's affairs and make fully informed decisions regarding them.

A strong co-op is built on a foundation of involved members. Without an active base of members who are willing to work towards the success of the co-op, the co-op is bound to fail.

Starting a cooperative can be a lengthy and somewhat arduous process. It can also be very rewarding to see the fruits of your labour turn into economic and social benefits for you and your community.

The steering committee takes responsibility for seeing the organizing process through to the end. Be patient and give yourselves the time to conduct each development stage carefully.

Don't get discouraged if the process appears to get bogged down. Bring in outside technical assistance as needed, and solicit advice from others who have been down the same road.

Additional Information Related to Starting a Cooperative

Bylaws, Membership Application, Member Meetings

Bylaws

Bylaws are the rules and regulations that govern the day-to-day working and regular functioning of a cooperative society. They are equal to the Articles of Association followed by a private company. A bylaw can be amended to suit the needs of the cooperative.

Bylaws state how the cooperative will conduct business and must be consistent with both State laws and the articles.

Bylaws usually have membership requirements and lists rights and responsibilities of members; Grounds and procedures for member expulsion; how to call and conduct membership meetings, methods of voting, how directors and officers are elected or removed, and their number, duties, terms of office; time and place of directors meetings; requirement to conduct business; handling of losses; treating non-member business; dissolution of the cooperative; and the process for amending the bylaws.

Also covered is how the board is structured to represent the membership, given geographical distribution and size of the membership and the scope of business and function of the cooperative. Directors may be selected to represent areas based on membership density, to reflect commodities or services to be handled, or some other basis that provides equitable representation. The organizing committee's recommended management structure should include the basis for director representation, voting methods, and board officers, and their terms.

An outline of the major topic areas that the bylaws should cover appears below.

Membership

Identifies the qualifications for eligibility and procedures for joining the cooperative, including requirements for purchase of stock, if any. Describes the procedure by which membership may be ended, either voluntarily or involuntarily.

Meetings of Cooperative Members

Identifies the date for the annual meeting; how and when any special meetings may be held; requirements for notice of upcoming meetings; procedures for voting and requirements for a quorum; order of business at the annual meeting.

Directors and Officers

Specifies the number and qualifications of directors; procedures for electing directors and length of terms; election of officers by the board; frequency of board meetings and requirements for notice of board meetings; any special meetings; compensation of board members and requirements for a quorum.

Duties of Directors

States the director's specific powers and responsibilities, including: guiding the cooperative and articulating its mission, goals, and policies and periodically reviewing those goals. Authorizes directors to employ a manager, define the manager's duties, determine his or her compensation and evaluate his or her job performance. Specifies the director's responsibility to maintain an appropriate accounting system and have the co-op's books audited or reviewed annually. This section also specifies the board's responsibility to indemnify directors, officers and management against liability.

Duties of Officers

Specifies the duties of the president, vice president, secretary, and treasurer. Also describes the terms of officers and excused absences from board meetings.

Membership Capital Contributions

Specifies the required equity contribution by members and the method by which the co-op will collect the contribution; what type of stock the cooperative has the authority to issue; and any requirements regarding the co-op's stock certificates.

Profits and Losses

Specifies how the co-op's profits, if any, will be distributed based on each member's patronage with the co-op. In addition, any losses experienced by the co-op must be allocated across the membership.

Non-member Business

Specifies how the cooperative will distribute the benefits, if any, resulting from business with non-members.

Dissolution

Identifies a procedure for dissolving the cooperative, and specifies the distribution of any remaining assets.

Amending the Bylaws

Specifies a straightforward method by which the bylaws may be amended.

Contents of bye-laws

The bye-laws *must* contain:

1. The name and the trade name of the cooperative, which may be freely chosen, as long as there is no confusion possible with the name of another cooperative already registered and as long as the public is left in doubt about the limited financial liability of the members;
2. The locality of the head office, its postal address and possibly the conditions for a transfer;
3. The definition of the objective (including the indication of whether the cooperative is a single or a multi-purpose cooperative);
4. The conditions and procedures for admission, resignation, exclusion and suspension of members as well as eligibility criteria. These must reflect the particular character of the cooperative in question, as also reflected by its being a primary, a secondary or a tertiary cooperative;
5. The value and minimum number of the shares to be subscribed by each member. The GA ensures that the economic means of the least affluent members form the basis for the decision;
6. The procedure and conditions for the subscription and payment of the shares and, possibly, of additional shares. Shares may be paid in cash, kind, labour, service or by leaving the share of the surplus, to which a member is entitled, with the cooperative;
7. The type of financial liability of the members for the debts of the cooperative the administration of the registers;
8. The conditions and procedures for convening GAs (form of notice, fixing and notifying the agenda, election of the president of the session, preferably not a member of the board of directors, quorum and voting, number of delegates by section or by region if any, etc.);
9. The size of the board of directors and, possibly, of the supervisory committee; the conditions of eligibility to the various offices, the duration of the mandates and their possible remuneration; rights and obligations of officers, mode of decision taking;

10. The conditions and procedures for convening the board of directors and, if any, the supervisory committee (quorum, voting, etc.);
11. Financing: capital formation, constitution of the legal and of the statutory reserve funds;
12. Surplus distribution and contribution to cover losses;
13. The distribution of the capital in case of resignation, exclusion or liquidation;
14. Definition of the financial year;
15. Auditing;
16. Conditions and procedures for voluntary dissolution;
17. Arbitration procedure;
18. Decision making;
19. Specification of any other legal matter; and finally
20. The procedure for modifying the bye-laws.

Article 11 of the Cooperative Proclamation 147/1998

The above Article, explains the following relating to the bylaws of a cooperative in Ethiopia.

1. Every society shall have its own bylaws;
2. The contents of the bylaws shall include the following particulars:
   (*a*) Name and address of the society;
   (*b*) Objectives and activities of the society;
   (*c*) Working place of the society;
   (*d*) Requirements necessary for membership of the society;
   (*e*) The rights and duties of members of the society;
   (*f*) The powers, responsibilities and duties of management bodies;
   (*g*) Conditions for withdrawal and dismissal of membership;
   (*h*) Conditions for selection, appointment, term of office and suspension or dismissal of members of the management committee or other management bodies;
   (*i*) Conditions for calling of meeting and voting of the society;
   (*j*) Allocation and distribution of profit;
   (*k*) Auditing;
   (*l*) Employment of workers;
   (*m*) Other particulars not contrary to the Proclamation.

3. Bylaws of a society may be amended by the special resolution of the general assembly. However, the amendment of the bylaws of the society shall be effective on the date of its submission to and registration by the appropriate authority.
4. When the society decides on the amendment of the bylaws, 3 copies of the amendment and the special resolution of the society made in accordance with this Proclamation shall be submitted to the appropriate authority within 30 days from the date of the decision.
5. The appropriate authority shall register the amendment and give evidence or its registration to the society where it is satisfied that the amendment of bylaws was made in accordance with this Proclamation and regulations issued for the implementation of this Proclamation.

Membership Application

The application, signed by the member and approved by the board of directors, is the legal proof that a patron is a member. A cooperative should have a completed membership application on file from every member. Membership and the amount of business done with members and non-members are important factors for certain activities. A membership certificate may be issued to each member as evidence of entitlement to all of the rights, benefits, and privileges of the association.

Member Meeting

Further action is usually needed to accept those members who have subscribed for shares or agreed to become members.

If members of the first board of directors have not been named in the bylaws, they should be elected at this meeting or the steering committee can be converted as Board of Directors.

Here are some suggestions for selecting the first board of directors:

- Use a nominating committee to develop a panel of candidates for the board;
- Select only members as candidates;
- Nominate two candidates for each position; and
- Vote by secret ballot.

Implementing the Business Plan

Officers of the cooperative are elected and directors assigned to individual or committee responsibilities to implement the business plan. Members may be assigned to committees, but at least one board member should be on each committee to enhance communications. Target dates are established for important events such as groundbreaking, construction completion, dedication or open house, and full-capacity operations.

The board needs to act immediately on some specific items:

- Conduct a membership drive;
- Adopt a form of membership application or subscription;
- Acquire capital;
- Initiate steps to hire a manager;
- Authorize officers or employees to handle cooperative funds and issue checks;
- Design and install an accounting system.
- Provide for bookkeeping and auditing services;
- Print bylaws, and other member documents for distribution to all members;
- Bind officers and employees in accordance with bylaws.

Membership Drive

Cooperative normally have open membership. Initially they may have a selective membership policy. Members should feel a responsibility to recommend other believed to be qualified users. That's why it's important for members to understand what their cooperative is, how it operates, its benefits, and its limitations.

People join cooperative primarily for economic benefits-services and increased income. Most people want to be shown the advantages of cooperative membership. If those benefits are not evident, few prospects will join and even if they do, they probably won't regularly patronize the cooperative.

New members may be asked to join by purchasing shares or paying a membership fee and signing and application. The applicant should get a receipt for funds collected. The cooperative must follow up with membership and related material.

Accurate accounting of money is an extremely sensitive issue. The cooperative should retain an independent accounting firm to assist in recording funds prior to the collection of substantial amounts of money.

Now, we can look into the rights and responsibilities of members, board of directors, chairman, vice chairman, manager and chief account in the Ethiopian context.

Elections

Elections are conducted routinely as per the bylaws of the cooperative. Every year one-third of the directors will be relieved and elections will be conducted for the post of the directors. Elections can be conducted during the ordinary general assembly meeting as well as during the special general assembly meeting. The members must be given prior intimation by the presiding officer (usually the chairman of the cooperative) relating to the date of election and the nomination by the members. Elections to the posts of president, vice-president, secretary and other office bearers will be conducted among the members of the board of directors.

Members, General Assembly and Board Members

Cooperative management starts with membership, members formulate the broad general policies of the cooperative and elect the Board of Directors to supervise the execution of these policies. The manager and his staff put into practice the policies prescribed by the members under the guidance of the Board of Directors. This division of activities places important responsibilities on members, which should not be taken lightly.

The Obligations and Rights of Members

Obligations

Principle

Membership is linked to rights, these being conditioned by the discharge of obligations. The law and subsidiary legislation must ensure that this rule is respected, even in cases where social rules tend to override these rights and obligations.

In no case, must the social mechanisms based on family ties, race, age, religion or any other affiliation to a group affect the independence and the equality of the members.

Personal Obligations

By belonging to a cooperative, members commit themselves to:

- respect the bye-laws as well as all the decisions taken in the general assembly, whether they voted for their adoption or not;
- abstain from any activity detrimental to the objective of their cooperative.
- Membership in several cooperatives having the same objective and territory must not automatically be considered as harming the cooperative(s).
- participate actively in the life of the cooperative. This obligation may not, however, be
- enforced.

Financial Obligations

Membership in a cooperative implies the following financial obligations:

- Each member must subscribe to and pay for the minimum number of shares fixed by the bye-laws;
- Each member is financially liable for the debts of his or her cooperative. This liability is at least equal to the amount of shares subscribed.

In order to compensate, at least in part, for the financial weakness inherent to most cooperatives, the law or the bye-laws may impose an obligation on the members to make supplementary payments in case the cooperative is unable to pay its debts. This may result in an unlimited financial liability of the members.

The amount of these supplementary payments may be the same for each member, it may be determined as prorata of the transactions made by each of the members, according to the method used to distribute the surplus, or according to the number of shares held by each member. If not specified in the law, the type of financial liability of the members must be explicitly dealt with in the byelaws in order to protect the interests of third parties.

Because of the status of legal personality of cooperatives, this financial liability commits the members towards their cooperative only, and not towards the creditors of the cooperative. It extends beyond the termination of membership, during a period to be specified in the law. As a rule, a member must contribute to the discharge of only those debts which show in the balance sheet at the time of the end of his or her membership.

Other Obligations

One might envisage obliging the members to use, to a certain extent at least, the services of their cooperative. Although favouring in the short run the development of the cooperative, such a rule would in time have a negative influence on the competitiveness of the cooperative and it might violate competition law.

Rather than reasoning in terms of legal obligations, one might consider that cooperators have the moral duty to work with their enterprise. Furthermore, it is up to the cooperative itself to offer sufficiently attractive services to its members. In order to guarantee a certain stability in specific cases, the cooperative might have to conclude individual contracts with each of its members.

Furthermore, exceptions are possible particularly in the case where the members decide to make an important investment, the success of which depends on the members using that facility. Members could then temporarily be forbidden to look elsewhere for the rendered services.

Rights

Personal Rights

Each member has the right to:

- use the installations and services of the cooperative;
- participate in the general assembly, propose a motion therein, and vote;
- elect or be elected for an office in the cooperative;
- obtain at all times, from the elected bodies of the cooperative information on the economic situation of the cooperative;
- have the books and registers inspected by the supervisory committee.

Jointly as a group(minimum number to be determined), the members can also:

- convene a general assembly and/or have a question inscribed on the agenda of that GA;
- ask for an additional audit.

Financial Rights

The members have the following financial rights:

They receive a share of the surplus in the form of a bonus, calculated as prorata of their transactions with their cooperative (patronage bonus), and/ or a limited interest on the paid-up shares.

When terminating their membership, they can ask that the paid-up shares be reimbursed. Losses or devaluations may be deducted from the nominal value of these shares.

In the case of liquidation, members receive a share of the remaining sum, if any, unless the bye-laws stipulate that this must be credited to another cooperative or to a charitable organization.

Article 14 of the Cooperative Proclamation 147/1998

As per the above Article, the rights and duties of members of a cooperative in Ethiopia are as follows:

1. Any member of a society shall have the following rights:

   (*a*) To obtain services and benefits according to his participation in the society;

   (*b*) To participate in the meetings of the society and to vote;

   (*c*) To elect and be elected;

   (*d*) To withdraw from the society on his request with payment of benefits.

2. Any member of a society shall have the following duties:

   (*a*) To respect the bylaws, directives and decisions of the society;

   (*b*) To perform those activities which ought to be performed in accordance with the bylaws and directives of the society;

   (*c*) To pay for share capital and registration fee;

   (*d*) To protect the common property of the society.

Members participate in management in a number of ways. The most important are when they:

(*a*) Adopt and amend by-laws;

(*b*) Elect and remove Board of Directors;

(*c*) Approve changes in capitalization and major additions to plants and services;

(*d*) Decide on the appropriation of net surplus;

(*e*) Approve annual activity plan and budget;

(*f*) Make a decision on audit reports;

(*g*) Consider the annual report of the Board of directors controlling committee and making a decision;

(*h*) Become active in the cooperative affairs by attending meetings, serving on committees, accepting special assignments, and genuinely backing the cooperative;

(*i*) Abide by the decision of the majority;

(*j*) Keen informed about the cooperative by studying annual reports, talking with board of directors anf employees;

(k) Defend the cooperative and its management when it is unjustly criticized or attacked.

In order for cooperative members to exercise control, they must take action by legally called meetings. They by-laws should specify the procedure to be followed in calling meetings. The highest body in the cooperative is the general meeting. All members of the cooperative should attend meetings.

Self-learning Activity

Try to answer the following questions on your own.

1. Discuss the basic steps involved in organizing a cooperative?
2. What are the duties and rights of members of a cooperative?

Summary

- Bylaws of a cooperative give the guidelines to run a cooperative. Conducting the day-to-day affairs and running of a cooperative are clearly explained in the bylaws. Bylaws can be amended according to the needs of the members of the cooperative.
- After bylaws are prepared members are issued member application and members meet to elect the first board of directors.
- The first board has to go through the business plan. A business plan tells the future business activities in terms of figures and targets. A business plan is needed for a financing institution to appraise the credit worthiness of a cooperative.
- A membership drive must be undertaken by the new board to increase the capital structure and the volume of business. A cooperative should see that all the individuals or families in the area of operation of a cooperative are enrolled as members of the new cooperative.
- Members have their own rights and responsibilities which are explained in the bylaws of the cooperative. They have to actively participate in the deliberations of the cooperative to increase the financial resources of the cooperative. They must also actively participate in the elections, to select right persons to the board.

9 Do's and Don'ts in Organizing Cooperatives

Do's of Organizing Cooperatives

While organizing a cooperative and start running a cooperative, the following points must be taken into consideration by the promoters, steering committee/board of directors, and the leaders of cooperatives.

1. *Homogeneity of membership:* Cooperatives are organized by like-minded people and who have common problems. In the earlier days, in European countries, cooperatives were formed by trade union members, farmers, and labourers who have like-minded objectives and problems in life. If like-minded people are not selected, the cooperative may have to face lot of leadership, organizational, and functional problems in the future activities.
2. *Unanimity:* In running the cooperatives and in electing the committee members and leaders, there must be unanimity among the members. As far as possible the choice of selecting the committee member or the president must be unanimous. Any division or election in selecting the leaders may lead to division in the society from the very beginning. So, it is better to elect leaders unanimously by all members.
3. *Minimum membership:* Though the cooperative proclamation and the bylaws may prescribe 10 people as the promoters to organize a new cooperative, having only ten members, a cooperative cannot run viably. It is better that promoters should take efforts to enlist ten times more than the prescribed minimum membership. Only having higher level of membership, a society can raise more resources and can operate successfully.
4. *Electing honest leaders:* From the very beginning, the members must elect honest and dedicated leaders to their cooperative. The initial success of a cooperative depends on the hard work and dedication of the cooperative leaders. They have to work honorarily without expecting

any benefit or return from their cooperatives. They have to follow the principle of each for all, all for each and unity among diversity.

5. ***Following the sequence of events:*** While starting a cooperative, the following sequences must be looked after by the promoters:

   (*a*) Hold meeting of leading members to discuss an economic need that the formation of a cooperative might fulfill;

   (*b*) Hold the first member meeting. Vote whether to continue. If affirmative, select a steering committee;

   (*c*) Conduct a member survey as a basis for determining cooperative feasibility;

   (*d*) Hold second general meeting to discuss the results of member survey, vote on whether to proceed;

   (*e*) Conduct a market or supply and cost analysis;

   (*f*) Hold third general meeting to discuss the results of the market or supply and cost analysis. Vote whether to proceed this time by secret ballot;

   (*g*) Conduct a financial analysis and develop a business plan;

   (*h*) Hold fourth general meeting to hear the results of the financial analysis. Vote again whether to proceed. If affirmative, vote a second time on whether the steering committee would remain intact or changes be made.

   (*i*) Drafting a cooperative bylaw—call a meeting of members to adopt a bylaw. It is a good idea to invite all the members to ratify the bylaw and elect board of directors;

   (*j*) Call the first meeting of the board of directors, assign responsibilities to implement the business plan;

   (*k*) Acquire capital, including developing a loan package;

   (*l*) Hire the manager and staff;

   (*m*) Acquire the facilities;

   (*n*) Start the operations.

6. ***Prepare feasibility plans:*** Before starting a cooperative, a feasibility plan or a survey must be prepared by the cooperative. This feasibility plan will contain the size of the society, location of the society, number of members to be enlisted, capital to be mobilized, market for the product or service of the cooperatives, the type of competition, personnel to be hired, etc. Feasibility can be prepared by the experts or consultants who have vast experience in the field of running a cooperative society.

7. ***Prepare business plan:*** A business plan is one, which tells the future business activities of a cooperative and such business plan is prepared for the financers of the cooperative. A business plan will tell the business operations like purchasing and selling by a cooperative month-war, quarterly, half-yearly, and annually. The achievable targets of business operations will also be fixed by the business plan. A business plan also be prepared by experts or consultants. If experienced members have the knowledge, they can also prepare a business plan.

8. ***Conducting meetings often:*** During the initial periods, the general assembly meetings and the board meetings can be conducted very often, more than the minimum required period put in the bylaws. Usually, the general assembly meeting can be convened once in a year and the committee/board meeting can be convened once in a month. But during the initial stages, such stipulation can be waved and the meetings can be convened very often. Once through such frequent meetings the members can be clarifications and controversies can be avoided.

9. ***Competition strategy:*** A new cooperative may be inexperienced in its business operations. Naturally, it has to face tough competition from the private sector and the public sector organizations. From the very beginning, a cooperative has to plan a competitive strategy to promote the interest of the cooperative. Only a competitive strategy can help the cooperative to attain viability and sustainability. A competitive edge can be provided by means of customer attraction measures and cost effective service.

10. ***Marketing strategy:*** Number of cooperative are undertaking marketing activities. Input marketing, output marketing, and services marketing are some of the important marketing activities undertaken by cooperatives. While purchasing inputs like consumer goods, farm inputs like seed, fertilizer, and pesticides, the cooperative must go for bulk purchase and distribute the goods for a lower price to the members. While undertaking output marketing, by better marketing practices, the cooperative must provide a higher price than the market price to the produce of the farmers. While undertaking services marketing, like the field of banking and insurance, lower charges must be made from the members and the cooperative must provide higher rate of interest to the deposits and a lower rate of interest to the loans of the members.

11. ***Plan vertical and horizontal growth:*** A cooperative must plan, from the very beginning the horizontal growth and vertical growth. A vertical growth denotes the increase of business turnover of a cooperative every quarter and every year. Every month, there should be improvement in the business transactions of the cooperative. For this purpose, a

cooperative must prepare business plan for every month, every quarter, and every year. With regard to horizontal growth, a cooperative must add more and more new services on a planned way. An agricultural cooperative can start with providing credit and can add marketing services, processing services, hiring services, consumer services, etc at various stages. Ultimately, a primary cooperative should become a multi-purpose cooperative and all-round service provider.

12. ***Self-reliance in resources:*** Cooperatives are raising their resources by way of owned funds and borrowed funds. As far as possible, a cooperative must raise resource through owned funds. Raising of resources through owned funds and by deposits alone can provide self-reliance. Owned funds are formed by share capital and reserve funds. Borrowed funds are formed by deposits and borrowings from external agencies. Though deposits from borrowed funds, for all practical purposes, they are considered to be owned funds. Deposits are cheaper compared to the borrowings from external agencies.
13. ***Federal structure:*** When cooperative are organized around the places, the next step would be the organization of central societies at regional level and federal cooperatives at the national level. A federal structure consisting of primary cooperatives, central cooperatives, and national cooperatives can strengthen the particular cooperative movement like credit cooperatives, marketing cooperatives, consumer cooperative, etc. Through federal cooperatives, resource mobilization and guidance for the lower level cooperatives would be easier.
14. ***Amendment of bylaws:*** Wherever possible a cooperative must take steps to amend the bylaws. When a cooperative grows and the business operations expand, naturally, there is need to amend the bylaws to suit the expanding operations of the cooperative. While amending the bylaws, the acceptance of not only the majority of the members, but also the acceptance of all members must be invited.
15. ***Welfare of the employees:*** A new cooperative must select experienced manager and employees. Their welfare must be taken care from the very beginning. They must be paid market wages and other fringe benefits. If possible, they must be provided with free transport, communication, housing, educational, medical, and other welfare facilities. A cooperative should become a model employer, then only we can expect fuller devotion from the employees.
16. ***Training:*** Training is a continuous process in cooperative and training must be given to the members, leaders and the employees. All employees and all members must be given training on a routing basis and a phased manner. The cost of training must be borne by the cooperative and a

cooperative should not hesitate to invest money on training. Training on areas like cooperative management, cooperative accounting, marketing, financial management, new business techniques, etc can be arranged.

17. ***Exposure visits:*** All the members of the cooperatives, leaders, and the employees of the cooperative must be taken to the exposure visits to the nearby cooperatives and at the national level cooperatives. By means of exposure visits, one can come to know the activities of other cooperatives and they can compare the working of their cooperative with other cooperatives. Exposure visits help the cooperatives to rectify their mistakes and find solutions to the problems.
18. ***Profit distribution:*** During the initial years, a cooperative must distribute lesser amount of dividend. Allocation for reserve funds and retained earning can be higher. By means of allocating more funds for reserves and retained earnings, a cooperative can plough back additional resources for next years' investment. The farmers have to make sacrifice towards this purpose.
19. ***Recovery of dues:*** One of the important activities to be done by a cooperative is to recover the dues in the form of loan, interest, etc from the members regularly. In many developing countries, the challenge for the agricultural cooperatives comes from the non-recovery of loans in time. Ultimately, many cooperatives have become sick and unable to serve the members. From the very beginning, the members can be careful in collecting the dues in time. Loans can be provided on a joint basis, which can allow mutual repayment of loans by members in time.
20. ***Viability and sustainability:*** The cooperatives must create viability from the very beginning. Viability denotes the minimum business operations to be undertaken in a year and the earning of an income needed to manage the expenditures. When a society attains viability, sustainability will be attained naturally. Sustainability denotes the long-standing function of a cooperative without any external help.

Don'ts of Organizing Cooperatives

While organizing and running a cooperative, the promoters, members, the leaders, and other stakeholders must avoid certain activities noted below. Then only they can run their cooperative successfully and make it a viable unit.

1. ***Membership:*** While organizing a new cooperative, it is better to avoid controversial members and members who may not work for a common cause. When controversial members are admitted as members, they may lead to division of a society from the very beginning. Division may take

place during the times of elections. Likewise, more number of members must be admitted. In many cooperatives the promoter and few members may not allow new members to be admitted. Likewise, the gender disparity in the form of not admitting women members must also be avoided. Women members must be given representation in the membership and leadership. In the board, representation to women must be given.

2. ***Locational factors:*** A basic precondition for the success of a cooperative is the location of the particular cooperative. The location must be a center place, which can be convenient to all the members and must have proper transport and communication facilities. A wrong location of a cooperative may ultimately lead to the failure. Cooperatives like marketing cooperatives, processing cooperatives and industrial cooperatives must be located in the center place of raw material or producing centers. This alone will make the movement of goods and services easier to the members.

3. ***Low capital:*** A cooperative must be careful that adequate capital must be raised from the members from the very beginning. Having low capital, a cooperative cannot make a good start. So, the cooperative must admit more members and in due course the existing value of shares can be raised. Even the individual maximum share holding can be raised to a particular level. Only by means of having strong share capital base, a cooperative can raise borrowed funds in the open market. A strong capital base will be guarantee for the lending institutions of a cooperative.

4. ***Multipurpose activities:*** A primary cooperative must ultimately undertake multipurpose activities for the members. But at the beginning a cooperative should not immediately go for undertaking various multipurpose activities. It has to add business activities once in every year or once in two years. Only by means of stabilizing the existing business, a cooperative can go for new service and supply functions.

5. ***Unanimous elections:*** Cooperative democracy denotes the conduct of elections freely, frankly using the principle one man, one vote. During the initial years, it is better to select the board members and leaders unanimously. If elections are held, there will be a division among the members, which may perpetuate in future also. Any divisions of membership at the beginning may create lot of problems for the future functioning of a cooperative.

6. ***Avoid failures:*** A cooperative should take steps to avoid failures from the very beginning. Proper planning of activities is necessary. A cooperative must undertake feasibility studies, market surveys, and business plans to make their operations successful. Rochdale Pioneers

made their consumer cooperatives successful by means of learning lot of lessons from the previous failures of consumer cooperatives. Hence, a new cooperative must look into the causes for previous failures and they must take steps to avoid such failure reasons.

7. ***Don't allow vested interest:*** Vested interest means, selfish interest. In a cooperative, a member or a leader must work for all the members. Members who are having selfish interest should not be selected as leaders of cooperatives. Vested interest may lead to corruption, malpractice, and enjoying the service of cooperative by a few.

8. ***Outside finance:*** While mobilizing the resources, the cooperatives must as far as possible, raise resource from the members and the depositors. Outside borrowings from commercial banks and other agencies will be very costly and a cooperative must try to avoid outside borrowings. If outside borrowing is cheaper, then they can go for such borrowings. For example, sometimes borrowings from government will be cheaper, on such occasions such borrowings can be entertained.

9. ***Cost-effective service:*** Cooperatives must provide service at a lower cost. Otherwise, they cannot get the continued loyalty of the members. The cost of operations of the cooperative must be kept lower by means of efficient services. If the cost of service is higher, steps must be taken to reduce them.

10. ***Remunerative price:*** A cooperative must charge lower price for the inputs supplied to the members and must provide a higher price to the produces or articles sold by the members. Then only they can get the continued patronage from the members. To provide a higher price, a cooperative must go for bulk purchase and purchase by central cooperative agencies.

11. ***Enlightened staff:*** While recruiting the manager and other staff, a cooperative must be careful. They must be experienced and have adequate knowledge about the business activities of the cooperative. They should have the hard work mentality and a mentality to do service to the members. For this purpose, the employees must be paid a reasonable salary and welfare services. On no account a discouraging working condition for the staff members should prevail in a cooperative. Otherwise, the workers in cooperatives will move out of the cooperative and the job turnover rate will be high.

12. ***Training:*** Many cooperative are not worried about training to the members, leaders, and employees. Money spent on training to the above people is an investment and a cooperative should have broad mind to depute people for various types of training and exposure visits. By means of undergoing various training and exposure visits to other cooperatives,

people will become familiar with problem solving mechanism. Training will provide new input for the effective functioning of a cooperative.

13. *Loyalty of the members:* Loyalty of the members denotes the continued patronage of the members to their cooperative in the form of providing more share capital, keeping their deposits with the cooperative and by selling their produces through the cooperatives. This is quite applicable in the case of processing cooperatives. Processing cooperative like the sugar cooperatives, cooperative spinning mills, fruit and vegetable processing cooperatives, etc face problems of raw material shortage due to disloyalty of the members. The private sector will be careful to undermine the importance of cooperatives by providing a higher price for a shorter period. The members should show their loyalty by supplying the raw materials continuously, even during the times of crisis.

Self-learning Activity

Try to answer the following questions on your own.

1. Write about do's regarding competitive and marketing strategy?
2. What do understand by vested interest?

Summary

- While organizing and developing cooperatives certain measures must be taken care and certain steps must be avoided, which are discussed as do's and don'ts of organizing cooperatives.

10 Past Experiences in Organizing Cooperatives in Ethiopia

Traditional Cooperatives

Traditional cooperatives are established to provide help or assistance in regard to scarce resources supply such as labour, which are very difficult for an individual to obtain them within a short period of time without external cooperation. On top of this, such types of cooperation are a means for sufficient resource use, namely timely ploughing, weeding, harvesting or building of houses, fence, streets and bridges.

Equib

Equib is a self-help traditional form of saving (credit) cooperative of individuals practiced in both the urban and the rural areas of the country. It is a voluntarily organized money saving cooperation, where each week or month, members get together; collect a fixed amount of money (agreed upon) from each member and hand over the money to a member waiting for his turn. The collected money goes to each member in rotation to serve a defined purpose—such as for the construction of a house, the purchase of a household furniture, clothing, investment on income generating ventures—trade or to meet any other financial obligations.

Eddir

Eddir is properly applied to local associations whose primary, and usually only function is to provide assistance in time of death, but now-a-days it also includes participation in wedding ceremonies of the member.

Eddir associations in larger towns are organized in neighbourhood basis, while in smaller towns and villages this need not be a factor. Within a given area people will join a particular eddir for a variety of reasons. As noted by Markakis (1974), although eddirs in towns are not ethically segregated, most people prefer to join one that includes a fair number of people from their own ethnic group. Given the religious aspect of the ceremonial functions of this kind of associations, Christians and Muslims have separate eddir associations.

In a few years, the neighbourhood-oriented eddirs have begun to broaden their scope to include matters of general interest to the locality. The status of the new eddir includes general community welfare among their objectives.

Mahiber and Senbete

Mahiber and senbete are found both in urban and rural areas. The membership of the mahiber meets in periodic feast held at each member's house successively. Whereas in the case of senbete members prepare food and local drinks and fetch to the church where members get together every Sundays. The feast takes place in the church compound. As stated by Markakis (1974), while normally membership tends to ethnically homogeneous, it is not unusual to include friends and co-workers who belong to different ethic groups, provided of course they are Christians. This traditional form of organization is established not only for feast purposes but for mutual assistance in time of death and happiness.

Meredaja Mahiber

It is a self-help development association that bears the name of a particular area, region or ethnic group whose development they seek to foster. Their membership is drawn from among the residents who belong to that particular ethnic group or originally came from that particular region.

We can see that there are many different types of traditional social cooperation among the Ethiopian people for various economic and social reasons. Thus the Ethiopian population has got a long standing and experience in pooling resources and working together for mutual benefit.

Modern Cooperative Movement in Ethiopia

History of cooperative movement in Ethiopia shows that cooperatives play an important role in the country's economic development. Even though this is what have movement of cooperatives. This was mainly due to different socio-economic policy of the country followed. To fit those policies different cooperative legislations were enacted. The first decree No. 44/1960 has declared the conditions to form the farm workers cooperatives.

Under this proclamation cooperatives were organized for the following objectives:

(*a*) arrange for cooperative production, processing transportation and marketing of agricultural products;

(*b*) operate and administer livestock and agricultural and other machinery owned by the cooperative for the benefit of its members;

(*c*) promote goods farming and agricultural practices;

(*d*) promote cooperation among members of the cooperative;

(*e*) promote cooperation among cooperatives generally by the pooling of common resources and the taking of other action to this end.

In 1966 the decree of 1960 was replaced by cooperative society proclamation No. 241 of 1966. The main objective of this proclamation was improving the standard of living of the farmers, better business performance and improved methods of production. By:

(*a*) Reducing cost of credit;

(*b*) Reducing the cost of goods and services for production and consumption;

(*c*) Minimizing and reducing the impacts of risks and uncertainties;

(*d*) Spreading knowledge of practical technical improvements;

(*e*) May otherwise contribute to achieve the above-mentioned objectives.

In actual sense the formulation of this proclamation has benefited wealthy commercial farmers.

This proclamation has led to the organization of different types of cooperatives such as:

- Multipurpose and farm cooperatives;
- Thrift and credit cooperatives;
- Handicrafts and small scale industry cooperatives;
- Consumer cooperatives; and
- Other forms of cooperatives.

Modern cooperative movement has started at the beginning of 1960s. During this period emphasis has been placed on the need to establish multi-purpose agricultural cooperatives as a major means of:

- providing rural credit;
- storing and marketing farmers' crops;
- providing goods and services for production and consumption; and
- promoting savings.

The Ministry of National Community Development and Social Affairs was responsible for the organization and development of cooperatives through its Cooperative Department. In 1960, the cooperative movement was started by the enactment of the 'Farm Workers' Cooperative Decree' to promote the establishment of modern cooperative institution for farm workers.

However, this decree was limited in scope only to farm workers. Thus, later it was considered desirable to broaden the scope for cooperative development beyond farm workers; and a new legislation was issued in 1966. This legislation was called the 'Cooperative Societies Proclamation'. While the new law and regulations may help to expand the cooperative movement, the establishment of agricultural cooperative has been slow and restricted to cash crops growing areas such as Sidamo, Kaffa (including Jimma and Agaro) and Wolloga. This was mainly geared towards earning cash and foreign currency.

In general the history of cooperative movement in Ethiopia goes back to the history of 1960 when the first indication of the movement was carried in the 2nd five years development plan (1960/64—1967/68).

Lots of efforts were made to establish and develop cooperatives of various types in the 2nd and 3rd five years development plans. The plans visualize a comprehensive use of different forms of cooperatives with the objectives of:

(*a*) increase in productivity of different resources;

(*b*) raising the saving potential from part of individuals income for the purpose of expanding investment and consequently production and income of the members;

(*c*) improvement of the living conditions of the members through realized income from members production;

(*d*) expand and provide social services such as health, education, and pure water supply to the members;

(*e*) protect the right of all citizens and have equal opportunity of contributing to the economic and social progress.

In the establishment, development and expansion of cooperatives was given due emphasis to both urban and rural (agricultural) areas. In the urban areas, more emphasis was given to the saving, credit, handcrafts and consumers cooperatives.

In the plan, it was also stressed that successful implementation of the cooperative program was to be assisted by the government. The assistance was also to include the set up of a legal framework to provide fund for training of cooperative supervisors, field workers, or organizers and members. Arrangements were made to provide productive credit facilities and other supportive measures.

The target of the effort was to establish and make a self-reliant of at least twenty cooperatives of different types and carry out all the preparatory works on the basis of the experience gained from the next five-year plan period.

The third Five-Year Development Plan (1968 - 1973) tried to continue emphasis on the role of cooperative as the best way of mobilizing the latent organizations and use the under utilized resources such as land and labour. The attention given to agricultural cooperatives was much higher than the other sectors with an overall aim of increasing the capacity of the farmers and the artisan people in cottage and small scale industries.

By the, an ambitious and exaggerated target of no practical ground was laid down to establish about 300 different types of cooperatives in the country. To achieve the target laid down, various arrangements were made including the following:

(*a*) Establishment of national cooperative board consisting of concerned organizations in the expansion of cooperative advice on future course of cooperative development in different parts of the country.

(*b*) Establishment and development of cooperative training centers where organizers, managers, members, supervisors, etc are trained on how to deal with cooperative establishment or organization and further development.

After the arrangement of the above prerequisites, hopes were placed to mobilize and pool quite good sum of money from the contribution of the members.

In 1978 the proclamation of 1966 was replaced by cooperative societies proclamation No. 138/1978. Under this proclamation cooperatives were organized for the following objectives:

(*a*) to develop self-reliance and to promote interest of their members;

(*b*) to put the means of production under the control of cooperatives and to transform them gradually to collective property as may be necessary;

(*c*) to increase production;

(*d*) to expand industries;

(*e*) to conduct political agitation;

(*f*) to eliminate reactionary culture and customs;

(*g*) to participate inn the building up of a socialist economy;

(*h*) to accumulate capital and to mobilize human resources to sustain economic development.

This proclamation was enacted on the ground of socialist ideology and centralized economic planning system. This has led to the complete collapse of the previous cooperatives.

Cooperatives organized as a result of this proclamation were:

- Producer cooperatives
- Service cooperatives
- Thrift and credit cooperatives
- Housing cooperatives

The proclamation of the edict entitled, Public Ownership of Rural Lands, completely abolished private ownership of land and made "... all rural lands...the collective property of the Ethiopian people". The preamble of this Proclamation, No. 31 of 1975, has this to say:

> *... in countries like Ethiopia where the economy is agricultural a person's right, honour, status and standard of living is determined by this relation to the land... (and) several thousand gashas* of land have been grabbed from the masses by an insignificant number of feudal lords and their families as a result of which the Ethiopian masses have been forced to live under conditions of serfdom; ... it is essential to fundamentally alter the existing agrarian relations so that the Ethiopian peasant masses... may be liberated from the age old feudal oppression, injustice, poverty and disease, and in order to lay the basis upon which all Ethiopians may hence forth live in equality, freedom and fraternity ... the development of Ethiopia of the future can be assured only by instituting basic change in agrarian relations, which would lay the basis upon which, through work by cooperation, the development of one becomes the development of all...*
>
> (Proclamation 31 of 1975, p. 93)

The proclamation had 6 chapters and 33 Articles, with Chapter 3 devoted to the creation of institutions, i.e. the "Establishment of Associations for the Implementation of the Proclamation". Article 8 of the Proclamation states that "to carry out the provisions of this Proclamation a peasant association shall be formed ... within a minimum area of 800 hectares". It was in this article that the idea of organizing marketing and credit cooperatives was mentioned for the first time as one of the objectives of the peasant associations.

According to 1985/86 report of the Ministry of Agriculture (MOA), the total number of Peasant Associations (PAs) in Ethiopia by the end of June 1985 was 20,157 with a total membership of 5,594,018 households. Considering 4.4 people as the average size of households in the rural areas, the PAs contain 66 per cent of the total rural Ethiopian population using the 1984 census. This grassroots peasant institution has become the basis for creating the various types of rural cooperative organizations.

---

* gasha = 40 hectares

As part of the process of implementing land reform and organizing the peasantry, Proclamation No. 71 of 1975, a "Proclamation of provide for the Organization and Consolidation of Peasant Associations", was declared eight months after the Land Reform Act. This proclamation found it necessary, among other things:

> *... to organize and develop cooperatives in all places and at all levels in order to lay down the foundation for socialist agriculture so that the peasantry may benefit from joint labour;... to give legal personality to peasant associations;... and to define by proclamations and regulations to powers and duties of judicial tribunals, cooperative societies, women's associations and the like;*
>
> (Proclamation 71 of 1975, p. 107)

It was in this proclamation that the roles of cooperatives as the basis for socialist agriculture were strongly emphasized.

Moreover, this proclamation for the first time introduced the two types of cooperative societies, the Agricultural Service Cooperative, and the Agricultural Producers Cooperative Societies. It also outlined the organization, membership, objectives, powers and duties of the two types of cooperatives.

Agricultural Service Cooperatives

Regarding the Agricultural Service Cooperative Societies, "not less than three and not more than ten peasant associations may form a service cooperative society ... which will be supervised by the district peasant association".

Among the objectives, powers and duties of Service Cooperatives are the following:

1. to procure crop expansion services;
2. to market the produce of members at fair prices;
3. to give loans at fair interest rates;
4. to supply consumer goods to the members according to their needs;
5. to give an education in socialist philosophy and cooperative work in order to enhance the political consciousness of the peasantry;
6. to provide political education, with a view to establish agricultural producers cooperative societies by forming, promoting and consolidating mutual aid teams ... (Proclamation 71 of 1975, p. 109).

An elaborated proclamation was later declared concerning cooperative societies. This was Proclamation No. 168 of 1978 "A proclamation to provide for the Establishment of Cooperative Societies".

All types of cooperatives need to be registered if they are to have legal protection. These cooperatives are registered with, and supervised by, different institutions of the state: the agricultural service and producers cooperatives under the Ministry of Agriculture; the artisans' service and producers' cooperatives under the Handicrafts and Small-scale Industries Development and Housing; thrift and credit societies under the National Bank of Ethiopia. The broad guide-lines in each of these cooperatives and the manner in which the surplus is appropriated for reserve and other funds are left to the respective societies.

The agricultural service cooperatives have increased in size during the last ten years. According to a report of the Ministry of Agriculture (MoA), in 1985 there were a total of 3964 service cooperatives, which embraced 394 (or 84 per cent) Peasant Associations.

These service cooperatives encompass 4.6 million peasant households or 82 per cent of the total households that are members of peasant associations.

The service cooperatives are registered with the MoA if the cooperatives have shown managerial competence, developed an accounting system and provided satisfactory services to the rural community. Registration gives them the status of a legal entity, which will help them so secure loans and credits from banks and agricultural credit agencies. By the end of June 1985, there were a total of 1190 registered service cooperative societies. This was 30 per cent of the existing service cooperatives in the country.

The procurement of consumer goods for the rural population is one of many functions of the service cooperatives. In the fiscal year ending June 1985, the service cooperatives distributed consumer goods worth Birr 77, 370,758*; however, this was 31 per cent less than in 1984. Regarding the marketing of produce from the member peasant associations, the service cooperatives sold 815,806 quintals of grains and 88,098 quintals of washed coffee to the state-owned Agricultural Marketing Corporation (AMC). Although lower than the amount sold in 1984, the service cooperatives controlled 71 per cent of the total grains marketed to the Agricultural Marketing Corporation. The 1985 reductions in the supply of consumer goods and the amount of grains sold to AMC have been attributed to the lack of foreign exchange and to the fall in the productivity of the agricultural sector.

Agricultural Producers Cooperatives

A comprehensive policy edict about producers' cooperatives was issued by the Provisional Military Administrative Council (PMAC) in June 1979. Prior to issuing this policy edict, attempts were made, first in 1975 and later

* Birr 2.07 = US$ 1

in 1978, to define the objectives, powers and duties of the agricultural producers' cooperatives. the June 1979 Edict is different from its predecessors in that it lays out in detail the development of cooperatives, the use of the means of production, membership, organizational structures and guidance, planning, manpower allocation, villagization in the cooperatives, relations between producers cooperatives and mass organizations, and the support they get from the government.

The national agricultural producers cooperative policy defines a producer cooperative (PC) as an economic organization whereby individual peasant proprietors willingly combine their means of production, in part or in whole, under one economic management and into collective ownership. The objectives of the PC are the following:

(i) to bring to an end to capitalist exploitation and to see that it is not reinstated in the rural areas, and to do away with the exploitation of man by man;

(ii) the use of modern agricultural technology to transform fragmented and small-sized farms to large-scale farming and to develop small-scale industry;

(iii) by creating socialism in the rural areas, to safeguard the political, economic and social rights of the peasantry;

(iv) to prepare the ground for national planning.

A producer cooperative can be established by a minimum of three people who have willingly agreed to give their (oxen) implements of production into collective ownership and who, at the same time, have understood the benefits of a cooperative. Such cooperatives can be registered and attain legal rights if they have a membership of at least 30 peasant households.

Membership is open to all members of peasant association and to the members of their families, both male and female above the age of 18. People outside of a peasant association can apply for membership if they are unemployed and if their living conditions are poor. They can become members if they are approved by the general assembly. Dismissal from membership is decided by the same body.

The degree of the development of a PC is measured by the extent to which the means of production in the cooperatives have been collectivized. Accordingly, there are three developmental stages of producers' cooperative organizations, namely: the primary level of the Producers Cooperative, the *Melba**; the secondary level of the Producers' Cooperative, the *Welba**; the *Weland** is the Advance level of the Producers' Cooperatives, resulting from an amalgamation of *Welbas*. Each Welba becomes a Habre or a production brigade of a *Weland*.

In the *Malba* stage, each member retains 2000 sq.m. for private use but combines the rest of his holdings with those of other cooperative members. Draught animals used in the production process, e.g., oxen for ploughing, donkeys for transportation, etc, are still under private ownership. However, they can be used by the PC and the rental cost for the use of the animals is paid to the owner by the cooperative. The main objective of the first stage of PC, as the policy states, is not to realize "from each according to his ability to each according to his work", but to transform the means of production from private ownership, i.e., ownership by the members of the producer cooperative.

The *Welba* stage is the one into which the *Malba* transform itself. There are many forms and paths of transformation to the *Welba* stage, one of which is if members of a peasant association decide to create the secondary stage of a PC; they can do so without forming the first stage of the PC. In the *Welba* stage all the means of production, including the draught animals, which were under private ownership become the property of all the members of the PC. The individual member's household retains 1000 sq.m. for gardening and private use. Here, all the means of production have become *Ye Wel Nibret*, implying that the property of the collective and the socialist principle "from each according to his ability to each according to his work" has been realized.

The Welbas reach a certain level of development where their production is high and they begin to specialize and use higher level technology, then a merger can take place between the Welbas. The level of the PC organization that is created by the amalgamation of the two or more Welbas is referred to as the Weland.

Organizational Structure and Decision Making

The main organs of a PC are: the General Assembly, the Executive Committee, and the Inspections and Control, and Development Committees.

The General Assembly meets at least twice a year and decides the important issues of the PC. Among its functions, the General Assembly:

(i) drafts and amends the guiding principles and regulations of PC;

(ii) elects and dismisses the Executive, the Inspections and Control Committees, the Chairman, etc.;

---

* These terms are neither abbreviations nor do they have root words in any of the languages spoken in Ethiopia. Most likely they are coined from the *Amharic* words and phrases related to cooperative work and ideas. *Manlba* is coined from *Ye Mehiberna Ye Gil*, to mean owned privately and by cooperative; *Welba* coined from *Ye Wel*, to mean belonging to collective; *Weland* coined from *Ye Welbawoch Andenet* to mean the amalgamation of *Webas*-commune.

(*iii*) accepts new members and dismisses those not worthy of being cooperative members;

(*iv*) approves the budget and production targets that have been presented by the Executive Committee;

(*v*) determines the division of labor and the points system in the cooperative;

(*vi*) determines the amount of money that is to be reserved as a collective fund, etc.

In any PC, after all payments have been made to the members, the net income of the cooperative distributed in the following way: 60 per cent for investment, 13 per cent for social welfare, 2 per cent for prize awards (incentives) and 25 per cent for contingencies.

Members of the Executive Committee will spend 75 per cent of their time in the same kind of production as any other member of the cooperative, and only 25 per cent in handling administration and other tasks.

After the implementation of the 1979 National Policy of Cooperative Organization, Agricultural Coöperatives have increased in size and membership, particularly in the period between 1980/82 - 1984/85.

According to reports from the Ministry of Agriculture, the Agricultural Producers Cooperatives (APCs) by the end of June 1985 numbered 1856, of which 1255 are the Melba, primary stage, 601 are in the *Welba*, secondary stage, and none in the *Weland*, advanced stage. The number of agricultural producers' cooperatives has increased by 71 per cent compared with five years ago. Membership in the cooperatives has also reached 132,872 households. This is 3.4 times the 1980/81 producers' cooperative membership figure. Taking the Central Statistical Office data 4.4 as the average household size in rural Ethiopia, the producers' cooperatives contain 1.5 per cent of the 1984 rural Ethiopia population and 2.4 per cent of the rural population who were organized under peasant associations.

In June 1985 the Agricultural Producers' Cooperatives owned 491,324 hectares of arable land, of which 44 per cent was cultivated. The total acreage owned increased by 57 per cent and the cultivated land by 30 per cent over that of 1984. Each producer cooperative owned, on average, 264 hectares of land, of which 115 hectares was cultivated land. Each household, on average, owned 3.7 hectares of the total land and 1.6 hectares of the cultivated land.

The new market Liberalization policy launched by the government has necessitated the formulation of new cooperative legislation. This was agricultural cooperative societies proclamation No. 85/1995.

(*a*) To improve the living condition of members by increasing production and productivity;

(*b*) To promote self-reliance among members;

(*c*) To solve problems collectively which a peasant cannot personally achieve;

(*d*) To make members obtain modern technologies products which are capable to increase agricultural production and materials necessary for their livelihood easily and at fair price;

(*e*) To satisfy the needs of a community and increase the income of a peasant by processing agricultural products.

(*f*) To promote the cultures of the members by teaching and training.

The above proclamation was replaced by the Cooperative Proclamation No. 147/1998. The detailed provisions of this proclamation have been discussed elaborately in Module one.

Cooperative movement has crossed 160 years of service to the society. In European countries it did service for more than a century. In Asian, African and South American countries cooperatives did service for more than a century. The cooperative started in European countries succeeded due to the economic and social factors like high rate of literacy, leadership, conducive industrial atmosphere, etc. On the other hand in the developing countries of Asia, Africa and South America, in many countries cooperatives faced failure or the expected growth of cooperatives was not attained.

Causes for Failure of Cooperatives in African Countries

According to Manzi Bakaramutsa of Zaire (1982), causes for failure of cooperatives in African countries are as follows — their origins under colonial rule as agencies of cash crop production for export, their continuation under bureaucratic control after independence, the incorporation and actual exploitation of cooperatives by state and parastatal enterprises. But to these he adds some secondary causes of failure, which will need to be noted if independent cooperative associations are to be successfully revived. These include misappropriation of funds, where clan pressure no longer operates, inadequate accounting systems, lack of training and even illiteracy among cooperative members, which leads them to hand over responsibility to managers without democratic accountability.

According to World Bank Report (World Bank Discussion Paper Number 121, 1994) the causes for failure of cooperatives in Sub-Saharan Africa were as follows — high operative costs, low margins, low turnovers, narrow inventory stocks, fluctuating seasonal demand and trading patterns, and weak infrastructure. In many instances, private entrepreneurs have not found it profitable to break into these markets, yet cooperatives have been expected to succeed.

Professor Hans Munkner, the famous cooperator, has pointed out the causes for failure of cooperatives as follows:

1. Cooperatives were created on a large scale without much preparation, by offering short-term incentives, e.g. access to loans in cash or in kind which otherwise would not be available.
2. In some countries administrative and political pressure was used to impose a model of cooperation on peasants, by creating monopolies for the supply of inputs and the marketing of produce or by making membership compulsory. In all these cases, the intention of the promoters of cooperatives focussed on priorities of national development rather than on the interests of the individual members.
3. Cooperatives were conceived primarily as instruments of government for carrying out plans made by Government officials, financed with government funds and accordingly government controlled. The citizens called upon to cooperative (mainly peasant farmers) were seen as persons who were unable to organize themselves without guidance, outside assistance, supervision and control.
4. The models of organization were (and still are) predetermined in almost every detail (e.g. model by-laws are prescribed from which people are not supposed to deviate), government intervention and government control left (and still leaves) no room and no incentive for active participation by cooperative members. But there is also little reason why members should actively participate in such cooperatives.
5. (*a*) Their share contribution and liability (if any) are usually purely nominal, so that members do not have to commit themselves and thus have no stake in the cooperative.

   (*b*) Often the rules according to which 'their' cooperatives are operating are not known to them (e.g. by-laws available only in the official language, which they cannot read and understand; by-laws containing complicated procedures which are different from their rules and values). As a result, there is no member control over office-bearers and employees of cooperatives, many of whom are elected, appointed or seconded from government staff in undemocratic ways.

   (*c*) Control exercised by government officers is usually ineffective either because it does not reach the societies due to lack of qualified staff or due to lack of transport, or it does not curb malpractices because of powerful vested interests, and government officers teaming up with influential leaders for their own benefit.

(*d*) Income that could be earned by cooperatives is either siphoned off by high prices for inputs and low prices for produce, by embezzlement and corrupt practices, which go undetected or unpunished, or remain low because of losses due to lack of storage facilities, transport or capacity for processing. Under such conditions it is not surprising that persons refuse to join cooperatives or if compelled to join, show little interest in actively participating in their affairs. Such 'Cooperatives' deserve the bad reputation that they have earned themselves.

6. In all countries of Africa self-help activities have found other venues for organization such as traditional rotating savings and credit associations (ROSCAs) adapting themselves to the conditions of a money economy, mutual aid working groups of young people (e.g. Nnoboa in Ghana, Nam in Burkina Faso), young farmers' clubs, saving clubs, informal village groups, women's groups, for production and processing of food crops and handicrafts.

Causes for the Failure of Cooperatives during Imperial Period (1960-1974) and during Derg Period (1974-1991)

Causes for the failure of Cooperatives during the Imperial Period

The first cooperative society in Ethiopia was started during the Imperial Period in 1960. Efforts were taken to introduce and strengthen cooperatives during the planning period. The stipulated target to establish three hundred and twenty cooperatives during the second (1963/64 - 1967/68) and the third five-year development plan (1968-73) were not achieved. Only 112 different types of cooperatives were organized and registered up to the end of the third-five year development plan. Among the total number of cooperatives organized, 76 were farmers' cooperatives; while the rest consist of different sectors mainly handcrafts and marketing cooperatives.

Even though, various efforts were made the goals were not that much realized as anticipated. Several factors are accounted for the failure, including:

1. Oppressive land tenure system and domination in the agricultural sector. To be successful in farming, a cooperative should be established by farmers who own resources of which land is the major factor of production in agriculture. By then majority of farmers were tenants or share croppers. This enabled the rich and affluent farmers and landlords to play a leading role in the establishment of cooperatives to adjust the conditions to their own benefit. The have-nots were thus, pushed away to the corner of poverty line and were demoralized to participate in cooperative development.

2. Inadequate trained manpower to propagate the idea on how to organize and manage cooperatives.
3. Inadequate budgetary allocation for the purpose of promoting of cooperatives which reflects poor interest of the government to the expansion of cooperatives. On top of this, the bank credit and collateral policy was not convenient for the poor farmers to get credit for cooperative and farm development. Actually, the farmers as such did not have access to bank credit. Subsistence and traditional forms of production with no surplus production for the formation of reserve capital was thus, among the farmers' problems of the time to limit the expansion of cooperation throughout the country.
4. Lack of efficient marketing system:
    - Low price of farm products;
    - High price of inputs;
    - Inadequate transport services.

Though, there were many convenient situation for organization, development and further expansion of cooperatives in Ethiopia (such as land reform and establishment of Peasant Association—as training school for collective work), there were various problems that contributed for the failure of cooperative movement, including:

1. Distorted training system of manpower

   Cooperative organizers were trained in socialist political ideology than in cooperative discipline who were known as 'production and political cadres'.
2. Lack of coordination between cooperative principles and state policy

   Cooperative principles clearly show ways and of means of organization cooperatives, the place and time of organizing cooperatives, the pre-requisites of organizing cooperatives.

   Whereas,

   (*a*) ambitious cooperative organizers (government agents), neglected pre-requisites and jump to higher forms of cooperatives (e.g. from Malba to a complete collective form of Wolba), step-by-step and gradual development of cooperatives (elementary and simple forms of cooperatives could have been used to introduce and show advantages of cooperative work and train collective work);

   (*b*) neglecting of cooperative principles especially voluntariness (free will), conviction of membership, rather used forced cooperativization method, especially following a quota system in different peasant associations and woredas.

(*c*) Interference of the government in production and marketing of agricultural outputs of the cooperative members.

Instead of following a competitive marketing system, the government used a complete centrally controlled marketing.

For example, the government used to fix prices of agricultural outputs of cooperative members.

The observed consequences were:

- Low supply of goods and services by suppliers;
- High demand of goods and services;
- Black markets (and skyrocketing prices);
- Quota system of supply; and
- Food/goods rationing.

This action has demoralized the farmers and they considered that a cooperative to be the most hated agency serving the government.

However, prices are not of stimulating factors of production, but in the case of Ethiopian cooperatives, prices were highly demoralizing and frustrating. Because the government fixes prices of farm products without considering cost of production and imposes quota system of supply.

For example:

- The Agricultural Marketing Corporation (AMC) used to buy food crops at low prices and farmers were obliged to give their quota and this also was in initiation of black markets.
- The Ethiopian Coffee Marketing Corporation (ECMC) used to buy coffee from the farmers on quota basis at low prices. Thus, farmers in some regions (such as Hararghe) replaced their coffee farms by chat an food crops.

3. Credit availability

   Credit was not available at the desired time and place for all cooperatives. Only very few favoured cooperatives with legal status could get credit.

4. Poor record-keeping

   Even if there were some formats prepared by the Ministry of Agriculture, they were too complex and inappropriate to the farmers. For others credit was not accessible and the interest rate was incompatible with their level of income generation.

5. Premature start of cooperatives

Cooperatives usually started before studying their feasibility in the community (see the methods of organizing a cooperative)

6. Inadequate member support

   This problem stems from:

   - Poor communications on a cooperative as a whole;
   - Poor business performance;
   - Lack of members' appreciation of what they can and cannot expected the cooperative to accomplish.

7. Cooperatives were frequently imposed from above

   Even where and when the rural population has no idea as to what a cooperative is and has no interest in cooperatives, the government used to force farmers and other producers to establish cooperatives.

8. Cooperatives were misused by the government

   The government used cooperatives:

   - As a means of imposing or pushing forward specific policy objectives.
   - To perpetuate government control or even to extend political control to the village level.

For example:— farmers' producers' cooperatives were used as an instrument for the expansion and consolidation of socialist ideology in the farming community.

9. Cooperative were charged with inappropriate tasks, which conflict with interests of the members

   For example cooperatives were used as a means of:

   - Ideological work;
   - Forcing individuals for membership;
   - Tax collection—as an agent of the government.

10. Cooperatives take more of the character of bureaucratic governmental institutions than of organizations of/for their own members.

Thus, from this one can conclude that, cooperatives in Ethiopian were no longer pretend to be politically neutral because:

- Cooperative leaders were supporters (members) of the workers party of Ethiopia of the Derg regime and most are members of parliament;

- All important decision and actions were ordered and directed by the party and its instrument—the state;
- Cooperatives had lost their internal autonomy as well as their freedom of action;
- Cooperatives had become the obedient servants of the state.

Precautions for the Future

Suggestions for the Speedy Growth of Cooperatives in Ethiopia

During the Imperial Period the progress of the cooperatives was very slow and vast majority of the cooperative became failure due to mismanagement, corruption, poor accounting system, lack of leadership, etc.

With the political change during 1974, cooperatives were given a new shape in the form of Proclamation No. 138/1978, which replaced the proclamation of 1966. This proclamation was enacted on the ground of socialist ideology and centralized economic planning system. This has led to the complete collapse of the previous cooperatives.

Again a political change took place in the year 1991, which had its effect on cooperatives also. A new cooperative proclamation 147/1998 came into existence and all previous cooperatives legislations became null and void. Again Proclamation No. 274/2002 made provisions for the establishment of cooperative commission and to manage it a commissioner for cooperatives was created. But under the new democratic setup the cooperatives could not achieve the things expected from them. Certain amendments were made to the Cooperative Societies Proclamation No. 147/1998 by Cooperative Societies (Amendments) Proclamation No. 402/2004. Compared to other neighbouring countries like Kenya, Tanzania, and Nigeria, the cooperatives in Ethiopia were moving very slow and stagnation exists at present. To revitalize the cooperatives and the cooperative movement, the following suggestions are offered:

1. ***Organization of cooperative banking structure:*** Ethiopia lacks a prominent cooperative banking structure with tier systems, which is very popular in other countries. Only with a strong cooperative banking structure, the cooperative movement can raise resources of its own and be self-reliant in resources in order to protect the cooperative democracy intact. Cooperative banking should be organized from primary level (kebele level), zonal level, regional level, and at national level. At present in regions of Oromiya and Amhara, Regional Cooperative Banks have been established with branches since 2004. But these banks are not pure cooperatives but they are registered as share companies. Without the permission of the cooperative bureau or the cooperative commission

the word '*Cooperatives*' should not be allowed to be used. Further, there is an immediate need in Ethiopia to institute a *National Cooperative Bank of Ethiopia*. Such bank can be floated directly by the cooperative commission or by the existing cooperatives around Ethiopia. This national cooperative bank can mobilize resources and inculcate banking habits in rural areas by means of opening branches throughout the country. It can also play a balancing function role to other cooperative banks and can guide the activities of all other existing and future cooperative banks in Ethiopia. Moreover, the national cooperative bank can act as a spokesman for the cooperatives in Ethiopia and can create link with international organizations like ICA (International Cooperative Alliance), ILO, FAO, etc.

2. ***Creation of separate Ministry of Cooperation:*** Ethiopia is one of the few countries where there is no separate department for cooperatives. At present the subject cooperation comes under the jurisdiction of the Ministry of Agricultural and Rural Development. In order to give special attention to the growth of the cooperatives (which can provide employment opportunity to vast number of educated youth) a separate ministry for cooperation must be created and a senior and experienced politician must be appointed as the Minister for Cooperation. With the creation of separate ministry of cooperation, lot of funds available with foreign cooperatives and international cooperative agencies can be brought to Ethiopia. Like the federal government the regional governments must also create separate Regional Bureaus.

3. ***Arrangement for cooperative education and training:*** In the cooperative proclamation of 1998, provisions have been made to organize separate structure for cooperative education and training. Again only in Ethiopia at the national level or at regional levels a separate agency is lacking for the provision of cooperative education and training. Only by means of creating a strong cooperative education and training structure, the employees can be given continuous training and the cooperative members can be given training in leadership, management, etc. At present, four educational centers of Ambo College, Ambo; Debub University, Alemaya University, and Mekele University offer degree programmes in cooperation by means of creating a separate department for cooperatives. As a transitional arrangement the existing four departments can undertake the training of cooperative employees also by means of creating separate wing for cooperative training. At the national level a separate training institute must be organized immediately. In this respect, the help of the International Cooperative Alliance's, Regional Office for East and South Africa located at Nairobi can be resorted.

4. *Increase in Agricultural Prosperity:* As Ethiopia is a major agricultural country; the prosperity of the country depends on the prosperity of agriculture. It is a country, which grows specialized crops like coffee and has enormous potential for the future growth of agriculture. But due to lack of irrigation facilities, land ownership rights, marketing problems, etc the country is yet to move towards self-reliance in food grains. Food security and agricultural prosperity can give a guarantee for the organized growth of cooperatives. On the other hand, cooperatives can make agriculture prosperous, as has been shown in other developing countries.

5. *Participation of Women in Cooperatives:* For the future growth of cooperatives in Ethiopia, the participation of women is very much needed. Women forming part of half of the population, has been very much neglected in the membership of cooperatives, leadership and management of cooperatives in Ethiopia. There is an immediate need to promote the women membership in cooperatives and to encourage and motivate their participation in the cooperatives. Special types of cooperatives like cooperative banks, consumer cooperatives, dairy cooperatives, etc can be exclusively organized for women to improve their role and employment opportunity.

6. *Revising the Cooperative Proclamation:* In all countries where cooperatives are fast developing, the respective cooperative legislations have been revised from time to time in order to incorporate the latest trends that are taking place in the cooperative movement. The Cooperative Proclamation of Ethiopia must also be revised from time to time in order to suit the changing needs of the cooperative movement. This also warrants a need to have a separate Ministry of Cooperation at the federal government level.

7. *Coordination with International Cooperative Agencies:* International cooperative agencies like International Cooperative Alliance (Headquarters Geneva, Regional Office Nairobi), ILO, FAO, other countries national level cooperatives are offering unlimited funds and exchange programs for employees. Unfortunately, these facilities from international cooperative agencies have not been used by Ethiopian cooperatives at present. This was due to a lack of spokesman for the cooperatives at the national level and lack of a separate ministry of cooperation. So the time has come in Ethiopia to organize national level cooperatives like National Cooperative Bank, National Cooperative Training Institute, National Federation of Consumer Cooperatives, National Federation of Dairy Cooperatives, etc.

8. ***Organization of New Cooperatives:*** At present in Ethiopia only producers' cooperatives and service cooperatives are functioning. Other types of cooperatives like marketing cooperatives, consumer cooperatives, cooperative banks, dairy cooperatives, labour cooperatives, etc are completely absent. There is an immediate need by the thinkers of cooperatives and government to start about such cooperatives to avail locally available resources, to increase the employment opportunities, to increase agricultural and dairy production, to empower the women-folk and to ameliorate the living conditions of the farmers.

9. ***Using the Words Cooperation and Cooperatives:*** The words cooperation and cooperatives denote a corporate sector called cooperative movement. In other countries strong legal measures have been taken to use above words. Without the permission of the concerned cooperative authorities like cooperative commissioner nobody should use the words cooperation and cooperatives. But in Ethiopia cooperation and cooperatives are used by all people who do not form cooperatives or come under the purview of the cooperative commission. *So, the time has come in Ethiopia to use the words cooperation and cooperatives on a restrictive manner only with the permission of the commissioner for cooperatives.* Suitable amendments to the cooperative proclamation, and even the federal constitution must be made towards this objective.

Self -learning Activity

Try to answer the following questions on your own.

1. Discuss about Eddir?
2. What are causes of failure of cooperatives in Ethiopia?
3. Can you suggest some measures to make cooperatives successful in Ethiopia?

Summary

- Ethiopian cooperative movement in terms of traditional cooperatives and modern cooperatives is discussed.
- The causes for the failure of cooperative movement in Africa and Ethiopia are given.
- Suggestions for speedy growth of cooperatives are listed.

Part—II

Promotional Roles of Agencies

11 Role of Federal and Regional Bureaus in Organizing Cooperatives

Sponsored Cooperative Agencies

The subject Cooperation is coming under the Ministry of Agriculture and Rural Development in Ethiopia. There is no separate Ministry for Cooperation. The Cooperative Agency is the policy making authority relating to the cooperatives and cooperative legal system in Ethiopia. The Cooperative Proclamation is coming under the purview of Cooperative Agency. The organizational set up of the Department of Cooperation is given below, in the order of hierarchy.

1. The Federal Cooperative Agency
2. Regional Cooperative Promotion Bureau
3. Woreda (District) Cooperative Promotion Bureau

Certain General Features

1. Cooperatives are autonomous bodies:

   Though efforts have been taken by the Government to introduce the Cooperative movement in Ethiopia, the people themselves have organized the real cooperatives voluntarily. Because during earlier periods, cooperatives initiated by the government became a failure.

2. Cooperatives can receive government help:

   Unlike other developing countries, where government assistance to cooperatives is enormous, in Ethiopia, the help rendered by the government to the cooperatives is very meager. But in future, the government may come forward to help the cooperatives on a wider scale.

3. Federal Cooperative Agency:

   In Ethiopia, the Federal Cooperative Agency, which was appointed under the Proclamation No. 274/2002, is the Supreme authority for the cooperative movement. It has greater say in organizing, guiding, and regulating the cooperative movement.

4. General Director for Cooperatives:

   He is the Supreme authority for the cooperatives and appointed by the Federal Government. He is empowered to implement the programmes of the Cooperative Agency. His post is equal to that of Registrar of Cooperative Societies in other developing countries.

5. Deputy General director and Subordinate Officials:

   The Deputy General Director and the subordinate officials who work under the General director for Cooperation form the core of the officials of the Department of Cooperation in Ethiopia. The Department is at its infant stage and is yet to expand in future.

6. Cooperatives come under the Ministry of Rural Development:

   In Ethiopia, a separate Ministry for Cooperation is yet to come. At present, cooperatives are coming under the Ministry of Rural Development. There is a need to have full-fledged Ministry of Cooperation in future.

Role of Federal Cooperative Agency

The federal cooperative agency, previously known as federal cooperative commission, is the highest body for the cooperative movement in Ethiopia. The General Director is the authority formerly known as the commissioner for cooperatives. Under him there are several other officers in different wings of administration and management like personnel office, plan and project office, internal audit, registrar, RUFIP, administration and finance service, vice-general director, cooperative promotion unit and capacity building and human power study unit.

The vision of the Federal Cooperative Agency is "to see the Ethiopian cooperative societies enhance the livelihood of the communities being self confident and sustainable socio-economic institution in the coming 20 years".

The mission is "to enable the society solve its economic and social problem by using local resources and by organizing itself on voluntary basis in terms of different type and standard of cooperatives have modern management system, promote and expand marketing, saving and credit services. Build up the professional capacity of cooperative leaders, employees and experts through creating conducive legal environment and enabling the cooperative societies to directly participate in the process of the country's development and hence improve the livelihood of the society".

Office set up of Federal Cooperative Agency

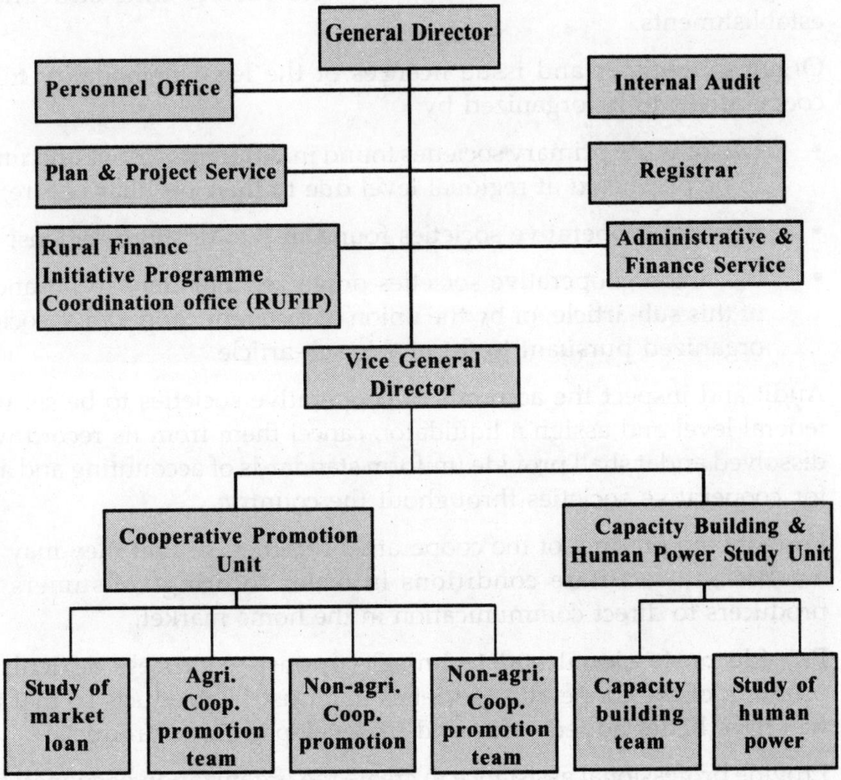

Duties and Functions

The following are the duties and responsibilities of federal cooperative agency in organizing and promoting cooperatives in the country.

(*a*) Formulate policies and prepare draft laws for the activities and development of cooperative societies and submit the same to the giovernment and follow-up their implementation;

(*b*) Encourage that the organization of cooperative societies be in accordance with the Cooperative Proclamation and in line with the International Principles of Cooperative Organisations;

(*c*) Direct and supervise cooperative training institute to be set up at the federal level;

(*d*) Undertake research and study to promote traditional and local self help associations to modern cooperative societies, it shall make known and disseminate the results of the study and follow-up the implementation thereof;

(*e*) Make that the values, principles, organization and benefits of the cooperatives be further known by the society and educational establishments;

(*f*) Organise, register and issue licences of the legal personality to, the cooperatives to be organized by:

- two or more primary societies found in different regions and unable to be organized at regional level due to their peculiar nature;
- regional cooperative societies found in two or more regions;
- the union cooperative societies organized pursuant to (a) and (b) of this sub-article, or by the union of different cooperative societies organized pursuant to (b) of this sub-article.

(*g*) Audit and inspect the accounts of cooperative societies to be set up at federal level and assign a liquidator, cancel them from its record when dissolved and it shall provide uniform standards of accounting and audit for cooperative societies throughout the country;

(*h*) Promote the product of the cooperative societies, so that they may find market and facilitate conditions in order to bring consumers and producers to direct communication in the home market;

(*i*) Provide professional and technical support to process agricultural products of the cooperative societies to industrial products so that they will have better added value and to develop artisans products;

(*j*) Provide professional assistance to create the organization of cooperatives based on the culture and experiences of pastoralists and which enables them to improve their living conditions;

(*k*) Facilitate in cooperation with regions as may be necessary, means to provide support for societies by studying and preparing projects suitable for the development of cooperative societies;

(*l*) Facilitate conditions to enable the cooperative societies in different regions to exchange their products and information about the market and to share experiences with one another;

(*m*) Provide technical and professional assistance for the bureaus and cooperative societies to be set up in the regions;

(*n*) Establish relationship with concerned local and international organizations in order to expedite the progress and the activities of the cooperative societies;

(*o*) Formulate and distribute model by laws of societies which may vary according to the type and level of societies;

(*p*) Submit reports on its performance to the concerned government organ;

(*q*) Own property, enter into contracts, sue and be sued in its own name; and

(*r*) Carry out other duties helpful for the implementation of its objectives.

Role of the General Director for Cooperatives

Being the highest authority for the Cooperatives in Ethiopia, the General director for Cooperation is expected to play a promotional and effective role in developing the cooperatives like the Registrar of Cooperatives in Developing Countries.

(*a*) He is the Chief Executive of the Agency:

The General Director for Cooperatives is the Chief Executive of the Cooperative Agency and the Federal Government appoints him.

(*b*) He discharges the duties and powers of the Co-operative Agency and works for the promotion and welfare of the cooperatives.

(*c*) He employs and administers the staff for the Cooperative Agency. In other words, he is expected to recruit staff to his Department, give them training and motivate them for the all round development of Cooperatives in Ethiopia.

(*d*) He draws up work programme and budget. Based on these, he has to implement the same in the same in the interests of the cooperatives.

(*e*) The General director for Cooperatives can effect expenditures incurred for the Cooperative Agency and on employees. This is a privilege given to the Cooperatives and an expanded scope is expected from him.

(*f*) The Cooperative General director represents the Cooperative Agency in dealing with third parties and on matters relating to the development of cooperatives. This includes in contact with the Federal Government and various Ministries of Federal Government.

(*g*) He presents reports annually and during periods required by authorities on the activities of the cooperatives and Cooperative Agency.

(*h*) The General director may delegate any of his powers to the Deputy General director and other subordinate officials. He may direct them to discharge the duties on behalf of him.

(*i*) The General director can have his own budget and the income for the Agency shall be drawn from the budget allocated by the Federal Government. He can also avail the help provided by domestic and foreign sources.

(*j*) The General director shall keep books of accounts relating to the cooperatives in Ethiopia. The Auditor-General shall audit the books of accounts or Auditors assigned by him.

Powers of the General Director for Cooperatives

The General Director for Cooperatives of Ethiopia is to implement the Cooperative Societies Proclamation No. 147/1998. His powers are specified as follows:

1. Formations and Registration of Cooperative Societies:

   Under the Cooperative Societies Proclamation No. 147/1998, the General director is empowered to register new cooperatives under Article 6. He can register societies from Primary level Federal level. (The procedure for the registration of cooperative societies is given in *Article 9*).

2. Amendment of By-laws:

   Any cooperative society can amend its by laws. The amended by law must be sent to the General Director and he may approve it under *Article 11*.

3. Amalgamation and Division of Societies:

   Any cooperative society can be amalgamated with other societies and any society can be divided. But the General Director under Article 12 must approve amalgamation and division of societies.

4. Calling the General Assembly:

   The General director for Cooperation under Article 22(3), is empowered to call the General Assembly of a society as and when he desires.

5. Audit:

The General director is expected to undertake auditing on all cooperatives under Article 36, once a year.

6. Inspection:

   The General director can undertake inspection of cooperative societies under *Article 37*. But this must be done at the request of the majority of the executive members or at the request of one-third of the members.

7. Loss of Property or Funds of Society:

   If any loss arises for any of the cooperatives, the General Director is empowered to take action on concerned people under *Article 39*.

8. Dissolution of a Society:

   When a society is dissolved, the society must inform this matter to the General Director under *Article 40*. Only after getting the approval of the General Director, such a society can be dissolved.

9. Liquidator:

   When a decision is taken to dissolve a society, the General director can appoint a liquidator under *Article 41*. The liquidator will complete the process with the knowledge of the General director.

Role of Regional Cooperative Bureaus

One of the subdivisions of the Federal Cooperative Agency is Regional Cooperative Promotion Bureau. There are fourteen regional bureaus in Ethiopia. The bureau play a key role in organizing and promoting cooperatives in the respective region. It is here that the policies are implemented and transferred downwards. The regional bureau is the link between the central agency and the cooperative societies, the organizers, promoters, auditors, and others who are engaged in the organsiation and promotion of cooperatives in the region.

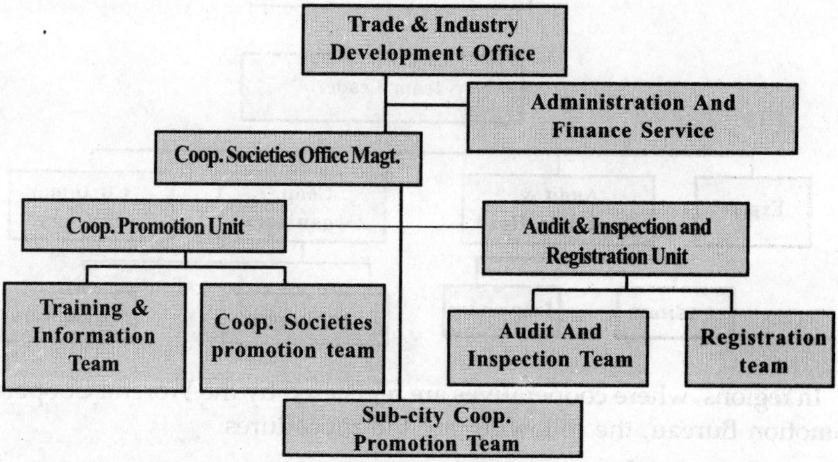

The functions of the regional cooperative promotion bureau:

1. Regional bureau through the promotion team performs duties and responsibilities in organizing and promoting the cooperatives in the region;
2. Organisation of cooperatives in the region;
3. Develop and promote cooperatives in the region;
4. Encourage the organizers and promoters to organize different types of cooperatives and promote them;
5. Registration of cooperative societies in the region;
6. The regional bureau is performing the arbitration duty;
7. Other legal formalities as specified in the Cooperative Proclamation.

Role of Woreda Cooperative Promotion Bureau

Registration of Cooperative Societies

In Ethiopia registration of cooperative societies, differs from region to region. In some regions societies are registered by the Regional Cooperative Promotion Bureau and in several regions registration is done by Woreda Cooperative Promotion Bureau.

Office set up of the Woreda (District) Cooperative Promotion Bureau

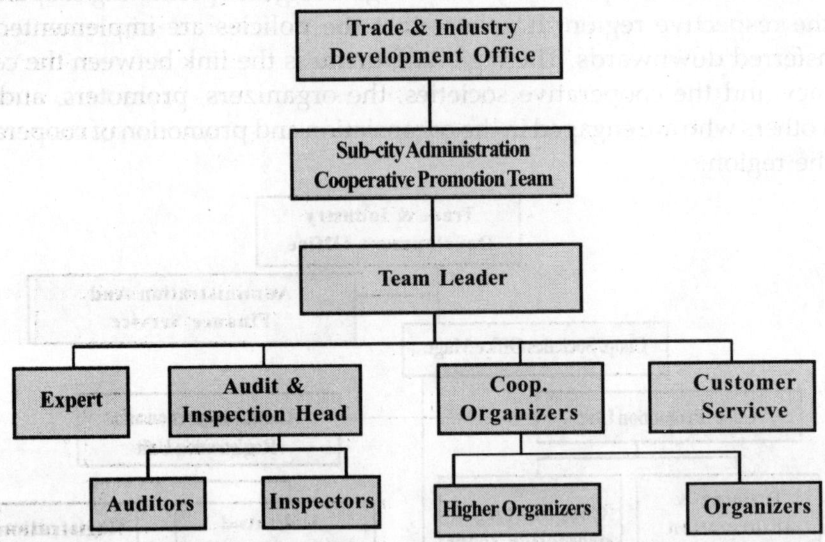

In regions, where cooperatives are registered by the Woreda Cooperative Promotion Bureau, the following are the procedures:

The Bureau has three categories of staff viz., Organisation and Promotion Experts, Market Experts and Audit and Inspection Experts. Each wing has a team leader and specified duties and responsibilities. A manager directs these wings.

Duties and responsibilities of Organisation and Promotion Team Experts

1. Helps the farmers cooperative societies in the preparation of annual plan and their functional strategy and assists in its implementation.
2. Follow-up whether basic documents of the societies are completed.
3. Provides farmers cooperative societies with professional assistance and follows their day-to-day activities.
4. Follow-up if the activities undertaken by the management committees, control committees during the movement of the societies are based on the byelaws and directives of the societies.

5. Selects farmers cooperatives and provides assistance pursuant to the criteria sent by Zonal Bureau and Woreda Bureau.
6. Conducts socio-economic research to organize new cooperatives.
7. Provides education to members and facilitates conditions to get consecutive education and information.
8. Encourages cooperative societies to conduct annual general assembly and provides important support by attending the general assembly.
9. Prepares monthly, quarterly report about the movement of societies.
10. Participates in different training, annual work plan and budget.
11. Collects the annual work plan based on the format passed on plan collection by the Zonal Promotion Bureau.
12. Undertakes other necessary activities entrusted by the manager.

Duties and Responsibilities of Market Experts Team

1. It provides professional assistance to cooperative societies to enable them to enter into the business of consumer goods, inputs and agricultural products to satisfy their members.
2. It helps societies to get loan and have insurance for their properties.
3. It ensures whether the loan need of the societies is in accordance to the operational area and size, follows the loan process and collects information regarding these activities.
4. Provides professional assistance to societies in preparation of annual work plan with marketing and loan.
5. Provides inland and international market information to cooperatives from different market sources.
6. Participate in marketing, loan and insurance research and makes supportive information for the study to be collected.
7. To provide support to societies to solve members problems, sound and reliable market and loan services and follow the implementation.
8. Facilitates conditions to promote income source of the societies and their members to get better price for their produce.
9. Coordinates the societies to utilize modern technology, quality of products and supply of such products through different markets.
10. Offers suggestions and proposals by studying the problems faced by the societies in marketing, loan and insurance.
11. Undertakes other necessary activities entrusted by the managers.

Duties and responsibilities of Audit and Inspection Team experts

1. Ensures that the accounts of these societies in the Woreda are closed monthly, prepared trial balance and whether the financial statement prepared is correct.
2. Prepares and provides training of accountants, storekeepers, control committee members of societies about book keeping and inventory management.
3. Helps cooperative societies to organize modern accounting system and provides professional support.
4. Takes part in studying modern accounting system and collects important information.
5. Formulates strategy of internal inspection system and follows up its implementation.
6. Checks whether there is cash fund loss by checking the balance sheet surprisingly.
7. Promoting accounting system by system documents, cards and records to be served as a full information source.
8. Ensures that financial statements are submitted accurately and informs the auditors to carry out inspection.
9. Inspects and checks whether the suspense documents are audited in time.
10. Ensures whether the bank accounts of the societies prepared monthly.
11. Pursues the defaults and recovers the amount due to the society.
12. Conducts checks if the societies annual proerty account is complete.
13. Follows the maintenance and keeping of the societies' fixed assets, storage and warehouse.
14. Follows up if transactions held by the societies are pursuant to the byelaws and directives.
15. It ensures whether loans given by the societies are based on the byelaws and directives and the documents under records are complete.
16. Facilitates the societies the audit and inspection reports to be submitted to the general assembly.
17. Participates in the societies' plan preparation and ascertains that the budget is maintained properly.
18. Prepares needed annual planned budget to carry out its activities.
19. Undertakes other necessary activities allowed by the manager.

Self-learning Activity

Try to answer the following questions on your own.

1. Discuss the role of regional bureau in organizing a cooperative?
2. What are the duties of promotion team experts?

Summary

- Under the new set up, a Federal Cooperative Commission was instituted with powers to organize various cooperatives and regulate the working of cooperatives. The chief of the Federal Cooperative Commission was the Cooperative Commissioner. During the year 2004, the Commission was renamed as Federal Cooperative Agency and the chief was renamed as General Director.
- In several regions the Regional Bureau has the authority to register new cooperative societies and in certain regions the Woreda Promotion Bureau has been entrusted with the powers to register new cooperative societies.
- For the future growth of the cooperatives in Ethiopia, a separate Ministry for Cooperatives must be established at the Federal and Regional levels. A strong cooperative banking structure must be developed. The movement must concentrate on training and cooperative education.

12 Role of Federal Government of Ethiopia

In developing countries the governments must take initiative to promote cooperatives by means of passing cooperative legislations, creating funds and subsidies, providing facilities for cooperative education and training, providing advisory service for cooperative members and office bearers, concentrate on improving physical infrastructure to facilitate the movement of goods and communication and to regulate the audit and inspection of cooperative societies.

The role of government in the development of cooperatives in Ethiopia can be divided into three parts, namely, Imperial Period, Derg Government Period, and Present Federal Government Period.

Imperial Period

During Imperial government period, the first cooperative movement was started during 1960. Provisions were made to give a place to the cooperatives in the Five-year Plans. But no worthwhile steps were taken to start cooperatives all round.

Derg Period

During this period land was nationalized and had its impact on cooperatives also. Peasants' Associations were formed and they floated Producers' Cooperatives. The cooperatives were officially dictated without any involvement of the actual members. Cooperatives became an instrument of the state. Several of such reasons led to the failure of cooperatives.

Federal Government

With the change of power in 1991 drastic reforms were introduced in the field of agriculture and industry. New cooperative proclamation was passed in 1998 and all the previous cooperatives were brought under the new cooperative proclamation. A cooperative commission was created and a cooperative commissioner was appointed to look after the growth and development of cooperatives. The cooperative commission along with the ministry of rural development was expected:

1. Administer the cooperative proclamation.
2. Giving guidelines to cooperative commission.
3. Organizing new cooperatives.
4. Reviewing the progress of cooperatives periodically.
5. Creating a section for audit and inspection.
6. Making arrangements for cooperative training.
7. Organization of national level cooperatives.

One of the important steps taken by the federal government of Ethiopia is to introduce a draft cooperative policy of Ethiopia. This draft policy is yet to be implemented, but it is under the process of implementation.

Features of Draft Cooperative Policy of Ethiopia

A Policy is defined as statement of a government as to what it intends to do with, for and about something of national importance and significance.

The Goal of the Cooperative Policy — Ethiopia has been managing the affairs of cooperatives without having any definite cooperative policy for the past decades. At present the Federal Cooperative Commission has issued a draft of such policy. It is stated in the draft policy that the goal of the cooperative policy is to create conducive socio-economic environment, legal and institutional framework both for the rural and urban dwellers of the population so that they can voluntarily organize cooperative societies by coordinating their knowledge, labour and wealth with which they can be the direct participants and users of the fruits of their movement.

Details of the policy objectives — The details of the policy objectives are:

1. Transformation of subsistence farming into modern commercial farming;
2. To create conditions for cooperatives to properly discharge their responsibilities in poverty reduction;
3. To coordinate government, private and cooperative efforts in providing for example, rural electricity and telephone services;
4. To enact cooperative legislations and regulations to assist the cooperative movement;
5. To establish the sustainable working relationship between cooperative movement and government, and non-government institutions;

6. Assist and support women, the youth and the physically disabled segment of the population to organize cooperatives to improve their lives.
7. To organize cooperatives fitting to the peculiar characteristics of the values and customs of the pastoralists to enable them properly utilize the resources of their respective region;
8. To conduct various studies and researches that can help hammer operational and implementation weaknesses and suggest future directions and solutions;
9. To create conducive environment for the relationship to be establish between the national cooperative movements and in other parts of the world and international organizations.

The draft cooperative policy includes the following major issues in order to transform the country's cooperative movement to an elevated level.

(A) Expansion and development of cooperatives;

(B) Cooperative organizational structure—primary, union, federation;

(C) Cooperative finance;

(D) Cooperative education and training;

(E) Cooperative audit and inspection system;

(F) Social participation by cooperatives;

(G) Role and support of the government;

(H) The relationship between cooperatives and other institutions;

(I) Policy implementation.

(A) *Expansion and Development of cooperatives:*

- Cooperative shall be established in any socio-economic sector of the economy without contradicting values and principles of cooperatives;
- Cooperatives shall be encouraged to improve both rural and urban marketing systems by supplying inputs to enhance the production and productivity of the farmers; they will arrange both local and foreign markets for the produces of the farmers so that the farmers could receive better price and efforts shall be made to prevail efficient credit system;
- Cooperatives shall be encouraged to curb the shortage of houses in cities in collaboration with the private sector and the government;
- Through continuous education and awareness traditional associations shall be encouraged to organize into cooperatives;

- To create a link between the consumers and the producers, consumer cooperatives shall be organised;
- Producers, traders and service providers in rural as well as urban areas shall organize cooperatives to enhance their economic capacity;
- To enrich the saving culture of the people, saving and credit cooperatives shall be established both in rural and urban areas;
- In the regions where livestock husbandry is the main stay, cooperatives shall be organised and involved in the production of exportable products, foodgrains, in the mineral and extraction and collection of wild adhesives;
- Cooperatives shall contribute towards establishing of agro-ecological based diversification and specialization production methods;
- Efforts shall be made to establish a national network of market information system to help cooperatives in all regions to assist each other in sharing experiences;
- The government shall offer its maximum support for cooperatives to have their own managers to effectively operate their business;
- In connection with the making use of appropriate technologies in the fields of artisanship and cottage industries, cooperatives shall be established in urban and rural areas;
- Notwithstanding international cooperative ceremonies that are celebrated by cooperative movements, 'Ethiopian Cooperative Day' shall be celebrated on Sunday annually the first week of July.

(B) *Cooperative organization and structure*

Cooperatives can be established at different levels depending on the type and functions performed by individual cooperatives, usually known as three-tier structure which include primary, union and federation cooperative structures. Primary and union cooperatives are particularly encouraged to be established to participate in the provisions of marketing and credit services. Primary cooperatives, unions and federations may establish a cooperative league.

The operational area of the cooperative societies established at different levels would be based on their economic benefits. The organisation of cooperatives from primary to the national level shall be free from duplication and competition but rather to obtain a better result.

(C) *Cooperative Finance*

- In cooperatives, because of the fact that members share capital is the primary source of finance, members shall be encouraged to invest in their cooperatives by buying additional shares. In line with this, members payments and other forms of participation shall be registered and maintained in an appropriate manner and system;

- Cooperatives shall be encouraged to save and allocate some of their earnings for the expansion of investments;
- The cooperative fund shall be established in order to let cooperatives access and obtain credit services from commercial banks;
- Cooperatives shall be encouraged to insure their properties against risks and uncertainties;
- Cooperatives shall contribute towards building investment capacity by providing additional saving and credit services;
- Cooperative banks shall be formed when cooperatives have gained financial strength through internal savings;

(D) *Cooperative Education and Training:*

- Basic cooperative education and benefits shall be included into curriculum of primary education. Further, regular cooperative programme shall be offered in higher education institutions;
- Programmes in cooperatives shall be disseminated through mass media both at regional and federal levels;
- With a view to enhance and assure the competitiveness of cooperatives in the free market economy, management, bookkeeping, business administration and other related skills improving training shall be offered in the short term and in the long term;
- Domestic and international experience sharing programmes shall be prepared to produce sufficient manpower trained in the cooperative profession. Capable cooperatives shall be motivated via different mechanisms;
- Cooperative Training Institutions shall be established at regional as well as federal levels;
- To support cooperatives to attain efficient operation and to make their products competitive in the world market, studies and researches shall be conducted in the field of cooperation.

(E) *Cooperative Audit and Inspection:*

- The government shall provide audit services until cooperatives have become self sufficient in affording to pay such services;

- A system of operation and management peculiar to one type of cooperatives shall be established. To support this effort various operational manuals shall be developed and implemented.

(F) Community service by Cooperatives:

- Cooperatives shall participate and would play their role based on the regulations in the effort to solve the problems of their community. Particularly cooperatives would contribute in expanding rural electrical activities, education and environmental health care, clean water supply, natural resource conservation, protection and inhormonizing cultural and traditional lives of the people with technological advancements;
- Cooperatives shall not be a forum for promoting political or religious objects. However, a member is entitled to follow or not any political or religious outlook on his/her own;
- The sustainability of cooperation is measured by the participation of younger generation in cooperative societies. In this regard cooperatives shall create job opportunities with the objective of refraining the youth from spending their time and energy inappropriately and to instill in them good attitude towards diligent by establishing youth clubs and formulating various income generating schemes.

(G) *The role and support of the Government:*

- The government will enhance the capacity of the rural cooperatives to help them transform subsistence farming into modern one through capacity building;
- The government shall play positive intervention role in organizing and expanding cooperatives in different sectors of the economy. It shall transfer this role to cooperative federations and league to be established in the future;
- Cooperatives shall participate in the rural, urban and industrial development and capacity building, and other development policies, strategies and programmes to bring about enhanced overall development;
- The government shall issue cooperative legislations, it provides technical supports and carries out appropriate supervision;
- Land shall be given free for cooperatives to carry out production, distribution and service provision and house construction;

- Cooperatives shall be encouraged to be involved in real estate development to alleviate shortage of housing;
- Cooperatives shall be entitled to participate in the marketing activities without additional permit requirement once they are legally certified and registered;
- The government shall provide legal protection to ensure that cooperative properties are not exposed for misappropriation.

(H) *Cooperative relations with other institutions:*

- The relationship between cooperatives and other private and governmental organizations shall be based on members approval and consent;
- NGOs can financially and materially support cooperatives in carrying out integrated development activities and in human resource development;
- Cooperatives can participate in development activities with private organisations either in concessions or inpartnership;
- These relationships with other institutions shall be checked that cooperative values and principles are maintained and the spirit of societies self help and autonomy are not violated.

(I) *Policy Implementation:*

- The ultimate beneficiary of cooperative policy is the people and without active participation of it, the implementation of this policy is unconceivable;
- Thus, based on the constitutional right given under Article 31 of the Federal Constitution, conducive conditions shall be prevailed to enable the people to benefit from this right;
- Different government structures at all level shall create conducive condition to ensure that this policy is appropriately implemented and to let the people make use of rights granted in the constitution;
- Federal and Regional governments shall render appropriate support in the endeavour to expand cooperatives in Ethiopia;
- Cooperatives that are organized from primary to federation shall mobilize their members in implementing this policy, they shall also generate policy improving ideas by carrying out studies and researches;
- All concerned cooperatives at all levels, government bodies and others involved in the sector shall meet and evaluate and discuss on performance and problems encountered;

- The Federal Cooperative Commission shall be responsible for presenting and getting it approved on policy improvements in collaboration with others involved in the sector and based on comments obtained from the people;
- An advisory board shall be established comprising members from the Federal Council of representatives, Rural Development Committee, Cooperative Institutes, mass media and from NGOs to oversee the implementation of the policy on established criteria.

Self-learning Activity

Try to answer the following questions on your own.

1. Discuss the role of government briefly in cooperative development?
2. What do understand on support of the government as per the Cooperative Policy?

Summary

- Like other developing countries, cooperative movement in Ethiopia was introduced by the government. The first cooperative movement was started during the year 1960.
- With the change of government during 1974, the previous cooperative legal system was modified and new Cooperative Proclamation was introduced in the year 1978 to promote producers cooperatives and service cooperatives.
- Again with the change of government during 1991, the previous cooperative proclamations were made ineffective and at present, the cooperatives are governed by the Cooperative Proclamation No.147/1998.
- The Federal Government is taking lot of steps to promote the cooperatives by means of enacting separate legal system for the cooperatives, instituting a Federal Cooperative commission and appointing a high level official to administer the cooperative proclamation and cooperative commission.
- The government has also introduced Draft Policy proposals to improve and strengthen the cooperative movement.

13 Role of Non-Governmental Organizations

Role of Non-Governmental Organizations in the Development of Cooperatives

What are NGOs?

Non-governmental organizations come in many shapes and forms, with differing goals and activities. Some concern themselves directly or indirectly with policy; others do not. The concept of NGOs is applied specifically to non-profit organizations rather than civil society in general. In addition, it does not include popular movements or community-based organizations. Rather, it describes that grouping of organizations that function between state and community—some at local level, some at regional or national levels.

1. Many NGOs are primarily concerned with poverty or disaster alleviation.
2. Others focus on local-level development projects, usually filling gaps government services have not met.
3. A third type of NGO strategy can be described as 'sustainable systems development. It is this type of NGO that is most likely to facilitate change at the level of policy or implementation.

As on 1989 there were 4000 NGOs in Organization for Economic Cooperation and Development (OECD) member countries. They work with around 10000 to 20000 developing countries NGOs. In Kenya as on 1990 there were 400 NGOs. In Ethiopia there were more than 400 international and local NGOs.

Features of NGOs

- Many of the NGOs form coordinating bodies, through which they pool resources to share technical services, transport services and create linkages with government to faster cooperation;
- NGOs play an important role in war-tone areas, in which government services cannot operate;

- NGOs actively participate in food security and agricultural development;
- NGOs promote village organizations, help village group to develop programmes and provide funds and technical assistance for projects, including village crafts, cereal banks, soil conservation, and reforestation;
- NGOs provide lot of technical information and encourage rapid dissemination of technical information in the fields of water harvesting, soil conservation, improved methods of agriculture, HIV/AIDS prevention, etc.
- NGOs have built regional networks to promote the dissemination of agricultural information;
- A large number of local level NGOs publish news letters and other publications carrying articles on a wider technical issues relevant to research and extension;
- NGOs encourage small farmers, operate under different conditions to organize themselves into commodity-based producer associations and cooperatives;
- Certain NGOs focus on agriculture technology and provide relevant skills both from their own experience and from the relevant literature;
- Above all, NGOs influence the policies and policy changes for the betterment of the population. The conventional wisdom in many sectors is that policy changes are decided on the basis of a rational assessment of possible options, given existing human and economic resources. This perspective is particularly espoused by those most directly responsible for policy development that is government technocrats, who define themselves as those with the technical expertise to advice government. Like-wise many transnationals put money into research for policy, and argue policy perspectives on the basis of research or international experience. This approach, described by policy analysis as a 'rational' approach, formed the basis for early frameworks for understanding the policy process. Initially articulated by Laswell in the 1950s, it presents a chronological set of decision-making stages or phases that usually include identification of the policy problem, agenda-setting, formulation of policy proposals, adoption of policies, implementation and, lastly evaluation.

NGOs and Cooperatives

The NGOs can help the cooperatives through the following means.

- *NGOs can influence policy making on cooperatives with government and similar agencies*—In many countries local NGOs and International NGOs help to introduce new policies and cooperative legislations. Through this process they pave the way for the development of cooperatives by giving institutional and legal status.

- *NGOs can float cooperatives*—NGOs are particularly interested in developing agricultural cooperatives. They concentrate on agricultural development and food security measures, for which cooperatives are the primary source of development. They are not interested much in organizing cooperatives at the urban areas. Their focus is mainly on rural areas.
- *Funding the cooperatives*—While organizing new cooperatives, NGOs provide seed money as a form of capital to activate the financial system of cooperatives. Such seed money is given free of interest and they are to be repaid after a period like five years.
- *Construction of infrastructure*—While starting the cooperatives, in certain areas NGOs provide grants for the construction of office buildings and storage buildings for the agricultural cooperatives. Such help is undertaken only on a selective basis and not on a wider scale due to their financial constraints.
- *NGOs can provide leadership to the cooperatives*—Cooperative leaders are identified and promoted by the NGOs. They are given training in various areas like cooperative management, accounting, financial management, marketing management, etc. Such leaders are given exposure visits to neighbouring cooperatives as well as to the cooperatives of other countries. The entire expenses on cooperative leaders training and exposure visits are met by the NGOs.
- *NGOs can provide managerial leadership needed for the cooperatives*—The employees of the cooperatives are also given training by the NGOs. They come into contact with training centers and consultants, and provide need based training to the cooperative managers and other staff of cooperatives. They are also sent for exposure visits to neighbouring cooperatives as well as cooperatives of other countries.
- *Promoting cooperative business*—Agricultural cooperatives like the marketing cooperatives are provided with business techniques in output marketing and input marketing. Applying modern management techniques and marketing techniques these cooperatives go for bulk purchase of inputs and distribute them for a lower price than the market price to the farmers. Likewise, in the case of output marketing, by providing better marketing facilities and transport facilities they provide higher prices to the produces of the farmers.
- *Improved techniques*—NGOs inculcate improved methods of agriculture, cultivation of commercial and horticultural crops in suitable areas. To market these products they create market linkage at regional level and national level.

- *Employment generation*—NGOs are particularly interested in creating job opportunities through the cooperatives to the young people. They promote SACCOs, irrigation cooperatives and seed multiplication cooperatives to increase agricultural production and employment generation.
- *Women empowerment*—NGOs encourage women to form cooperatives like SACCOs, dairy cooperatives and artisan cooperatives. Through these cooperatives women get employment opportunities and a standard income to them. Income and employment security empower the women to have secured family life.

NGOs and Cooperative Development in Ethiopia

Ethiopia has more than 800 NGOs international and local NGOs They are mainly engaged in agricultural development, food security measures, development of primary cooperatives, SACCOs, and cooperative unions and the prevention of HIV/AIDS.

VOCA Ethiopia

This is one of the leading American NGOs operating in Ethiopia since 1997. VOCA is a non-profit international NGO which provides technical assistance, training and managerial support in emerging markets in developing countries. It is owned and supported by the largest grower-owned supply and processing cooperatives and farm credit banks in the U.S.A. It has 40 years of experience in 127 countries around the world. At present it has programme in 40 countries including Ethiopia. It has promoted Adama Farmers Cooperative union in East Shewa, launched Oromia Coffee farmers Cooperative Union in 1999 and organized Sidama Coffee Farmers Cooperative Union in 2001. In January 2000, VOCA in collaboration with the Regional Cooperative Promotion Bureau launched a five year extension of the ongoing development effort to benefit small farmers in the four major regions of Ethiopia viz., Oromia, Tigrey, SNNP and Amhara. This programme is helping the establishment of secondary level cooperative unions.

The lessons learned by the VOCA on cooperatives in Ethiopia are as follows:

- *Cooperatives must be farmer owned and controlled*—In order to be successful, cooperatives must be supported by their members through direct investment and control. The cooperatives that do not meet the needs of their members do not receive support.
- *Cooperatives required the involvement and decision making of the members*—The need for member participation in decision making is very important for the cooperatives. As cooperatives become business organizations, members become self motivated in identifying areas for new business.

- *Cooperatives can adopt to the changing needs of their membership*—Cooperatives are able to increase their operations to meet the changing needs of the farmers by expanding their product lines, value added processing and moving into new type of business.
- *Cooperative unions build scale*—Cooperative unions provide the opportunity for increased integration of markets and increased empowerment of farmers in terms of regional and national influence.
- *Cooperatives can be restructured*—Cooperatives with sufficient member awareness, training and support can be restructured and reoriented to serve the needs of the members.

Self-Help Development International (SHDI)

The SHDI has worked in Ethiopia since 1987. In the early years of development, the organization initiated a number of area-based programmes focussing on food security, natural resource conservation and sustainable rural development. Building on the success of these area based progammes, the SHDI developed an Ethiopian country programme for the period 2003 to 2006. This aimed to build coherence between different area based programmes and the dimension of capacity building or support action at a regional level in order to institutionalize measures of support to a larger rural population and to expand the lessons learned from the area based programmes through cooperatives. The main objective is to develop and improve the financial, technical and managerial capacity and capabilities of the targeted farmers cooperatives, youth and women groups and government institutions.

The main focus of the SHDI is on the following four areas:

- Cooperative Development;
- Women Development;
- Youth Development; and
- Information and Communication Systems.

The main goal of the Ethiopia country programme is to establish food self sufficiency and food security at household level in particular and at community level in general through promoting stable agricultural production systems. It is to be noted that nearly 80 per cent of the Ethiopian population depends on agriculture, but Ethiopian farms are subsistence farms and they produce only 30 per cent as surplus production. The efforts of the SHDI are directed in two dimensions of the programmes:

- Direct action where the development issues are addressed in partnership with selected rural communities and authorities in an integrated, holistic approach through integrated conservation based area projects - the Area Based Programme;

- Support action where support is given to authorities and the wider rural community at national, regional and local levels in capacity building and resource provision to enable and empower them to respond to the challenges and opportunities inherent in the development process and to the initiatives promoted by authorities and agencies—the capacity Building Programme.

Role of Other Agencies in promoting Cooperatives

Self-Help Groups (SHGs)

Self-help groups are voluntary organizations promoted mainly by women. Their major activity is the mobilization of savings from women and lend them money for self employment and small business purposes. Such self help groups will be converted into cooperatives at later stages. So, cooperatives and self help groups have mutual interaction.

An ideal self help group may be defined as an unregistered body of people, preferably the disadvantaged, who willingly contribute an agreed sum of money periodically, based on mutual trust, with the understanding that the money so contributed would be lent at a price for a short period. India's National Bank for Agriculture and Rural Development has defined SHG as "is a homogeneous group of rural poor voluntarily formed to save whatever amount they can conveniently save out of their earnings and mutually agree to contribute to a common fund of the group to be lent to the members for meeting their productive and emergent credit needs".

Objectives of SHGs

- To prevent the bank neglected sections of the societies from falling into the debt trap of money lenders;
- To inculcate the habit of thrift and savings among the economically disadvantaged;
- To realize the importance repayment ethics and credit recycling;
- To facilitate improvement of the living conditions of the members and their families, especially women.

Principles of SHGs

- *Mutual Trust*—The cooperative philosophy of self help through mutual help can be seen operating more or less in a full-fledged manner in the case of SHGs.
- *Manageable groups*—Both the size and composition of the SHGs are determined by the members themselves. It is left to the members to increase their membership or limit it. The usual size of membership is 30 to 120.

- *Promotion of the spirit of Thrift*— "Little drops of water makes a mighty ocean", seem to be the guiding principle of SHGs. Every member contributes the barest minimum, and such savings increase in future.
- *Demand based lending*—Loans are provided according to certain priorities fixed by the members of the group. Such priorities are employment oriented or for the development of small businesses.
- *Regularity and discipline*—Whether in attending the periodical meetings, remittance of savings amount or repayment of loan amount, the members should be regular and be self disciplined.
- Lending without collateral—SHGs have made it a point to make a member establish his/her own credit worthiness through repayment performance. Members mutually offer personal security for the repayment of the loan.
- *Review, re-orientation and participatory credit management*—Through periodic review of credit and recovery situation within the SHG, in which every member participate, each one of them learns not to view the problems of SHG as different from his/her own. This participatory management of credit makes the credit programmes very effective.
- *Our money, their money: the vanishing distinction*—This principle hits at the very root of the poor people. The villagers have learnt to be more disciplined in dealing their own money compared to what is given to them from outside. SHGs made the members realize that financial discipline is an important character, irrespective of the source from where the money comes.

Success Factors of SHGs

The success of SHGs depends on the four factors viz., organizational, functional/financial, sustainability and replicabilitiy.

1. *Organisational Aspects*
   - A community gathering in which the representatives initiates the idea and promotes interaction. Such interaction leads to identification of prospective members. Community leaders also initiate such gatherings;
   - Members identified are facilitated to name their representatives for the purpose of specific orientation;
   - Representatives identified are oriented to various aspects of organizing a cooperative effort for a common cause;
   - Focussing on the family for the purpose of membership rather than on the individual. Particular emphasize is placed on the involvement of women members;

- In line with the wishes of the people, the group would get structured irrespective of the differences;
- Periodic meetings in which attendance by definition declared as compulsory, yet a practical minimum is indicated. To acquire eligibility for financial assistance, an attendance precondition is fixed;
- Like any registered body, a standard pattern of office bearers is followed including periodical elections.

2. *Functional/Financial aspects*
   - Savings first, credit next is the popular belief. A member may force herself to save in order to earn access to credit;
   - Demand based lending through peer decision on the basis of mutual trust, reinforced by borrower orientation, form the theme;
   - Simplicity in processing, openness, dependability, flexibility, and security of access to credit are the characteristics of SHGs;
   - The group fixes the rate of interest for the loan, if a higher rate is fixed it is to plough back an income to the group;
   - With regard to repayment the individual goal and the group goal coincide;
   - The pace, schedule and place of recovery of money from a borrower are fixed in full practical reality of the life of the borrower;
   - The role of the peer pressure is important in keeping the repayment on track;
   - Accounting system is simple enough for any one to understand.
3. *Sustainability*
   - While maintaining accounting procedures, training is offered in maintenance of accounts, bookkeeping, leadership, etc., to the representatives of SHGs;
   - Broad-based goals of the SHGs through the creation of various sub-committees in order to identify specific group needs;
   - Ploughing back earnings from different sources and also ploughing money into SHGs from external sources with a view to build financial sustainability;
   - Consortium of SHGs to cover a larger geographical area with a long term perspective, like that of a cooperative.

4. *Replicability*
   - *Participatory Approach*—It is essential to initiate the process through people's participation. Such an approach would help the people to realize what exactly they are forming part of a larger organization.
   - *Open decision-making*—The readiness on the part of the members to accept any decision, which is made openly.
   - *Participatory management*—When representatives of the members get trained in running the organization democratically their commitment to success and willingness to involve is appreciated.
   - *Limiting consumption credit*—As consumption credit is not productive, it is discouraged.
   - *Gender-based identity*—SHGs can be organized either by men or by women or by both.

Self-help Groups and Cooperatives

1. *Self-help groups can promote future cooperatives*—SHGs are promoted by people of limited means and who suffered poverty and unemployment. Cooperatives have been organized and made success in many countries having the above theme. So, many SHGs have promoted new cooperatives or they convert themselves into a cooperative through the registration process. Within the SHGs, handicraft cooperatives, consumer cooperatives, etc., have been organized.
2. *Self-help groups can provide leadership needed for the cooperatives*—Leadership is one of the basic necessities for the success of voluntary organizations. SHGs provide training and experience in various fields like management, accounting, bookkeeping, marketing, etc., which are very much needed to organize new cooperatives.
3. *Self-help groups can help the cooperatives in their resource mobilization and recovery of loans*—SHGs mobilize savings of small amount and relend them as loans to the members. The same concept can be applied when they convert the SHG into a cooperative or the same members organize new cooperative.
4. *Skill development*—When new cooperatives are organized by the members of SHG, various types of skills like financing, marketing, bargaining, etc., are transformed successfully for the new cooperative.
5. *Multi-purpose activities*—Cooperatives at the initial stage start with single purpose, like the agricultural credit cooperatives. At later stages they add many more functions and become multi-purpose units. The same concept can be applied by the SHGs and they can promote multi-purpose activities like marketing, consumer, dairying, housing, etc.

Impact of Self-help Groups

- For effective implementation of the self-help groups collaborative links must be established by women development departments, health and family welfare departments and other development agencies/ organizations.
- Members of Self-help Groups were made aware of their rights and responsibilities in the cooperative approach of the group activities. As an outcome of the adult education programs initiated by the Self Help Groups the members had started reading and writing simple sentences besides counting.
- All self-help group members have opened their bank accounts. The women feel economically strong and independent when there is an increase in her income, security of work and assets in her name.

Consumer Forums and Cooperatives

Consumer forums have been widely organized in almost all countries. They are registered bodies under the special Acts that prevail in countries. Such consumer forums have been given judicial powers to fight the exploitation against the consumers. They also uphold the rights of the consumers. Consumers enjoy several rights which are changed from time to time. John F Kennedy, the then President of USA has given four rights of consumers.

1. Right to safety
2. Right to be informed
3. Right to choose
4. Right to be heard

In addition to the above rights, the following rights of consumers could be added.

5. Right to seek redressal
6. Right to consumer education
7. Right to a healthy environment

These consumer forums provide education to the consumers. The importance of the consumer education are as follows:

- Helps a person to become a discriminating buyer who can distinguish needs from wants;
- Helps to develop skill and resourcefulness, the ability to seek out and solve problems and to find alternatives;

- Helps people to move from one initial responsibility of self and family towards a wider social responsibility to the community;
- Teaches youngsters to make a renewed appraisal of advertsising and other pressures to buy;
- Helps people to understand the imbalance between those who supply and produce and those who buy and use and to do something positive;
- Helps the national economy, if domestic consumers demand products of an accepted quality and standards, the whole economy of the nation benefits;
- Develops a person's ability to choose goods and services intelligently;
- Imparts skills for making enlightened decisions while purchasing goods or services;
- Provides knowledge about existing loss and standards for the benefit of the consumers;
- Guides and advices consumers in the use of these consumer protection services;
- Makes consumers aware of agencies which can help them to take appropriate action in a problem situation;
- Helps to cope with the rapid changes in the communication, production and marketing systems with new, complex products and service and with different ways of buying and selling;
- Prepares low income and physically disabled consumers to cope with problems through voluntary and governmental agencies;
- Prepares consumers to demand safe, reliable quality products and services at a fair price;
- Makes people aware of their rights and responsibilities in a society.

Consumer forums can help the cooperatives through the following means:

1. *Educate the cooperative members about their consumer rights*—Cooperative members are not expected to know the rights and responsibilities of ordinary consumers. Consumer forums can arrange meetings, conferences and seminars to impart the rights of the consumers over the cooperative members.
2. *They can help to distribute pure goods through cooperatives*—Consumer cooperatives are the best choice to distribute pure goods to the members and non-members. In many countries we could find that consumer forums themselves have promoted consumer cooperatives.

3. *They can help to bring down the market price*—One of the objectives of consumer forums is to avert exploitation by middlemen and provide reasonable prices to the consumers. Consumer cooperatives by means of following active price policy have brought down the market price.

4. *They can join the cooperatives in avoiding the exploitation of the consumers by the private traders*—The members of the consumer forums can either float separate consumer cooperatives or they can join the existing consumer cooperatives. The experience and awareness of the members of the consumer forums can be helpful to the consumer cooperatives to improve their service and competitive ability.

Women Associations

Women associations are formed to protect the rights of women. The empowerment of women is also undertaken by such associations. They have to take care of the education, health, etc of women and to take care of rural development and food security. These associations can help the increase of membership of cooperatives, in the management of cooperatives, etc as fifty per cent of the population consist of women.

Place of Women in Society

Women play an important role in developing the family and society by means of advancing the culture of the society and upbringing the values. The development of a family and children is mainly in the hands of women. They play the role of mother, wife, and other important roles. The place of women is discussed as follows:

1. ***Household worker:*** All the routine working in the family like cooking, washing, cleaning, etc are undertaken by women. Though in modern society, due to education and equality, men have come foreword to share the burden of women, the ultimate responsibility for the household work lie with the women.

2. ***Upbringing children:*** From time immemorial it is the duty of the mother to upbringing the children. In all societies the children are brought up by mother up to a stage, say teenage. Even after that stage the mother would like to take care of her children by means of taking interest in their welfare, health and growth.

3. ***Habits to family and society:*** Women as mother and responsible citizen bring good habits to the family and the society. The good name of a family is pronounced only by the hard work and good habits shown by women apart from men, who may play a very minor role.

4. ***Ethics and religion:*** Women inculcate good habits, virtues and ethics to their children and society. Such virtues form as ethics, which are the

basis for a cultured society. Likewise, women play an important role in practicing religion, taking the message of God to their children. Any religion cannot get purity without the involvement of women in the sacred affaires of religion.

5. ***Public administration:*** Women play a significant role in public administration in modern days. They actively participate in the civic and political administration as corporate, council members, legislators, ministers and administrators.
6. ***Labour force:*** Women form a major labour force in agriculture and related activities. In the organized sector women labour force has become very precious in the fields of education, health, social welfare, etc.
7. ***Women in decision-making:*** Decision making affairs relating to family, corporate sector and government are looked after well by women. Ethiopian women are still underrepresented in leadership and decision-making roles in community affairs. They are underrepresented in traditional structures. They hardly serve as elders or religious leaders in their community. In the field of education also the role of Ethiopian women is very negligible. Due to financial problems girls are often obliged to work as maids and street vendors. Cultural and social norms such as early marriage, abduction are major constraints, which hinder the capacity of the girl child to perceive education. Social norms, cultural factors and lack of education tend to contribute towards the lower status of women.
8. ***Agriculture:*** In many of the African countries, including Ethiopia women play the major role in the field of agriculture. Though they lack title to the land they do all sorts of agriculture work and make agriculture a success.

Women are exploited by the society by many ways. Inequality of women can be balanced by organization of cooperatives by women. The following are the areas of inequality of women:

- *Economic development and livelihood security*—According to the UN, women perform 53 per cent of all economic activities in developing countries, but only about a third of their work is currently measures and acknowledged in national accounts, compared with three quarters for men.
- *Human Development*—Research by the World Bank has shown that education for girls is the single most effective way of tackling poverty. Women with even few years of basic education have smaller, healthier families. Child mortality is lower the higher the number of years of education of the mother. Each additional year of female education is thought to reduce child mortality by 5-10 per cent.

- *Personal security and violence against women*—In parts of Africa and South and East Asia, some traditions see girls as a burden rather than an asset. Infanticide, sex-selective abortion, and preferential care for and feeding of boys, particularly in early childhood, appear to lie behind demographic data which show alarming evidence of "missing" women in some populations.
- *Empowerment and political representation*—Women are poorly represented at all levels of political life and decision-making processes, leading to the widespread neglect of women's priorities by politicians and bureaucrats. Figures published in 1999 show that women hold only 12.7 per cent of the world's parliamentary seats, and only 8.7 per cent of those in the least developed countries.
- *Disability*—Women with disabilities suffer multiple disadvantages and severe challenges with regard to the achievement of their human rights.
- *Rights of the child*—The sexual exploitation of children is particular abhorrent violation of child rights. It is estimated by the International Labour Organization that approximately 95 per cent of child prostitutes are girls. As many as 800,000 children in Thailand, 400,000 in Brazil, 100,000 in the Philippines and countless thousands elsewhere, have been forced into prostitution. Many others are compelled to work, from very early on in their live, to help their families fend off poverty. Therefore, when explaining women's state of poverty, it is not expedient to stress the poverty they face only at the household level. Even though the household is the first place where production, consumption, reproduction and socialization of identities merge according to sex, we have to recognize and understand that other social units can also play a role in perpetuating women's poverty.

Role of Cooperatives for Women Development and Vice-versa

Training, education, and information, have an important role to play in increasing women's involvement in cooperatives. But they would be more effective if: programmes were better adapted to women's broad concerns (health, electrification, housing...); more female trainers were available, making it easier for women to join in the courses; less stress were placed on written training materials, of little use to illiterate women; radio cooperative programmes were provided more in local languages (all too often they are in the 'colonial' language); timing took account of the women's daily schedules.

Women can also be groomed to play their rôle in mixed societies by first learning group leadership roles in exclusively women's cooperatives. Such cooperatives, and other rural groups, can also serve as training grounds in participatory development, teach methods of group decision-taking, and develop trust and self-assurance. They also provide a valuable apprenticeship in the conduct of business: successful women's groups demonstrate to skeptical men (and women) that women are capable of developing their own business and can thus be valuable participants in mixed societies.

As breeding grounds for democracy and participation, cooperatives could be used to empower women by enhancing and upgrading their specific knowledge and capacities. For instance, indigenous knowledge in areas such as traditional healing, frequently transferred through the female members of the family, is under severe threat from modern medicine. Cooperatives could institute programmes whereby such knowledge would be systematically called on and preserved, and proposed as a service where modern health services are being cut back.

With greater freedom to decide on the types of business to conduct through a cooperative, the way is open for the development of activities of specific interest to women such as small cooperative mills, food storage and preservation, production of household necessities like soap and clothing, small animal raising and handicrafts. More stress should also be laid on cooperatives' social function by organising services which would relieve women from certain of their tasks: child care services or drudgery-reducing activities, or assist with organising mariages and other ceremonies.

Such activities are already taking place through so-called informal groups: in Benin, while only 8 per cent of rural women are members of cooperatives, 90 per cent belong to traditional groups. An important reason for this apparent imbalance is that they keep control over their own money and can use it flexibly when it is channeled (invisibly) through women's groups. Experience has shown that women prefer to stay independent both of cooperative laws and more especially of interference and domination by men!

Finally, more active female participation in rural cooperatives will have an additional bonus. A debate on gender division of labour for agricultural and domestic tasks, especially in the light of evolving technologies, would almost certainly develop through the regular cooperative meetings. The male members may then become convinced that there are more efficient ways of allocating tasks and resources than the current ones, to the greater good of the whole village and household social and economic set-up.

Trade Union and Cooperatives

Trade unions are an essential part of modern industrial system. They are the organized associations of workers for the promotion of their common interests. The term trade union refers to the unification of labour for purposes of collective bargaining with the employers with a view to gain some economic advantage. Labour unions are the "associations of employed persons for collective bargaining about their conditions of employment and also for the provision of benefits, legal defense, and the promotion of their members' interest by brining pressure to bear on governments and parliaments and in certain cases political action".

Trade unions and cooperatives are identical institutions. In fact, the cooperative movements in England and other countries have been sponsored by the trade union leaders. Howarth Charles, the leading pioneer of the Rochdale Pioneers' society was one of the leading trade union leaders in England.

Similarities

Trade unions and cooperatives are identical in few respects because:

1. both have developed against distressing conditions generated by industrial revolution;
2. both are associations of individuals who are economically weak and need to be uplifted;
3. since they are exploited class, people come together to achieve a greater bargaining power. They are too weak to achieve the common end individually.

Dissimilarities

In spite of certain similarities, trade unions and cooperatives have lot of dissimilarities noted below:

1. *Coercion*—Trade unions are based on the theory of coercion. Trade union leaders coerce the employers to accede to their demands and they coerce the workers to join a particular organization and make the trade union movement more effective. They pressurize both the workers and employers for different purposes. But in the case of cooperatives, compulsion is absent. Voluntarism is the essential principle and no one will be compelled to join the cooperatives.
2. *Business*—Trade unions do not run a separate business, on the other hand cooperatives run various types of business activities. They compete with private sector organizations to do service to their members.
3. *Method of functioning*—To ensure that their movement yields quick results, trade unions resort to strike, indiscipline, etc. Cooperatives do not resort to such methods.
4. *Employer-employee relationship*—Through collective bargaining, trade unions attempt to get as much as possible from their employers. As a result, superior-inferior relationship continues between the employer and the workers. On the other hand, in cooperatives, the workers cooperative with the society and maintain good employer-employee relationship.

5. *Politics*—Majority of the trade unions are promoted by political parties. On the other hand, cooperatives do not allow politics. One of the earlier principles followed by Rochdale Pioneers was "Political and Religious Neutrality".
6. *Strategies*—The strategies utilized by workers' organizations and cooperatives are fundamentally different in general workers organizations try to improve their members' standard of living and quality lf life through negotiations collective bargaining and grievance handing while cooperatives establish joint business enterprises to provide common economic and social services such as the supply of consumer goods, savings and credit marketing channels, etc.

Promotion of Cooperatives by Trade Unions

Workers' organizations and mutual forms of cooperatives have traditionally shared common goals and objectives and in some countries a common history and even related organizational structures Both workers' organizations and such cooperatives are based on self - help, democratic organization mutual aid and solidarity They aim to solve their members' problems through group action In many European countries both the trade union and cooperative movements had similar origins in the wake of the social and economic upheavals brought about by the Industrial Revolution.

By promoting cooperatives, workers organizations help to advance the broad interests of their members For example consumer cooperatives that promote the sale of good quality products at reasonable prices directly benefit lower-income families Likewise, housing cooperatives can assist in the provision of good quality low-cost accommodation savings and credit cooperatives enable workers to save regularly and obtain loans at reasonable interest rates Insurance health and social welfare cooperatives all benefit workers and their families.

A significant example of trade union cooperative action is to be found in Singapore where the National trade union congress (NTUC) has initiated a significant network of cooperatives including the NTUC fair price consumers cooperative the NTUC income insurance cooperative the NTUC health care cooperative and the NTUC chidcare cooperative In Kenya most national trade unions support savings and credit cooperatives and have contributed to the establishment of the National Cooperative Housing Union (NACHU) In Turkey the largest trade union federation (TURK-IS) and its affiliates established consumer cooperatives (YOL-KOOP) and housing cooperative unions (KENT-KOOP) in the 1970s and 80s.

In the Philippines it is estimated that there are some 3,000 cooperatives initiated by trade unions including for example the LEAD-CO-TUCP which was established by the trades union congress of the Philippines (TUCP) to improve the lives of families living in a depressed coastal community called Degut-Dagestan in cloacae city It provides assistance to members to acquire home lots legalize their electrical power supply and rehabilitate their water supply.

A challenging aspect of cooperative action by workers' organizations is in the area of workers buy-outs of failing state or private enterprises In the United kingdom the Wales cooperative center was established by the wale Trade union congress in 1983 to assist workers form new enterprises in the face of redundancy and privatization In the Philippines the KASUCO workers Agricultural cooperative Inc (KWACI) was organized in 1991 by the beneficiaries of an agrarian reform programme and represents a buy-out by sugar company workers facilitated by the National congress of Unions in the sugar Industry of the Philippines (NACUSIP)

The south African National Union of Mineworkers (NUM) has promoted some 30 cooperatives for retrenched and retired miners They are active in agriculture horticulture brick making poetry-raising and so on The NUM considers cooperatives as a more advanced element within its overall employment promotion strategy

Trade unions may participate financially in the establishment of cooperative enterprises In Singapore trade unions are the main shareholders in NTUC cooperatives The Ghana Trades Union congress (GTUC) has established a fund financed out of members contributions for the establishment of cooperative and other types of enterprises by trade union members. The Danish labour movement's workers cooperative Financing Fund is another case in point as is the Unity Trust Bank a joint venture of the United kingdom's cooperative Bank and British trade unions.

Joint Effort by Trade Unions and Cooperatives

1. Trade Unions may provide information assistance education and training to members wishing to establish cooperatives Negotiating with employers to ensure check-off facilities for savings and credit of insurance cooperatives may be a useful service that trade unions can provide.

2. Trade unions may also assist workers in the informal sector to establish and develop their own cooperatives as a means of improving their working conditions and increasing their income.

3. Trade unions may participate together with employers' organizations and other interest groups in works council task forces and other bodies established at the central and local level to deal with issues that have an impact on the cooperative sector.

4. It could be of special interest for cooperative movements and trade union organizations to develop joint strategies for raising income and ensuring job security and social protection of informal sector workers. This could include cooperative organizations for home workers street vendors and casual labourers.

5. At the organizational level cooperatives and trade unions could undertake joint training of each other's elected officials develop joint training programmes and materials for members and develop joint financial services for their members such as savings loans insurance and pensions.

Self-learning Activity

Try to answer the following questions on your own.

1. VOCA Ethiopia and cooperative development—comment?
2. What is the importance of SHDI in cooperative development?
3. Discuss inter-relations between SHGs and cooperatives?
4. What is your opinion on Trade Unions and Cooperatives relationship?

Summary

- NGOs are playing a notable role in promoting the cooperatives. The notable international NGOs that have done commendable work in Ethiopia are the VOCA of USA and SHDI of Ireland.
- Like the NGOs, SHGs are also promoting cooperatives and using cooperatives like credit cooperatives to provide employment opportunities and increase the living standard of the population.
- Consumer forums in many countries are working hand in hand with cooperatives especially with consumer cooperatives. many consumer forums have organized consumer cooperatives to benefit the consumers.
- Women associations are fighting for the rights of women and work for the removal of inequality of women. Women associations also promote cooperatives. Cooperatives help the women to improve their employment opportunities and their prominent role in cooperatives is expected from the community.
- Trade unions and cooperatives are the outcome of the industrial revolution. Both are having lot of similarities and certain dissimilarities. Trade union leaders gave birth to the cooperative movement during 1844. Trade unions can promote cooperatives and can run cooperatives successfully.

14 Role of International Agencies

Role of UNO in Promoting Cooperatives

United Nations, the world body of nations is taking interest in providing peace among world countries. It is equally supporting the member countries financially through short-term and long-term investments on development projects through its organs International Monetary Fund (IMF) and World Bank. As cooperatives are popular non-governmental agencies and voluntary agencies, UNO is encouraging the cooperatives through many ways. Recently, the UNO has pointed out to participate the cooperatives in achieving the 'Millennium Development Goals'. These goals are to be achieved within the year 2015 by the member countries, especially by developing countries. The millennium development goals and targets are as follows (to which cooperatives are one of the stakeholders):

1. Eradicate extreme poverty and hunger

   Target for 2015—halve the proportion of people living on less than a dollar a day and those who suffer from hunger.

2. *Achieve universal primary education*

   Target for 2015—ensure that all boys and girls complete primary education.

3. *Promote gender equality and empower women*

   Target for 2015—Eliminate gender disparities at all levels (eliminate gender disparities in primary and secondary education preferably by 2005)

4. *Reduce child mortality*

   Target for 2015—reduce by two-thirds the mortality rate among children under 5.

5. *Improve maternal health*

   Target for 2015—reduce by 3 quarters by ratio of women dying in child birth.

6. *Combat HIV/AIDS, Malaria and other diseases*

   Target for 2015—halt and begin to reverse the spread of HIV/AIDS and the incidence of malaria and other major diseases.

7. *Ensure environmental sustainability*

   Target 2015—integrate the principles of sustainable development into country policies and programmes and reverse the loss of environmental resources. Reduce by half the proportion of people without access to safe drinking water.

   Target 2020—Achieve significant improvement in the lives of atleast 100 million slum dwellers.

8. *Develop a global partnership for development*

   Target—develop further an open trading and financial system that includes a commitment to good governance, development and poverty reduction—nationally and internationally. Address the least developed countries' special needs and the special needs of *land locked* and small island developing states. Deal comprehensively with developing countries' debt problem. Develop decent and productive work for youth, in cooperation with pharmaceutical companies, provide access to affordable essential drugs in developing countries. In cooperation with the private sector, make available the benefits of new technologies, especially information and communication technologies.

It is heartening to note that UNO and its agencies have already on several occasions acknowledged the contribution which cooperatives can make. The UN General Assembly Resolution 56/123 emphasized the importance of cooperative organizations in social development, poverty reduction, employment creation and participatory development. These recognize the cooperative movement as a distinct and major stakeholder in both national and international affairs. They advice member states to adopt a policy framework to recognize cooperatives as legal entities and to give cooperative organizations equality in relation to other associations and institutions.

Guidelines Aimed at Creating a Supportive Environment for the Development of Cooperatives

Objectives

1. Within the General Assembly and the Economic and Social Council, and at major recent international conferences, Governments have acknowledged the significance of cooperatives as associations and enterprises through which citizens effectively overcome a wide range of problems and achieve many of their goals. They have recognized the cooperative movement as a distinct and major stakeholder in both national and international affairs.

2. Governments recognize that the cooperative movement is highly democratic, locally autonomous but internationally integrated, and a form of organization of associations and enterprises whereby citizens themselves use self-help and self-responsibility to meet goals that include not only economic but social and environmental objectives, such as overcoming poverty, securing productive employment, and encouraging social integration.
3. Consequently, Governments seek to support the cooperative movement and to work closely with it to develop an effective partnership to achieve their respective goals. Policies setting out the objectives and means of support and collaboration are valuable instruments for ensuring that the potential of cooperatives for meeting the individual goals of citizens who are members, and through this the aspirations of the wider societies of which they are a part, is realized.
4. However, such policies can be effective only if they take into account the special character of cooperatives and the cooperative movement. This differs significantly from that of associations and enterprises not organized according to cooperative values and principles.
5. The objective of these guidelines is to provide advice to Governments that is appropriate to contemporary and anticipated conditions. Because of the expectations shown by Governments in recent years in respect to the cooperative movement, rapidly changing global conditions and changes in the cooperative movement itself, many policies in most of the States members of the United Nations might benefit from review, and in some cases from substantial revision. Given the relevance of cooperatives to many aspects of national life, as well as the special nature of cooperative organization, policy in respect to cooperatives may be complex and sensitive. It is the purpose of these guidelines to set out succinctly the principles on which national policy might best be based, and the scope and content likely to suffice as a framework for the necessarily more specific and detailed national policies which fall within the responsibility of each Government.

Policy in Respect to Cooperatives and the Cooperative Movement

6. The objective of policy is to ensure that cooperatives, recognized as legal entities, are assured real equality with other types of association and enterprise, and this equality is extended to all organizations and institutions set up by the cooperative movement. Enjoyment of such equality requires that the special values and principles of cooperative organization, expressed in the particular forms taken by cooperative organization, receive full recognition as desirable and beneficial to society,

and that appropriate measures are taken to ensure that their special qualifies and practices are not the cause of discrimination and disadvantage of whatever type.

7. To achieve this objective, government is concerned with creating - and then with maintaining as conditions change—a supportive and enabling environment for cooperative development. As part of such an environment, it is useful if every effort is made to create and maintain an effective partnership between Government and the cooperative movement.

A. Public Recognition

8. It is appropriate and useful for Government to acknowledge publicly the special contribution—in both quantitative and qualitative terms made by the cooperative movement to the national economy and society. It is also beneficial that Government acknowledge and publicize the purposes of all forms of partnership and collaboration between it and the cooperative movement. A number of specific actions may be useful of which one might be full participation in the annual joint observance of the United Nations International Day of Cooperatives and the International Cooperative Day organized by the International Co-operative Alliance, pursuant to General Assembly resolutions 47/90, 49/155 and 51/58; and appropriate participation in other celebrations of the cooperative movement.

B. Legal, Judicial and Administrative Provision

9. Appropriate provision is necessary within law and both judicial and administrative practice if these most important areas of the environment in which cooperatives exist are to contribute positively to the supportive and enabling nature of that environment Legal provision may take various forms appropriate to the national legal system, it should address the status, rights and responsibilities of cooperatives and the cooperative movement in general, as well as, if appropriate, those of special categories of cooperatives or of distinct aspects of cooperation.

10. *National Constitution*—This could acknowledge, if appropriate, the legitimacy of cooperatives and the cooperative movement and the utility of their contribution to national life.

11. *General Law on Cooperatives or the general section of a single Law on Cooperatives*—This should form the basic element in legal provision and the fundamental point of guidance for all judicial and administrative practice. Participation by representatives of the cooperative movement in its formulation would a valuable means to ensure its relevance and utility. It should acknowledge the nature of cooperation and its utility,

set out criteria for treatment of cooperatives in law and define the nature of governmental responsibilities as well as the rights and responsibilities of the cooperative movement. It should include the following basic set of acknowledgements, definitions and provisions, certain of which might be set out in a preambular section:

- acknowledgement that the organization of associations and enterprises on the basis of cooperative values and principles is legitimate;
- acknowledgement of the utility of the cooperative approach to association and enterprise, its contribution to national life and the status of the cooperative movement as a significant stakeholder within society;
- definition of cooperatives, using the 'Statement on the Cooperative Identity' adopted by the International Co-operative Alliance in 1995;
- recognition of the unique nature of the values and principles of cooperation, and hence the need for their separate and different treatment in law and practice;
- commitment that neither their distinctive nature nor their separate and different treatment in law and practice should be the cause of discrimination, intended or not;
- undertaking that no law or practice should restrict the rights of citizens to full participation in the cooperative movement in any capacity consistent with its values and principles and should not restrict the operation of that movement;
- provision that a general law apply to all categories of cooperative, but that in order to respond to the situation of certain categories of cooperative special laws might be enacted, consistent with the general law;
- stipulation that all judicial and administrative regulations and practices be based only on the general or special laws on cooperatives; that all regulations clearly identify the provision of the law on which they are based and the purpose for which they are made;
- recognition of the full autonomy and capacity for self-regulation of the cooperative movement;
- acknowledgement that intervention by Government in the internal affairs of the movement should be strictly limited to measures applied generally to all associations and enterprises equally in order to ensure their conformity with the law. Adjustments may be made only to ensure real equality in treatment;

- definition of the responsibilities of the cooperative movement for self-regulation in all matters distinctive to it;
- provision that the texts of laws and regulations be made available to all cooperative members and employees;
- provision that representatives of the cooperative movement participate fully in drafting special laws or judicial or administrative regulations and guidelines concerning practice;
- provision for the maintenance of a public register of cooperatives as a part of procedures for registration of all associations and enterprises;
- provision for procedures for continuous monitoring and regular review of law and practice which would include the full and equal participation of representatives of the cooperative movement and for encouragement of research on the effect of law and practice on the environment for cooperatives;
- establishment of the responsibility of Government to formulate and carry out a policy in respect to cooperatives that would seek to establish a supportive and enabling environment while avoiding any infringement of the autonomy of the movement and any diminution of its capacity for responsible self-regulation, and would seek also to engage in an effective and equal partnership with the movement in all matters where it is able to contribute significantly to the formulation and carrying out of public policy; recognition also of the value of governmental support for the international cooperative movement, including through intergovernmental activities;
- definition of the responsibilities of the cooperative movement as a major stakeholder in society, to the extent these may be consistent with its full autonomy. These include making available its experience in self-reliant, people-oriented and community-based organization of associations and enterprises.

12. ***Special Laws on Certain Categories of Cooperatives***—These must be consistent with the basic provisions set out in either a general law or in the preambular and initial sections of a single law where neither exist. Each special law should provide the same set of such basic provisions. They may be necessary when the distinctive nature of cooperatives require special provision in law to safeguard their autonomy while achieving their equal although different inclusion in generally applicable regulations. This is often the case in respect to financial cooperatives.

13. ***Judicial and Administrative Practice concerned Explicitly with Cooperatives***—These must be consistent with the general law on cooperatives, and specifically with its provisions concerning such practice.
14. ***All Other Laws and Practices insofar as they may have an effect on Cooperatives***—Many laws and judicial and administrative practices may affect the environment in which cooperatives operate, whether intentionally or not. Relevant governmental bodies should make every effort to exclude any discriminatory or prejudicial impact. Responsibility for identifying cases needing revision lies also with the cooperative movement. Government bodies should assist by making available the full text of drafts of proposed laws or regulations as well as any evaluation of their impact.
15. ***Monitoring, Review and Revision of Laws and Judicial and Administrative Practices***—This is necessary to ensure that their impact on the cooperative movement is entirely positive. If identified, discriminatory provisions should be rendered inoperative as quickly as possible pending enactment of revised laws or issuance of revised regulations and guidelines concerning practice. This process should have as its purpose the early and complete disengagement by governments form the internal affairs of cooperatives and the cooperative movement, where this still exists, and full operational realisation of the principles that cooperatives, although different, are equal to other business enterprises and civil associations.
16. For these purposes formal procedures for consultation and collaboration should be set up, and should include regular and full participation by the cooperative movement. Advantage may be taken also of the special programmes and guidelines offered by specialist international cooperative organizations and intergovernmental organizations.

C. Research, Statistics and Information

17. *Research*—Given the significance of the cooperative movement, its own research and development programmes and the active role of Government in supporting research generally, it is appropriate to undertake the following measures:
    - recognition of the contribution of the cooperative movement itself, and hence disengagement from any direct intervention other than that applied to any recipient of public funding;
    - provision for equal access with other types of association, enterprise or movement in respect to public funds;
    - collaboration between governmental and cooperative movement research on matters relevant to public policy; publication and wide

diffusion of research results, including those produced by the international cooperative movement and intergovernmental organizations, including the United Nations;

- Emphasis should be on applied research of immediate utility in improving the efficiency of cooperatives, extending benefits to society and improving partnerships between movement and Government.

18. ***Statistics***—Several measures may be undertaken to improve statistics for and about cooperatives:
    - extend technical support provided by the national statistical service to the cooperative movement to an extent at least equal to that provided to other major stakeholders;
    - assist in preparation of the annual report of the register of cooperatives;
    - undertake preliminary studies on which to base integration of statistics on cooperatives in regular programmes of the national statistical service, and participate in international efforts to improve cooperative statistics, including establishment of a uniform set of definitions for use by national statistical services.

19. ***Information***—Given that Government regulates and broadly influences information diffusion, a number of measures may be useful in expanding knowledge of the cooperative movement and of overcoming prejudices and misconceptions:
    - extension of technical and financial assistance to an extent equal to that made available to other stakeholders, ensuring that no discrimination exists because of the special nature of cooperatives;
    - equal and non-discriminatory access by the cooperative movement to all public media commensurate with its contribution to national life;
    - adoption of affirmative action to overcome prejudice and misinformation where the term cooperative is associated with a previous and inappropriate usage;
    - diffusion through public media of material on inter governmental activities undertaken in partnership with or in support of cooperatives;
    - dissemination of printed and computer-based information prepared by Government of intergovernmental bodies with the same priority and resources as allocated to information on other stakeholders.

D. Education

20. Given the important contributions of the cooperative movement to education, a number of supportive and enabling measures might be useful:

- acknowledgement of the contributions made;
- commitment to non-interference in the movement's own programmes other than those generally applied in order to maintain standards in all educational institutions; and avoidance of discrimination in certification and accreditation;
- support for all forms of collaboration and partnership between cooperative and public systems, and assurance of equality with other types of private education (where this exists) in respect to eligibility for public funds;
- consideration of the option constituted by cooperative organization in any programmes of privatization;
- encouragement of student self-reliance by facilitating their formation of cooperatives for the supply of goods and services, including accommodation;
- encouragement of formation by public educational institutions of purchasing, supply and common service cooperatives; and assurance of equal access by cooperatives with other suppliers.
- inclusion within the national curricula at all levels of the study of the values principles, history, current and potential contribution of the cooperative movement to national society;
- encouragement and support of specialist studies of cooperation at tertiary level.

E. Provision of Public Funds

21. Financial self-reliance, unrestricted self-responsibility and full independence are vital for effective cooperative enterprise. The best policy approach is one where cooperatives receive the same treatment as any other form of enterprise. A number of other measures are valuable:

- acknowledgement and protection of the special character of cooperatives, and avoidance in law or practice of any discrimination arising from the special financial status, organization and management of cooperatives;
- avoidance of any direct or indirect engagement in the internal financial affairs of cooperatives or of the cooperative movement and recognition of the self-responsibility of the movement for its own financial affairs;

- development of partnerships with cooperative financial institutions in such masters as community and regional development, drawing on their experience of mobilizing and managing capital in a manner and for purposes conducive to the public good.

F. Institutional Arrangements for Collaboration and Partnership

22. Many departments and bodies in Government will have contact with the cooperative movement, while a policy of enabling and supporting cooperatives and operating an effective partnership with the movement will involve actions by a wide range of governmental institutions. In order to ensure consistency with broad general policy certain coordinating functions within Government, as well as liaison with the cooperative movement, will be useful.

23. It is advisable that a single department or office assume central coordinating, focal and liaison functions, of which the following might be most important:

    - elaboration of a single national comprehensive policy in respect of cooperatives, formulation of guidelines for consistent execution throughout Government, and monitoring and review of that execution;
    - collaboration with legal departments in drafting the general and any special laws;
    - liaison, consultation and collaboration with the cooperative movement.

24. The most effective organizational location for the responsible entity would be within a department already charged with broad strategic and co-ordinating functions, such as the office of a prime minister or president, or that responsible for economic management of development planning.

25. An institutional arrangement appropriate to national conditions which would permit effective collaboration between Government and the cooperative movement would be valuable.

26. Liaison between intergovernmental programmes and the international cooperative movement should be supported, including particularly that achieved through the Committee for the Promotion and Advancement of Cooperatives (COPAC).

Role of ILO in Promoting Cooperatives

International Labour Organisation (ILO), a specialized agency of the UNO was established in 1919 to promote social justice and internationally recognized human and labour rights. The ILO has been actively engaged in supporting cooperative development since the establishment of Cooperative Technical Service in 1920. The ILO then and now has viewed cooperatives as important tools for improving the living and working conditions of both men and women. The ILO sees cooperatives as businesses that are based on a broad set of democratic and egalitarian values. ILO has its branches to promote the cooperatives in each continent, which is called as ILO-COOPNET.

Through the Cooperative Branch, the ILO provides a variety of services to ILO constituents by means of policy advise to member state, technical cooperation, documentation and information to increase public awareness about cooperatives and the promotion of cooperative methods to resolve a variety of problems. Technical cooperation activities cover a wider range of themes like:

- Cooperative Reform and Legislation
- Human Resource Development and Networking
- Job Creation
- Poverty Alleviation
- Local Economic Development.

It is one of the units of UNO and do some service for the cooperatives as follows:

- Creation of a special wing for cooperatives;
- Deals mainly with management of cooperatives;
- Preparing course materials on cooperative management;
- To take care of the welfare of cooperative workers; and
- To organize conferences at international level on cooperatives.

ILO Recommendation on Cooperatives

The ILO promotes universally recognized human and labour rights primarily through its standard setting functions. Its highest decision making body, the International Labour Conference (ILC) debates and adopts standards on labour rights, employment, human resource development and other ILO concerns. An ILO convention once rectified by a member state becomes binding for that country and the compliance becomes mandatory.

R193 Promotion of Cooperatives Recommendation, 2002

This is the new recommendation adopted at 90th session of the ILO in June 2002. This recommendation replaces the Cooperatives (developing countries) Recommendation of 1966 (No. 127).

The General Conference of the International Labour Organization,

Having been convened at Geneva by the Governing Body of the International Labour Office, and having met in its 90th Session on 3 June 2002, and

Recognizing the importance of cooperatives in job creation, mobilizing resources, generating investment and their contribution to the economy, and

Recognizing that cooperatives in their various forms promote the fullest participation in the economic and social development of all people, and

Recognizing that globalization has created new and different pressures, problems, challenges and opportunities for cooperatives, and that stronger forms of human solidarity at national and international levels are required to facilitate a more equitable distribution of the benefits of globalization, and Noting the ILO Declaration on Fundamental Principles and Rights at Work, adopted by the International Labour Conference at its 86th Session (1998), and Noting the rights and principles embodied in international labour Conventions and Recommendations, in particular the Forced Labour Convention, 1930; the Freedom of Association and Protection of the Right to Organise Convention, 1948; the Right to Organise and Collective Bargaining Convention, 1949; the Equal Remuneration Convention, 1951; the Social Security (Minimum Standards) Convention, 1952; the Abolition of Forced Labour Convention, 1957; the Discrimination (Employment and Occupation) Convention, 1958; the Employment Policy Convention, 1964; the Minimum Age Convention, 1973; the Rural Workers' Organisations Convention and Recommendation, 1975; the Human Resources Development Convention and Recommendation, 1975; the Employment Policy (Supplementary Provisions) Recommendation, 1984; the Job Creation in Small and Medium-Sized Enterprises Recommendation, 1998; and the Worst Forms of Child Labour Convention, 1999, and

Recalling the principle embodied in the Declaration of Philadelphia that "labour is not a commodity", and

Recalling that the realization of decent work for workers everywhere is a primary objective of the International Labour Organization, and

Having decided upon the adoption of certain proposals with regard to the promotion of cooperatives, which is the fourth item on the agenda of the session, and

Having determined that these proposals shall take the form of a Recommendation;

Adopts this twentieth day of June of the year two thousand and two the following Recommendation, which may be cited as the Promotion of Cooperatives Recommendation, 2002.

I. *Scope, definition and objectives*

- It is recognized that cooperatives operate in all sectors of the economy. This Recommendation applies to all types and forms of cooperatives.
- For the purposes of this Recommendation, the term 'cooperative' means an autonomous association of persons united voluntarily to meet their common economic, social and cultural needs and aspirations through a jointly owned and democratically controlled enterprise.
- The promotion and strengthening of the identity of cooperatives should be encouraged on the basis of:
    - cooperative values of self-help, self-responsibility, democracy, equality, equity and solidarity; as well as ethical values of honesty, openness, social responsibility and caring for others; and
    - cooperative principles as developed by the international cooperative movement and as referred to in the Annex hereto. These principles are: voluntary and open membership; democratic member control; member economic participation; autonomy and independence; education, training and information; cooperation among cooperatives; and concern for community.
- Measures should be adopted to promote the potential of cooperatives in all countries, irrespective of their level of development, in order to assist them and their membership to:
    - create and develop income-generating activities and sustainable decent employment;
    - develop human resource capacities and knowledge of the values, advantages and benefits of the cooperative movement through education and training;
    - develop their business potential, including entrepreneurial and managerial capacities;
    - strengthen their competitiveness as well as gain access to markets and to institutional finance;
    - increase savings and investment;
    - improve social and economic well-being, taking into account the need to eliminate all forms of discrimination;
    - contribute to sustainable human development; and
    - establish and expand a viable and dynamic distinctive sector of the economy, which includes cooperatives, that responds to the social and economic needs of the community.

- The adoption of special measures should be encouraged to enable cooperatives, as enterprises and organizations inspired by solidarity, to respond to their members' needs and the needs of society, including those of disadvantaged groups in order to achieve their social inclusion.

II. *Policy framework and role of governments*

- A balanced society necessitates the existence of strong public and private sectors, as well as a strong cooperative, mutual and the other social and non-governmental sector. It is in this context that Governments should provide a supportive policy and legal framework consistent with the nature and function of cooperatives and guided by the cooperative values and principles set out in Paragraph 3, which would:
    - establish an institutional framework with the purpose of allowing for the registration of cooperatives in as rapid, simple, affordable and efficient a manner as possible;
    - promote policies aimed at allowing the creation of appropriate reserves, part of which at least could be indivisible, and solidarity funds within cooperatives;
    - provide for the adoption of measures for the oversight of cooperatives, on terms appropriate to their nature and functions, which respect their autonomy, and are in accordance with national law and practice, and which are no less favourable than those applicable to other forms of enterprise and social organization;
    - facilitate the membership of cooperatives in cooperative structures responding to the needs of cooperative members; and
    - encourage the development of cooperatives as autonomous and self-managed enterprises, particularly in areas where cooperatives have an important role to play or provide services that are not otherwise provided.
- • The promotion of cooperatives guided by the values and principles set out in Paragraph 3 should be considered as one of the pillars of national and international economic and social development.
    - Cooperatives should be treated in accordance with national law and practice and on terms no less favourable than those accorded to other forms of enterprise and social organization. Governments should introduce support measures, where appropriate, for the activities of cooperatives that meet specific social and public policy outcomes, such as employment promotion or the development of activities benefiting disadvantaged groups or regions. Such measures could include, among others and in so far as possible, tax benefits, loans, grants, access to public works programmes, and special procurement provisions.

- Special consideration should be given to increasing women's participation in the cooperative movement at all levels, particularly at management and leadership levels.

❑ (1) National policies should notably:

- promote the ILO fundamental labour standards and the ILO Declaration on Fundamental Principles and Rights at Work, for all workers in cooperatives without distinction whatsoever;
- ensure that cooperatives are not set up for, or used for, non-compliance with labour law or used to establish disguised employment relationships, and combat pseudo cooperatives violating workers' rights, by ensuring that labour legislation is applied in all enterprises;
- promote gender equality in cooperatives and in their work;
- promote measures to ensure that best labour practices are followed in cooperatives, including access to relevant information;
- develop the technical and vocational skills, entrepreneurial and managerial abilities, knowledge of business potential, and general economic and social policy skills, of members, workers and managers, and improve their access to information and communication technologies;
- promote education and training in cooperative principles and practices, at all appropriate levels of the national education and training systems, and in the wider society;
- promote the adoption of measures that provide for safety and health in the workplace;
- provide for training and other forms of assistance to improve the level of productivity and competitiveness of cooperatives and the quality of goods and services they produce;
- facilitate access of cooperatives to credit;
- facilitate access of cooperatives to markets;
- promote the dissemination of information on cooperatives; and
- seek to improve national statistics on cooperatives with a view to the formulation and implementation of development policies.

(2) Such policies should:

- decentralize to the regional and local levels, where appropriate, the formulation and implementation of policies and regulations regarding cooperatives;

- define legal obligations of cooperatives in areas such as registration, financial and social audits, and the obtaining of licences; and
- promote best practice on corporate governance in cooperatives.

❑ Governments should promote the important role of cooperatives in transforming what are often marginal survival activities (sometimes referred to as the "informal economy") into legally protected work, fully integrated into mainstream economic life.

III. *Implementation of public policies for the promotion of cooperatives*

❑ (1) Member States should adopt specific legislation and regulations on cooperatives, which are guided by the cooperative values and principles set out in Paragraph 3, and revise such legislation and regulations when appropriate.

(2) Governments should consult cooperative organizations, as well as the employers' and workers' organizations concerned, in the formulation and revision of legislation, policies and regulations applicable to cooperatives.

❑ (1) Governments should facilitate access of cooperatives to support services in order to strengthen them, their business viability and their capacity to create employment and income.

(2) These services should include, wherever possible:

- human resource development programmes;
- research and management consultancy services;
- access to finance and investment;
- accountancy and audit services;
- management information services;
- information and public relations services;
- consultancy services on technology and innovation;
- legal and taxation services;
- support services for marketing; and
- other support services where appropriate.

(3) Governments should facilitate the establishment of these support services. Cooperatives and their organizations should be encouraged to participate in the organization and management of these services and, wherever feasible and appropriate, to finance them.

(4) Governments should recognize the role of cooperatives and their organizations by developing appropriate instruments aimed at creating and strengthening cooperatives at national and local levels.

- ❑ Governments should, where appropriate, adopt measures to facilitate the access of cooperatives to investment finance and credit. Such measures should notably:
  - allow loans and other financial facilities to be offered;
  - simplify administrative procedures, remedy any inadequate level of cooperative assets, and reduce the cost of loan transactions;
  - facilitate an autonomous system of finance for cooperatives, including savings and credit, banking and insurance cooperatives; and
  - include special provisions for disadvantaged groups.
- ❑ For the promotion of the cooperative movement, governments should encourage conditions favouring the development of technical, commercial and financial linkages among all forms of cooperatives so as to facilitate an exchange of experience and the sharing of risks and benefits.

IV. *Role of employers' and workers' organizations and cooperative organizations, and relationships between them*

- ❑ Employers' and workers' organizations, recognizing the significance of cooperatives for the attainment of sustainable development goals, should seek, together with cooperative organizations, ways and means of cooperative promotion.
- ❑ Employers' organizations should consider, where appropriate, the extension of membership to cooperatives wishing to join them and provide appropriate support services on the same terms and conditions applying to other members.
- ❑ Workers' organizations should be encouraged to:
  - advise and assist workers in cooperatives to join workers' organizations;
  - assist their members to establish cooperatives, including with the aim of facilitating access to basic goods and services;
  - participate in committees and working groups at the local, national and international levels that consider economic and social issues having an impact on cooperatives;
  - assist and participate in the setting up of new cooperatives with a view to the creation or maintenance of employment, including in cases of proposed closures of enterprises;

- assist and participate in programmes for cooperatives aimed at improving their productivity;
- promote equality of opportunity in cooperatives;
- promote the exercise of the rights of worker-members of cooperatives; and
- undertake any other activities for the promotion of cooperatives, including education and training.

❑ Cooperatives and organizations representing them should be encouraged to:

- establish an active relationship with employers' and workers' organizations and concerned governmental and non-governmental agencies with a view to creating a favourable climate for the development of cooperatives;
- manage their own support services and contribute to their financing;
- provide commercial and financial services to affiliated cooperatives;
- invest in, and further, human resource development of their members, workers and managers;
- further the development of and affiliation with national and international cooperative organizations;
- represent the national cooperative movement at the international level; and
- undertake any other activities for the promotion of cooperatives.

V. *International cooperation*

❑ International cooperation should be facilitated through:

- exchanging information on policies and programmes that have proved to be effective in employment creation and income generation for members of cooperatives;
- encouraging and promoting relationships between national and international bodies and institutions involved in the development of cooperatives in order to permit:
  - *(i)* the exchange of personnel and ideas, of educational and training materials, methodologies and reference materials;
  - *(ii)* the compilation and utilization of research material and other data on cooperatives and their development;
  - *(iii)* the establishment of alliances and international partnerships between cooperatives;

(iv) the promotion and protection of cooperative values and principles; and

(v) the establishment of commercial relations between cooperatives;

- access of cooperatives to national and international data, such as market information, legislation, training methods and techniques, technology and product standards; and
- developing, where it is warranted and possible, and in consultation with cooperatives, employers' and workers' organizations concerned, common regional and international guidelines and legislation to support cooperatives.

VI. *Final provision*

❑ The present Recommendation revises and replaces the Co-operatives (Developing Countries) Recommendation, 1966.

Role of ICA in Promoting Cooperatives

ICA—International Cooperative Alliance was started in 1895. It has its regional offices at Geneva (for Europe), New Delhi (for Asia), Nairobi (for East Africa), Burkina Faso (for West Africa) and Costa Rica (for Americas). An additional office is opened at Singapore. The headquarters was shifted from London to Geneva during 1995. The Each Africa's office was shifted from Tanzania to Kenya in the year 1998. At present ICA's membership exceeds 230 member organizations. ICA admits only member countries National Federations as its member.

The objectives of the ICA are as follows:

- To provide a forum for the world cooperatives.
- To expand the cooperative movement in all countries.
- To concentrate on cooperative education and training of member countries.
- Empowerment of women.
- Special attention to youth.
- Organizing regional and global level seminars and conferences on cooperative areas.
- Publication of cooperative literature and periodicals.

What Does ICA Do?

ICA's priorities and activities center on promoting and defending cooperative identity, ensuring that cooperative enterprise is recognized form of enterprise that is able to compete in the market place.

- ICA raises awareness about cooperatives. It disseminates information materials including the ICA Digest and other communication means and jointly celebrates with the United Nations the International Day of Cooperatives every year.
- ICA is the voice of the cooperative movement - ICA has special status with a number of multinational institutions including the UN agencies, Council of Europe, the regional development banks, and others.
- ICA ensures that the right policy environment exists to enable cooperatives to grow and prosper. It helps its members in their lobbying for new legislations and more appropriate administrative procedures that respect the cooperative model, its principles and values.
- ICA provides its members with key contacts and information on best practice. It facilitates contacts between cooperatives for trading purpose and intelligence sharing in a wide range of areas. It organizes meeting, workshops to address key issues affecting cooperatives and allows discussion among cooperators from around the world.
- ICA provides technical assistance to cooperatives. Through its development programs at global and regional levels, it promotes capacity building, advice, and financial support to the cooperative movement.
- It ensures that right policy environment exists to enable cooperatives to grow and prosper.

Fields of Action

Following are the important field activities emphasized by the ICA for the cooperatives:

- *Food and nutrition*—The activities of ICA are focussed to the increase of food production and offering of nutritious food to the population, especially in developing countries. It has been pointed out that 600 million people in rural areas of the developing countries lack access to land. Re-distribution of land through the cooperatives is suggested to increase food production.
- *Urbanization and cooperative movement*—It is estimated that by the year 2000, half of the population in the Third World would leave in urban communities. This presupposes the migration of rural population to urban population. Slum improvement is one of the urgent policy areas in developing countries. Here, there is large scope for the cooperatives in the fields of housing cooperatives and consumer credit.
- *Employment and industry* — Cooperative organizations must offer viable alternatives to other forms of industrial organizations and must

undertake labour-intensive production techniques through industrial cooperatives. Industrial cooperatives in urban areas can offer income-generating opportunities for both men and women. Such cooperatives can restrict the rural migration to the urban areas.

- *Savings, credit and insurance*—The cooperatives must raise considerable part of their resources from the members themselves. Cooperative banks can make contributions to the establishment and expansion of cooperative organizations in a financially sound way. The same is true for cooperative insurance societies.

Priorities for Cooperatives

The following priorities for cooperatives have been laid by the ICA:

- *Development towards self-reliance*—The governments in developing countries must provide time-bound plans to provide help to the cooperatives. Ultimately, the cooperatives must be self-reliant in financial and other resources.
- *Democracy*—In an effort to democratize the cooperatives organizations, enlightened membership must be built through cooperative education. In the cooperative educational activities, stress should be laid on the involvement of women.
- *Involvement of women*—The ICA shall assist in the attainment of true cooperative democracy and to allow the participation of men and women on equal terms. Supporting the programmes for women like literacy campaigns, nutrition education, income generating projects, and developing thrift and loan cooperatives.
- *Professional management*—Cooperative organizations must improve their services only through professional management. Therefore, an effective system of cooperative staff training is necessary.
- *Education and training*—The education and training for members as well as committee members are vital for the cooperative performance. Without these, the desired level of quality of popular participation in the control of cooperatives cannot be expected.
- *Effective personnel policy*—In order to retain the skilled staff, cooperatives must establish comprehensive personnel policies including adequate recruitment and training, competitive salary system, job security and career possibilities.
- *Promote national and apex organizations*—The promotion of national and apex cooperative organizations is an important part of the development of autonomous cooperatives.

- ***Research***—It is necessary that due attention must be given to the examination of the needs of technical assistance, project identification, feasibility studies, monitoring and evaluation of cooperative programmes.

These elements should be includes in all ICA supported projects, including seminars and conferences.

Regional Structures of the ICA

Internationally, the global cooperative movement is represented by the International Co-operative Alliance (ICA). This provides services to member organizations, and represents them in resect to intergovernmental bodies and to international representatives of closely related movements and entities, including the non-cooperatively organized business community, other employers organizations, farmers' associations, trade unions, consumers organizations, and organizations representing major sections of the population defined in terms of gender, age, socio-cultural characteristics, etc.

The ICA Regional Officers were set up primarily as part of programmes of technical assistance for cooperative development in the South which began in the 1950s and gained momentum in the 1960s. They were established largely with financial and technical assistance from cooperative development agencies in the North. Thus the Office for Asia and the Pacific was established in 1960 with support form the Swedish cooperative movement, as was that for Eastern, central and Southern Africa at Moshi, Tanzania in 1968. Later, the ICA Project Office for the Southern Cone of South America, in Argentina, was funded largely by one of the Italian national cooperative organizations.

A decentralized organizational structure of the ICA Took effect in 1993. This included a more formal regional structure, including new Regional Assemblies. The Regional Assemblies were to be constituted by national (and in some cases, by sectoral and even regional cooperative organizations) in the countries of the geographical region being served.

At the same time a process of rationalization affected the geographical basis fro the regional Assemblies: In May, 1993 for the first time a Regional Assembly for Africa met, bringing together formerly separate bodies for West Africa and for Eastern, Central and Southern Africa respectively. In 1995 a new Regional Assembly for the Americas was set up: previously there had been groupings for Central America and the Caribbean and for South America.

As part of this restructuring process, the Regional Offices of the ICA assumed considerable autonomy. They were to less donor-oriented and would regard themselves as networks to support the work of regional cooperative organizations, specialized bodies and members within the region. They were to be operated by specialists from the region in question, and increasingly financed form the national cooperative organizations which are members. While financial and technical assistance, including the secondment of specialists, is provided by cooperative movements in the North, and the ICA Head Office and Specialized Bodies, these programmes are development as partnerships with equal participation of the regional offices in their planning, implementation and evaluation.

The projects administered by the ICA's regional offices are largely funded by the cooperative movement itself: in 1993 two thirds of the development budget of the Regional Office for Asia and the Pacific was provided with the region (albeit largely from Japan and Australia). regional development plans are examined and agreed at annual planning meetings by the regional office and c(cooperative) donors.

One of the principal functions of the Regional Offices was to stimulate cooperative development in all countries in the geographical region. For example, a Development Forum held in conjunction with the session of ICA's Central Committee held in Madrid, Spain in September, 1990 concluded that in Latin America and the Caribbean coordination of the actions of different regional organizations was essential if resources were to be better used it would be necessary to improve economic collaboration, joint activities, concrete entrepreneurial projects and common management and operational training.

The ICA's head office and regional offices are located as noted below:

- ICA Head Office and Regional Office for Europe—Geneva, Switzerland.
- Regional Office for Asia and Pacific—New Delhi, India.
- Regional Office for Americas—San Jose, Costa Rica.
- Regional Office for Eastern, Central and Southern Africa—Nairobi, Kenya.

ICA and Africa

The first regional office for Africa was opened in 1968 in Moshi, Tanzania. In 1993 a branch office of ICA-Africa was opened in Nairobi, Kenya. In 1983, the ICA opened the regional office for West Africa in Abidjan (Ivory Coast). This office was later moved on to Ouagoudougou, Burkina Faso. In the year 2004, both offices were merged thus creating ICA-Africa having the head office at Nairobi, with a project office located in Ouagoudougou.

The aim of ICA-Africa is to provide a forum for cooperative to exchange the ideas and experiences to complement cooperative development programs with educational and financial assistance and to be a center of information on areas related to cooperation.

The ICA-Africa works by providing guidance and support to its members and regional associations through projects, services, and networks.

The main area of activity is in development. Development activities are designed to suit the needs of cooperatives in the region. It thus, provide facilities in selected areas, namely, agriculture, rural finance, housing and national construction policies, and addresses a number of key issues that cut across the focal areas of resources development, youth, emerging cooperatives, gender, food security, resource mobilization, cooperative image and public relations, environment, and social service delivery.

ICA has also a series of sectoral bodies noted below:

- *Fisheries*—International Fisheries Cooperatives Association
- *Banking*—International Cooperative banking Association
- *Consumer*—Consumer Coop International
- *Housing*—International Cooperative Housing Organisation
- *Worker Cooperatives*—Industrial Organisation of Artisanal and Service producers Cooperatives
- *Finance*—International Cooperative and Mutual Insurance Federation.

ICA and UNO

Since 1972 ICA has worked closely with the United Nations, as well as with the International Labour Organisation and the Food and Agricultural Organization of the United Nations, in the Committee for the Promotion and Advancement of Cooperatives (COPAC), as well as by means of many types of direct collaboration.

It was in recognition of the special character of the ICA and of the closeness of its collaboration with the United Nations that the General Assembly, in its resolution 47/90, proclaimed the first Saturday of July 1995 to be International Day of Cooperatives "marking the centenary of the establishment of the International Co-operative Alliance". In its resolution 49/155 the General Assembly invited Governments, relevant international organizations and specialized agencies, as well as national and international cooperative organizations, to observe annually the International Day of Cooperatives on the first Saturday of July starting from 1995.

The ICA celebrated its first hundred years of existence by holding a Centennial Congress in Manchester, United Kingdom, in September 1995, one year after the world wide celebration of the 150th anniversary of the foundation of the modern cooperative movement in nearby Rochdale, where 28 individuals set up the first consumer cooperative in 1844.

Complementarity of the goals of the International Cooperative Alliance and the United Nations and actual and potential contribution of the international cooperative movement to solution of the major problems currently addressed by the United Nations

Individual women and men establish their own cooperatively organized business enterprises, or join cooperatives already in operation, in order that they can deal more effectively with the economic situation which confronts them, increase their ability to operate within the market economy and within contemporary society, and obtain benefits of an economic, but also of a social and political nature, which they perceive would be more difficult to enjoy by any other means of economic organization.

By means of membership in purchasing and supply cooperative, business enterprises, individuals, and independent enterprises in all sectors, are able to secure supplies of affordable, appropriate and high quality inputs, either for use in their enterprises, or for household consumption. Individuals and enterprises are able to secure better returns from the market by organizing marketing cooperatives. By means of organizing production cooperatives in all sectors, groups of individuals are able to ensure that the returns on their labour are maximized and employment itself made more secure. Specialized cooperative enterprises provide their members with security in the deposit of their savings, in the management of their finances, in the provision of credit; they provide their member-owners—who are also their users, clients or customers- with utilities, infrastructure, housing, social services, and healthcare.

By these means, as the Secretary-General of the United Nations acknowledged in the conclusion of his latest report to the General Assembly on the status and role of cooperatives in the light of new economic and social trends (A/49/213 of 1 July 1994):

"Cooperative enterprises provide the organizational means whereby a significant proportion of humanity is able to take into its own hands the tasks of creating productive employment, overcoming poverty and achieving social integration. ...";

"Cooperatives contribute substantially to the common good in market economies, principally by improving the efficiency and quality of the economy, but also by assuring democratization and environmental rationality. They constitute a model for a people-centred and sustainable form of societal organization, based on equity, justice and subsidiarity" (para. 72).

In its latest resolution on cooperatives, 49/155, the General Assembly recognized that "cooperatives in their various forms are becoming an indispensable factor in the economic and social development of all countries, promoting the fullest possible participation in the development process of all population groups, including women, youth, disabled persons and the elderly".

The General Assembly, in this same resolution, also recognized the "important contribution and potential of all forms of cooperatives to the preparations for and follow-up to the World Summit for Social Development and the Fourth World Conference on Women: Action for Equality, Development and Peace, to be held in 1995 and the United Nations Conference on Human Settlements (Habitat II) to be held in 1996."

In fact individual citizens, using the cooperative business enterprises of which they are the member-owners, and collaborating together within nation-wide cooperative movements, are working toward the same goals as have been identified by Member States of the United Nations. Through their representative cooperative organizations they are collaborating actively with the United Nations in carrying out many of its current programmes and in implementing many of its recent strategic decisions.

In respect to achievement of certain other goals of the United Nations, the international cooperative movement already is active and contributes significantly, but close strategic planning or operational collaboration has not yet been established, although the potential for the contribution of the international cooperative alliance to the solution of problems currently addressed by the United Nations is clearly very large.

These many different areas of actual and potential close collaboration are identified additional information will be set out in a series of background information notes being prepared jointly by the International Co-operative Alliance and the United Nations Department for Policy Coordination.

ICA and ILO

MEMORANDUM OF UNDERSTANDING BETWEEN THE INTERNATIONAL LABOUR ORGANIZATION (ILO) AND THE INTERNATIONAL COOPERATIVE ALLIANCE (ICA)

As early as 1919, formal relations started between the ILO and the ICA, by inclusion of the ICA in the list of international organization having consultative status in the ILO's governing body and International Labor conference (ILO constitution Article 12/3), bearing in mind that the first Director—General of the ILO, Mr. Albert Thomas , came from the cooperative movement and served also on the ICA Board in 1920s;

Technical cooperation and collaboration started in 1920 between the ILO and the ICA in order to promote cooperatives with the establishment of the cooperative branch of the ILO;

The ICA worked together with the ILO and its constituents to support the adoption and implementation of the ILO Recommendation 127 (the Role of cooperatives in Economic and social development of Developing countries) in 1966, as well as its revision by Recommendation 193 (promotion of cooperatives) in 2002;

The ICA worked together with national and international organizations supporting the cooperative movement;

It is in the interest of the ILO and ICA to define more detailed rules for their relationships in the light of the past experience as well as the framework for technical cooperation, attached to this MoU;

A COMMON COOPERATIVE AGENDA FOR ILO/ICA JOINT ACTION

Background and Justification

In his address to the ICA General Assembly in Oslo, in September 2003, the Director-General of the ILO invited the ICA to develop, together with the ILO, a 'common cooperative agenda' and a technical cooperation programme for the promotion and strengthening of cooperatives in developing countries to crate jobs and reduce poverty The ICA president responded to this call positively, indicating that combining the efforts of the two organizations in the fight against poverty will have a concrete impact. Furthermore, the ICA General Assembly, in its final resolution, highlighted the continuation of working together with the ILO on the implementation of ILO Recommendation 193 on the promotion of cooperatives.

As indicated in Mr. Somavia's speech to the General Assembly, the ILO-ICA partnership has indeed technical, constitutional and historical roots the first ILO Director—General, Albert Thomas, who came from the cooperative movement and who created the ILO'S cooperative Branch in 1920 , explained this in the ICA congress in 1930 as follows:

"Our two organizations have been technically and constitutionally, linked together. But the thing that matters most is neither technique nor procedure it is the spirit which animates the organizations from within—the communion of the hearts"

The two organizations have been working together for many years in many fronts to promote cooperatives The recent successful collaboration was undertaken in the process of preparation and adoption of ILO Recommendation 193 In 2003, the two organizations began collaboration through a series of workshops in Africa and Asia in promoting decent work in rural areas and strengthening the process of Poverty Reduction Strategy Papers (PRSP) through inclusion of cooperatives.

According to the Director—General's report 'working out of poverty' most of the poorest of the poor live in rural areas where jobs are scarce and basic services are weak In these areas the nearest institutions to the poor are often local cooperatives. A strong partnership with the ICA and its cooperative member organizations could therefore increase ILO's contribution to poverty reduction in more than 100 countries and support the poor in their efforts to create decent jobs. At the national level, the ILO-ICA partnership will focus on improving the policy environment through the implementation of Recommendation 193.

The ILO-ICA partnership will also be beneficial for the ICA and its member organizations as they will be able to receive technical expertise of the ILO's specialist teams in vocational training, management, social security, programme design and implementation, and micro finance within the framework of specific projects, the ILO's field structure will assist the ICA's national cooperative organizations in further developing strategic partnerships with governments, workers' and employers' organizations.

The partnership between ILO and ICA is therefore important to both organizations as they work with people in rural areas to achieve their common objective to combat social exclusion and poverty through participatory and practical means.

Objective

The objective of this 'common cooperative agenda' of the ILO-ICA partnership will be to design and implement technical cooperation programmers aimed at achieving the Millennium Development Goals (MDGs) particular emphasis will be placed on contributing to the following specific MDGs and targets:

- Eradicate extreme poverty and hunger
- Achieve universal primary education
- Promote gender equality and empower women
- Reduce child mortality
- Improve maternal health
- Combat HIV/AIDS, malaria and other diseases
- Ensure environmental sustainability
- Develop a global partnership for development.

To do this, the ILO and ICA will

- design and implement technical cooperation support programmes with national co-op organizations aimed at reducing poverty and creating jobs in developing countries. These will be practical initiatives aimed at demonstrating to Government and development partners the power of cooperative approaches;

- work on scaling up successes to national level, in collaboration with national organizations and Governments;
- influence the PRSP process by working together to incorporate the needs, expectations and fundamental principles of cooperative workers and ways of working into PRSPs;
- clearly demonstrate, and provide and provide analytical information, at the national and international level about the contributions that cooperative alliances and solidarity groups can have on poverty reduction.

Basic Principles and Implementation Guidelines

The following principles and operational guidelines will apply during the process of planning, implementation and evaluation of this ILO-ICA technical cooperation programme:

1. Each national programme will be designed on the basis of existing successful local development projects in order to make them sustainable and scale them up. These programmers will be owned and managed by local communities and local apex organizations.
2. where there is no cooperative-type of organization established by the poor the national co-op organization will start working with local self-help organizations pre-cooperatives and local development NGOs.
3. Empowerment of poor people through organizing them in cooperatives will be the basic grassroots approach of the programme through group action, purchasing power of the poor will be increased and their legal rights will be protected under the registered cooperatives.
4. Establishment of cooperatives that provide social protection and basic social services to the poorest of the poor will be encouraged and supported These cooperatives will include savings and credit, micro insurance, community health services, traditional medicine, cooperatives of disabled, elderly and HIV/AIDS victims, indigenous and tribal peoples, etc.
5. where crisis exists, scope for cooperative action will include many other services from rebuilding communications (infrastructure construction housing electricity water and communications supply transport community health and pharmacy services schooling funeral services food and nutrition clubs); to re-establishing economic activity (migrant worker

services employment creation insurance mutuals, cereal banks agricultural supply livestock breeding and veterinary services machinery irrigation fishing handicrafts etc.)

6. The ILO and ICA will focus on 'facilitation' and capacity building establishing linkages with relevant government agencies and other development partners and replication of good practices.
7. The role of governments will be to provide the forum for linking practical lessons into policy in other words helping to create national level initiatives and movements The key instrument for this will be the PRSP process.
8. Decent work indicators will be used to gauge success.
9. In accordance with the ICA cooperative Identity statement annexed to ILO Recommendation 133, cooperative principles will be respected and promoted by all programme partners including primary cooperative societies.
10. ILO's fundamental labour standards will be respected and promoted by all pilot programmes.
11. Gender equality will be given top priority in all programme operations, particularly in job creation schemes our target will be for at least half of the programme staff to be women including equity at management level.
12. To the extent possible programme staff will come from the local communities, selected by the communities themselves and trained by the ILO - ICA National Facilitation Team.
13. Local costumes, languages cultural values and indigenous practices will be respected and where appropriate incorporated into the programme activities.

Fund Raising and Financial Management

The ILO and ICA will jointly organize a funding campaign among major multi-bilateral donors and other development partners The existing 'movement-to-movement' technical cooperation linkage between the cooperative movements of some industrialized and developing countries will be strengthened with the joint programmes' multi-bilateral funding For this purpose, summary programme outlines (SPROUTs) will be prepared attached to an overall document providing the background information about the ILO-ICA partnership and MoU.

ILO will be responsible for the management of funds, and transaction for pilot programme funding as well as ICA's technical inputs Financial reporting to the donors will also be under the ILO's responsibility The ILO

Cooperative Branch will keep the ICA informed about all financial transactions and will also be responsible for issuing payment authorizations Annual review/audit of expenditures in local programmes will be undertaken by the ILO area offices in the countries convened.

Cost of programme formulation and other pre-programme costs will be covered jointly from the ILO's and ICA's own resources.

Linkages with Other Development Partners

Development agencies supporting cooperative development, governmental and non-governmental will be kept informed about the ILO-ICA partnership and its pilot programmes and their technical and financial contributions will be sought Direct movement-to-movement assistance will be encouraged to strengthen national cooperative apexes of developing countries implementing pilot programmes.

Memorandum of understanding (MoU) will be prepared between ILO and ICA outlining this partnership this common Cooperative Agenda will be an annex to the MoU.

ILO and ICA have agreed as follows:

Article 1: Objective of the Memorandum of Understanding

The objective of this Memorandum of Understanding is to further the existing cooperation between the ILO and ICA in the area of promotion and strengthening of cooperatives through regular consultation, exchange of information and coordination of efforts in the fields of common interest, in accordance with the objectives and principles of the ILO and ICA , with particular reference to the promotion an implementation of ILO Recommendation on the promotion of cooperatives (NO. 193, 2002), fight against poverty and creation of decent jobs.

Article 2: Strengthening partnership

Taking into account the ILO'S constitutional basis with regard to its relationship with the ICA, to strengthen the exiting partnership, joint programmers and projects shall be developed and implemented to promote cooperatives worldwide.

Article 3: Exchange of information and experience

The ILO and ICA shall arrange for the exchange of information, publications and documents concerning cooperative development. To this effect, the parties shall be periodically sending to each other their list of relevant publications and documents so that the other party could request copies of these publications and documents.

Following the existing practice, each party shall inform the other party about the meetings that could be interest to other party.

Article 4: Cooperation and consultation

ILO and ICA agree that, with a view to facilitating the effective attainment of the objectives set forth in their respective constituent instruments, they shall act in close cooperation with each other, and shall consult each other periodically, with respect to matters of common interest In particular, each party shall inform the other, at an early stage, of any plans for the execution of development of its activities whenever this is required to secure effective coordination and to avoid duplication of efforts.

Article 5: Specific areas of cooperation

The ILO and ICA shall formulate a common cooperative Agenda, as annexed to this MOU, that will identify areas for specific cooperation and respond to the current priorities of each organization these shall include activities to contribute effectively to the attainment of the Millennium Development Foals of the United Nations, particularly with regard to regard to reducing poverty by the year 2015.

When parties define other areas of cooperation, they shall be specified in a separate document to be also annexed to this MoU.

Article 6: Working arrangements

The Director-General of the ILO and the director - General of the ICA may make appropriate working arrangements for the implementation of the provisions of this Memorandum of Understanding.

Article 7: Entry into force

This Memorandum of Understanding shall enter into force on the date of its signature.

Role of FAO in promoting cooperatives

Food and Agriculture Oganization (FAO) is one of the organs of the UNO and is located in Rome, Italy. FAO is primarily engaged in the following activities:

1. Promotion of agriculture development in developing countries.
2. Providing technical assistance to member countries in the field of agricultural development.
3. Providing agricultural extension services to member countries.
4. To coordinate the activities of international agricultural research institutes located in various countries.

5. To organize forums, conferences and seminars frequently inviting the Ministers of Agriculture and Agricultural Scientists from various countries.
6. To produce literature in the field of agriculture and publishing the journal 'Ceres'.

FAO has a long history of working with primary rural cooperatives. Its technical assistance is focused on three areas:

1. Design of national Policies, Strategies and Legislation to enhance the role of cooperatives in Rural Development.
2. Support for the coalition building and partnerships.
3. Institutional capacity building for cooperatives.

In 1998, FAO produced a Training manual for Trainers on Agricultural Cooperative Development, recently revised. The FAO has also updated and revised in 2004, New Strategies for Mobilizing capital in Agricultural Cooperatives.

Role of International Cooperative Federations/Agencies in promoting cooperatives

Committee for Promotion (COPAC)

Established in 1971 as an inter-agency committee, the Committee for the Promotion and Advancement of Cooperatives is an ongoing partnership between three United Nations agencies and four international non-governmental organizations, representatives of the cooperative movement:

(a) United Nations;

(b) International Labour Office (ILO);

(c) Food and Agriculture Organization of the United Nations (FAO);

(d) International Cooperative Alliance (ICA);

(e) International Federation of Agricultural Producers (IFAP);

(f) International Union of Food, Agricultural, Hotel, Restaurant, Catering, Tobacco and Allied Workers' Associations (IUF);

(g) World Council of Credit Unions (WOCCU).

It aims to promote and coordinate development initiatives through policy coordination, information exchange, advocacy and a variety of services. The members of COPAC collaborate with each other to promote and coordinate sustainable cooperative development through policy dialogue, technical cooperation, collection and dissemination of information. Members meetings are held twice yearly and seminars and other meetings are organized on specific topics concerning cooperatives. In response to the UNO Resolution A/RES/51/58, COPAC has started to draft guidelines for cooperative development. The guidelines contain a series of recommendations that should be considered when establishing a policy with regard to cooperatives and the cooperative movement. These include public recognition of the cooperative movement, legal, judicial and administrative provisions; research, statistics and information; education, provision of public funds and institutional arrangement for collaboration and friendship.

World Council of Credit Unions (WOCCU)

It is a body of World Credit Unions. This organization provides technical assistance and training to credit unions in developing countries. As on 2002, the membership of this organization consists of 40258 credit unions, having individual membership of 118 million. The credit unions, according to World Bank's estimate sent back remittances by migrant workers as much as $ 88 billion in 2002.

International Cooperative and Mutual Insurance Federation (ICMIF)

The ICMIF was founded in 1922 today represents 240 cooperative and mutual insurance societies belonging to 100 member organizations in 61 countries. 60 per cent of the French market for non-compulsory insurance has been covered by the insurance cooperatives. In Japan, insurance cooperatives cover insurance for 10 million employees. They emphasize the maintenance of health, information and participation of the choice of treatment of the members. The federation has a re-insurance service which enables cooperative insurance societies throughout the world to exchange re-insurance business. The third supporting body of the organization, Allnations Inc., which had mainly concentrated on providing loan guarantees required by new formed insurance cooperatives, is now assuming a more active role in assisting cooperative insurance facilities.

International Cooperative Banking Associations (ICBA)

This was established in 1922 by National Cooperative Banks and financial organizations in order to exchange information, promote cooperation among cooperative banks, promote the development of new cooperative banks through advise and assistance and research and study subjects of common interests such as capital formation and cooperative values as applied to banking. The ICBA has 68 member organizations from 40 countries. The ICBA central executive maintains close contacts with the Association of European Cooperative Banks in Brussels, the World Council of Credit Unions (WOCCU) and the International Raiffeisen Union (IRU).

The CICOPA's members are producers cooperatives from different fields such as construction, industrial production, general services, transport artisanal activities, health and social care. It has a membership of over 70 Apex Cooperative Organisations from 57 countries. CICOPA supports commercial and technical links between producers cooperatives through the exchange of goods and services, the provision of education and training, the exchange of experiences, the study of issues specific to producers cooperatives and the circulation of recommendation for the solution of cooperative problems in the industrial sector.

Inter-Coop

It was founded in 1971, is an association of 10 National Consumer Federations in 9 countries viz., Finland, Hungary, Israel, Italy, Japan, Norway, Slovakia, Sweden and UK. INTER-COOP aims at promoting commercial cooperation between its member organizations in order to increase their competitive power in the market place. INTER-COOP's activities include the exchange of information and know-how among member retail organizations, several permanent and ad hoc working groups have been set up specifically for this purpose. In addition, INTER-COOP organizes an education and management development programme for senior managers of member organizations.

Self-learning Activity

Try to answer the following questions on your own.

1. Write short notes on UNO's research agenda on cooperatives?
2. Discuss the field of action of ICA?
3. Describe COPAC?
4. What is WOCCU?

Summary

- United Nations, the world body of nations, which has been organized to promote peace and prosperity among nations is also taking keen interest in promoting the cooperatives.
- The UNO has fixed Millennium Development Goals to be achieved by nations by the year 2015. Cooperatives are also expected to join the other agencies in fulfilling the Millennium Development Goals.
- Frequently, UNO is giving guidelines for the promotion of cooperatives. It has promoted a special agency called COPAC to act as a linking process to promote the cooperatives.
- ILO is one of the oldest international agencies established in 1919. It has opened a special branch of cooperatives called Cooperative Technical Service during the year 1920. Now ILO is taking a lead in promoting the cooperatives.

- The latest ILO Recommendation No.193 (2002) has given elaborate guidelines for the governments of member countries to encourage and promote cooperatives.
- ICA was started in the year 1895. It is the mouthpiece of cooperatives of more than 120 countries. The major objectives of ICA are: to promote cooperatives among the member countries, to encourage the federal structure of cooperatives in member countries, to provide forum for the world cooperatives, to encourage the interaction between world cooperatives for their trade and development, etc.
- ICA has its headquarters in Geneva. It has regional offices for continents, which are located in Geneva for Europe, Costa Rica for Americas, New Delhi for Asia and Pacific, and Nairobi for Africa.
- ICA is closely associating its activities with the UNO. The liaison with UNO is provided by the COPAC. The UNO has informed the member countries to promote cooperatives and take the help of ICA. UNO has informed the member countries to celebrate International day of Cooperatives on first Saturday of July starting from the year 1995.
- ICA and ILO are mutually working for the development of cooperatives. Recently, a Memorandum of Understanding (MoU) has been signed between the ILO and ICA in 2004. This commits both organizations to formulate a common cooperative agenda among other things, focus on ways in which cooperatives can contribute to the achievement of Millennium Development Goals.
- The FAO is one of the important organs of UNO engaged in the development of agricultural development among member countries. FAO has a long history of working with primary rural cooperatives. It helps the member countries to design national policies, strategies and legislation to enhance the role of cooperatives in rural development. FAO has also produced a training manual for trainers on agricultural cooperative development.

Part—III

Scope for Organizing Cooperatives

15 Management of Working Capital

Working capital is the day-to-day finance required to run a business. Otherwise known as the excess of current assets over current liabilities representing the capital immediately available for free and continues running of a business. Scientific management of working capital is important in maintaining the financial health of any enterprise. Management of working capital is concerned with the management of cash, inventories, marketable securities, accounts receivable and payable, investor's pre-paid expenses, wages payable, etc. In this context, financial management has to take decisions on the following aspects frequently:

1. What is the procedure to be followed to manage the cash of the firm?
2. What must be the inventory policy and the level of inventory?
3. To whom credit may be given?
4. What should be the structure of firm's current debt and future debt?

Cooperative executives pay much attention for the management of working capital. One of the serious reasons for the failure of small-scale business enterprises is the lack of working capital. Without considering the importance of working capital the small-scale business enterprises invest all their resources on the office establishments, plant and machineries. While running their business they could not stand in the vicissitudes of business cycle due to lack of working capital. That's why the banks have a separate scheme for providing working capital assistance to the firms. Lack of working capital makes it difficult to the firm to cope up with the environmental changes due to change in macro economic scenario. Further deficiency in working capital prevents the enterprises to take advantage of opportunity cost. At the same time excess of working capital decreases the profitability of the firm.

Factors Determining Working Capital

The following factors decide working capital needs of organizations including cooperatives:

1. *Nature of Business*

   A firm's working capital requirements are basically related to the kinds of business it conducts. Public utilities have the lowest requirements for current assets because they have only cash sales and supply services not product. In manufacturing companies, stock–in-trade represents a large investment. Trading and financial firms require a large sum of money as working capital.

2. *Size of Business*

   The size of business also has an important bearing in determining working capital needs of a firm. A firm with large-scale operations will need more working capital than a smaller firm.

3. *Manufacturing Process*

   If the manufacturing process in an industry entails a longer period because of its complex character, more working capital is required to finance that process. An extended manufacturing time span means a larger tie up of funds in inventories and higher amount of working capital.

4. *Business Fluctuations*

   Business variations affect the working capital requirements, especially the temporary working capital requirements of the firm. In a boom period the sales will increase. Correspondingly, the firm's investment in inventories and book debts will also increase and some firms may make additional investment in fixed assets. This act of the firm will require further additions to working capital. When there is a decline in the economy, the sales will fall and consequently the levels of inventories and book debts will also fall. So the need of working capital will be less in this period.

5. *Turnover of Circulating Capital*

   The speed with which the working capital completes its round i.e. conversion of cash into stores, inventory of raw material and stores, inventory of raw materials into inventory of finished goods, inventory of finished goods into book debts or account receivables, and book debts into cash accounts, plays an important role in judging the requirement of the working capital.

6. *Growth and Expansion of Business*

   A growing firm has to invest funds in fixed assets in order to sustain its growing production and sales. This will increase investment in current assets to support enlarged scale of operations. It will require more working capital.

7. *Volume of Sales*

A firm maintains the current assets because they are needed to support the operational activities, which result in sales. As the volume of sales increases, there is an increase in the investment of working capital, in the cost of operations, in inventories and in receivables. The increase in current assets will result in increase in the requirement of working capital.

8. *Terms of Purchases and Sales*

If the credit terms of purchases are more favorable and those of the sales are less liberal, less cash will be invested in inventory. A firm, which can get credit on favorable conditions, will require less amount of the working capital than a firm with out such a facility.

9. *Cash Requirements*

Cash is one of the current assets, which is essential for the successful operation of the production cycle. Cash should be adequate and properly utilized. Adequate cash is also required to maintained good credit relations.

10. *Profit Margin and Profit Appropriation*

The net profit is a source of the working capital. A high net profit margin contributes towards the working capital pool. The requirements of the working capital are also influenced by the tax liabilities and the firm 's policy to retain or distribute products. A high tax liability will impose an additional strain on the working capital. Payment of dividend consumes cash resources and therefore reduces the firm's working capital to that extent.

11. *Change in the Technology*

Technological developments related to the production process have a sharp impact the need for working capital. Changes in technology will need additional amount of the working capital due to fresh investment in new fixed assets.

12. *Inventory Turnover*

With a better inventory control, a firm is able to reduce its working capital requirements. If the inventory turn over is high working capital requirements will be low.

13. *Other Factors*

Absence of the coordination in the production and distribution policies in the company leads to the high demand for the working capital. The import policy of the government may also affect the requirements of the working capital for the companies as they have to arrange for the funds for importing goods at specified times.

Advantages of Adequate Working Capital

A cooperative should maintain adequate working capital to run the business smoothly. It is the life-blood of the business and claims the following advantages:

1. It creates a feeling of security and the confidence in the management or officials of the company.
2. It is 'must' for maintaining solvency and continuing production by making the payments in time in this era of the cutthroat competition.
3. It increases goodwill and debt capacity of the business.
4. Easy loans from banks can be obtained without any security.
5. Distributions of dividend in cash are not possible in spite of good profits, in the absence of adequate working capital.
6. Meeting unseen contingencies such as depressions, etc.
7. It increases fixed assets efficiency because of its proper maintenance.
8. High morale of the executives because of an environment of certainty, security, and confidence, which is a great psychological factor.

Increase production efficiency by maintaining continuous flow of raw materials.

Dimensions of Working Capital Management

Management of working capital covers the following three functions:

1. Management of Receivables.
2. Mangement of Inventories.
3. Management of cash.

Management of Receivables

Selling goods on credit is the most prominent form of modern business. The firm adopts this method of selling goods to protect it from the competitors and to attract the customers to buy its products at favorable terms. When firm sells goods or services on deferred payment basis, it is said that the firm has granted trade credit to customers. Trade credit in other words, is known as receivables or book-debt. The book debt has three characteristics, viz., *(i)* it involves an element of risk; *(ii)* it is based on the economic value. It – means goods/services passed on to the buyer have the economic value and the equivalent will be received in future by the seller; and *(iii)* the cash payment or equivalent will be made in the future. The book debts are also called debtors and represent the firm's claims on asset.

The financial management, in managing the receivables is concerned with maintaining the receivables at the optimum level and review the credit policy and procedures accordingly.

Management of Inventory

Inventory management has become unavoidable in the present day manufacturing process. The basic managerial objectives of inventory control are two-fold: first to avoid over-investment and under investment in inventories and the second to provide the right quantity of goods of right quality at proper time and at proper value. The objectives of inventory management are given below:

Availability of the Materials: The first and the foremost objective of inventory management are to make all types of materials available at all times whenever they are needed.

Minimizing the Wastage: Inventory control is essential to minimize the wastage at all levels.

Promotion or Manufacturing Efficiency: The manufacturing efficiency of the enterprises increases the right type of raw materials is available for the production department at the right time. It reduces wastage and cost of the production and improves the morale of the workers.

Better Services to the Customers: In order to meet the demand of the customers, it is the responsibility of the concern to produce sufficient stock of the finished goods to execute the orders received. It means a flow of production should be maintained.

Control of the Production Level: Proper control of the inventory maintains buffer stock. Any eventual production variation can also be avoided through proper control of the inventories.

Optimum Level of Inventories: It helps in maintaining optimum level of the inventories keeping in view the operational requirements. It also avoids the out of stock danger.

Economy in Purchasing: Proper inventory control brings certain advantages and economies in purchasing the raw materials. Management makes every attempt to purchase the raw materials in the bulk quantity and to take advantages of economies in purchasing the raw materials in the bulk quantity and to take advantages of favorable market conditions.

Reasonable Prices: Management should ensure the supply of the raw materials at a reasonably low price but without sacrificing the quality of it. It helps in controlling the cost of the production and the quality of finished goods in order to maximize the profits of the concern.

Minimizing Cost: Inventory costs are the part of cost of the production. Hence controlling the inventory costs can also minimize the cost of the production.

Management of Cash

Cash is importance to start a new venture, whether it is a banking organization or production unit. Initial investment made in the from of cash ultimately leads to the investment in the form of fixed assets like land, building, plant and machineries. The investment of cash must continue till the unit earns a surplus in the form of profit.

Cash is needed to meet the day-to-day expenses in firms and to meet the demand of the depositors in banks. If enough cash is not maintained daily the banks may have to face the risk. Cash is needed for:

1. Payment of expenses
2. Liquidation of creditors
3. Purchase of fixed assets, raw materials and supplies
4. Payment of dividend, interest, wages and taxes
5. Repayment of loan

Functions of Funds Management in Cooperatives

The basic function of funds management in any organization including the co-operatives is to maintain liquidity and profitability. But cooperatives eschew profit and strives to earn a surplus to earn a surplus. Following are the important functions of funds management in cooperatives:

1. ***Raising Funds:*** Co-operative Banks raise their funds by way of owned funds and borrowed funds. Owned funds consist of share capital and Reserve funds. Borrowed funds consist of deposits and borrowings from other agencies. Co-operative banks must concentrate on raising more deposits in the open market.

2. ***Deployment of Funds:*** The funds raised must be employed for more productive purposes, proper 'credit planning' must be applied.

3. ***Forecasting Cash Flows:*** Cash inflows must match cash outflows. The banks must forecast the timing of inflows and use them to pay its creditors and loan operations.

4. ***Cost Control:*** When money is spent on various items the cost of such investment must be noted periodically.

5. ***Pricing:*** Pricing a product or a banking service is another aspect of financial function. The financial manager can supply important

information's on costs, changes in costs of production or services and profit margin. This helps to follow an ideal price policy which can help to market a product of service and to maintain a profit margin.

6. *Measuring Cost of Capital:* Each different source of funds received by a firm or a bank may have different condition and cost. Short term debt may be costlier than long term debt. This must be measured and a return must be assured for capital.
7. *Forecasting Profits:* A successful financial management must predict future profits. For this the current costs and variable costs must be calculated to assure a reasonable profit.
8. *Managing Assets:* A firm's assets must be carefully managed and a number of decisions must be made on their use. The financial manger coordinates his activities with other managers and decides to increase or stabilize assets.
9. *Managing Funds:* Funds are the liquid assets of firm. Cash and liquid assets come under the category. The financial manager must guarantee to finance receivables and inventories and must make arrangements for the purchase of assets. Management of funds has both liquidity and profitability aspects.

Self-learning Activity

Try to answer the following questions on your own.

1. Write short notes on management of receivables?
2. Write about fund management in cooperatives?

Summary

- Any organization, including the cooperatives needs strong working capital to manage the operations. There are several factors like the nature of business, size of business, volume of sales, cash requirements, etc., that decide the volume of working capital needed by an organization.
- Working capital has certain advantages to the organizations. Adequate working capital is needed to run the business smoothly. It is the life blood of an organization.
- Working capital covers three major functions viz., management of receivables, management of inventory and management of cash.

16 Owned Funds and Borrowed Funds

Owned Funds

Owned funds of a cooperative consist of paid up share capital plus various reserves created by the cooperative. The committee on cooperative credit of India stated the importance of owned funds as "The owned funds of an institution are regarded by the creditors as the margin of security for their lending and in that context, a larger margin should prove conducive to the creation of more confidence in the minds of the outside creditors. What the owned funds are to a limited liability society, the net assets of the members or to an unlimited liability society". The importance of owned funds is as follows:

1. ***Owned funds indicate the self-reliance of a cooperative***—One of the problems faced by the cooperatives is lack of funds. Only by means of mobilizing enough owned funds, a cooperative can free itself from outside influence. Borrowings from outside will always introduce restrictions and interference in the freedom and autonomy of a borrower. Hence, enough owned funds can make a cooperative to stand on its own legs.
2. ***The maximum borrowing power of a cooperative bank is fixed on the basis of the owned funds***—A cooperative can raise funds through owned funds an borrowed funds. Borrowed funds consist of deposits and loans from various agencies. In many developing countries, the cooperative laws declare that outside borrowings should be based on the owned funds of the cooperative. So, to raise huge borrowed funds, the internal funds by way of owned funds must also be increased by a cooperative.
3. ***Owned funds act as a shock absorber during the times of financial crisis***—Financial crisis for a cooperative may arise when there is shortage of cash. When money is borrowed from outside agencies as loans, sometimes cooperatives may default repayments due to lack of cash and liquidity. Owned funds can provide liquidity to the cooperative and any temporary cash arrangement could be made by having adequate owned funds.

4. A sound owned fund structure could create good confidence in the minds of the investors, especially depositors. Cooperatives' financial strength and stability is decided by the owned funds. Among the shareholders, customers, public, government, and other stakeholders, the credibility of a cooperative is decided by its financial strength that too owning of sound owned funds.
5. *To improve the business*—Cooperative engaged in business activities and lending operations may need money in the form cash to manage crisis that may arise very often. If adequate cash is not available, there may be work stoppage in producers' cooperative and cooperatives like marketing cooperatives cannot undertake procurement operations. By means of having adequate owned funds, the business operations of a cooperative can move fast.
6. ***Sustainability***—Sustainability denotes the continued growth of a cooperative without any interruption. Owned funds can provide sustainability because the growth of owned funds would be on the higher level year after year, on any account it will not come down. On the other hand, borrowings from other agencies may go up or come down depending on the business operations.
7. ***Viability***—The financial viability for a cooperative could be provided by strong owned funds. This viability can help the cooperative to balance its operations and to invest the money in ventures needed to the members.
8. Apart from servings as margin of security, the creditor looks to the owned funds as absorbers of the impact of overdues, which to some extent are inevitable in agricultural finance. The larger the owned funds of a society, the greater is the ability to absorb overdues, so that repayment of the dues to outside creditors may be ensured.
9. Owned funds are equally important from the point of view of the society in maintaining a continuous flow of finance to it from outside creditors. If the shock of overdues is not adequately absorbed by the owned funds, and the society defaults to the creditors, further finance to it may be delayed. The owned funds are thus import for the creditors and the borrowing society.

Paid-up Share Capital—Capital is collected, primarily from members as well as from other cooperatives, government, and voluntary agencies. The importance of share capital is as follows:

1. ***Holding a share alone signifies the membership in a cooperative***—A member can assert his right as a member only by holding minimum number of shares. In a cooperative, irrespective of the number of shares held by a member, only one vote is given. This makes the precious nature of holding even minimum shares.

2. ***Share capital can be increased by means of increase in the value of shares***—In many countries cooperatives after certain years use to increase the value of shares in order to mobilize more amount of money.

3. ***In cooperatives, a member cannot take any number of shares; a ceiling is fixed for the individual maximum***—Unlike the corporate sector, in cooperatives a member cannot take any number of shares. In the bylaws of cooperatives, the maximum number of shares to be taken by a member is fixed in the form of ceilings.

4. ***The number of shares to be allotted for other cooperatives and government will be very high***—In countries where governments are allowed to participate in the shares of cooperatives, higher number of shares are allotted to government.

5. The major part of owned funds in a newly established cooperative would be formed by share capital. Till the reserve funds are increased, only share capital forms the major base of owned funds.

Share capital can be increased by the following ways:

- ***By admitting new members***—A cooperative is expected to increase its membership year after year and at one stage, they have to cover all families in the area of operation, especially in rural areas. By means of admitting new members, a cooperative can increase its share capital.
- ***Increasing the present value of shares***—As noted earlier, a cooperative can increase the quantum of money by means of increasing the present value of shares. Proper amendments must be made in the bylaws of the cooperative society to increase the value of shares.
- ***Linking of shares to borrowings***—In credit cooperatives and cooperative banks, the borrowings of members can be linked to the share capital. That means, if a member wants to take higher amount of loans, he must have higher amount of share capital. In non-credit cooperatives, the shares can be linked to the individual business operations of a member.
- ***Allotting shares to other cooperatives***—A primary cooperative or other types of cooperatives can allot shares to the neighbouring cooperatives. Through this process, the cooperative can increase its capital base. Because cooperatives can take more number of shares than the individuals.
- ***Institutional allotment***—Cooperatives can allot shares to government and local bodies to increase the share capital. But care should be taken to see that such agencies are not given any influential power in voting in the form of allowing 'veto power'.

Reserve Funds—All cooperative institutions according to their bylaws must distribute their net profit every year and set forth a portion of their net profit for reserve fund and other forms of reserves. Reserve funds can be used for the business purpose of a cooperative or it can be invested in other cooperatives. The importance of reserve funds is as follows:

1. Reserve fund is created compulsorily out of the net profit. So, it is increasing year after year. In many countries cooperative laws provide provisions to create reserve funds even if the society is facing loss.
2. It helps to increase the owned funds of the cooperative and the maximum borrowing power of a cooperative. In countries like Ethiopia, the cooperative proclamation and the bylaws allow the cooperatives to use the reserve funds for their business purposes.
3. Like the share capital, reserve funds also provide a cushion to the bank and acts as a shock absorber. Because entire reserve funds can be used for the business purpose.
4. If reserve fund is invested outside, it will fetch a rate of interest to the cooperative. But many cooperative make it a point to invest the reserve funds for their business operations.
5. Unlike other funds, reserve funds will not go diminished every year. On the other hand, reserve funds will be going on increasing every year due to the increase in profit and the distribution of profit for various purposes.

Borrowed Funds

A cooperative bank/society has to depend more on owned funds to self-reliant in resources. But there are limitations in raising the owned funds and hence, the cooperative have to resort to borrowings. Borrowings consist of deposits and other borrowings from higher cooperative agencies, government, and commercial banks.

1. ***Easy to mobilize***—Borrowings are the easiest sources to mobilize in the open market. If a cooperative has strong standing in the market, and shows a good performance, it will not be a difficult thing to mobilize more borrowed funds.
2. ***Customer attraction***—If a cooperative bank provides attractive customer facilities, like quick service, higher rate of interest for deposits, etc, it will not be a difficult thing for the cooperative to raise borrowed funds.
3. Compared to the owned funds, the volume and size of borrowed funds will be very high. Having only funds, a cooperative cannot expand its business activities fast. Owned funds have their own limitations like limitation to increase them in the short period, difficulties in increasing membership, etc. During such occasions, a cooperative can resort to borrowed funds.

4. *Availability*—Borrowed funds like deposits would be available to the cooperatives at any time in the open market. The only problem is they have to compete with other agencies to mobilize resources.
5. *Cheaper nature*—If cooperatives could borrow funds from government and NGOs, the rate of interest will be lower. The volume of credit will also be very high to meet the emerging needs of the cooperatives.

Limitations of Borrowed Funds

Borrowed funds, though attractive, have lot of limitations, which are noted below:

1. *Costlier nature*—Borrowed funds will always be costlier compared to the owned funds. The rate of interest provided for the loans will be naturally higher than the rate of interest to be provided to the share capital of the members.
2. *Administration cost*—Administration cost or the cost of borrowing and managing the funds would be higher in the case of the borrowing funds. Such administrative costs are apart from the rate of interest to be provided to the lending agencies.
3. *Freedom*—The democratic freedom of a cooperative will be affected by the borrowed funds. A cooperative has to abide the rules and regulations of a lending agency.
4. *Self-reliance*—Self-reliance of a cooperative can be created only by means of raising more owned funds. On the other hand borrowed funds will show the liability of the cooperative.
5. *Repayment difficulties*—Very many times, cooperatives are unable to repay the loans borrowed from lending agencies. During such occasions, they are put under difficulties like payment of penal rate of interest for delayed payment of loans. Such costs will add to the cost of operations of the cooperative.

Deposits—Cooperatives raise deposits from members and non-members. In many cases the deposits raised from non-members are more than from members. Cooperatives raise various deposits like current deposits, fixed deposits, recurring deposits, and savings deposits. The significance of deposits is as follows:

1. Deposits also promote the self-reliance of resource of a cooperative, because it is raised in the open market. Because they create the relationship applicable to banker-customer relationship in ordinary banking world. They honor the claims of the depositors and do normal banking services without affecting their internal work.

2. Cooperatives raise their deposits in rural areas and semi-urban areas thereby they promote rural banking. In developing countries, the established commercial banks shun the rural areas, which prevent the rural population to take the modern banking services. On such occasions, the cooperative banks can go to the rural areas and mobilize deposits.
3. Cooperatives, by attracting various deposits or providing banking services to the poor people and the rural people. Increased income and increased rate of literacy in rural areas allow the rural people to learn modern banking services. Only cooperative banks can go to the rural areas and provide the needed modern banking services to the rural population.
4. While utilizing the deposits as loanable resources, the cooperatives have to follow the rules and regulations of the central bank of the country. This allows greater confidence in the minds of the depositing public.
5. The deposits collected by the cooperatives, after keeping a part of the deposits as cash reserves, can be employed in the business operations of the cooperatives. But cooperatives, as established banking institutions, have to abide by the regulations of the central bank of the country. The central bank of the country fixes the rate of interest, regulations regarding the deposits, amount of cash reserves to be kept, etc.

Borrowings—A cooperative can borrow loans from higher cooperative institutions, government, and commercial banks. Borrowings have several advantages noted below:

1. Borrowings from agencies, though costlier, will be available at any time to a cooperative society. Funds mobilization cannot be quickly arranged through owned funds resources.
2. Borrowed funds have lot of flexibilities. According to the needs of a cooperative, money can be borrowed for short periods, medium periods, or long periods. Likewise, the rate of interest will also vary from lending agency to lending agency. A cooperative banker can choose an agency, which is lending money for a lower rate of interest.
3. Heavy investment needs could be satisfied only by means of borrowings. Cooperatives like industrial cooperatives, processing cooperatives, dairy cooperative need heavy working capital and long-term capital. Such heavy capital cannot be easily mobilized from the members. They have to borrow from other financial agencies.

Compared to other resources, borrowings are costlier as they fetch a higher rate of interest. Hence, cooperative must avoid borrowings and can raise resource by way of deposits. The other drawbacks of borrowings are as follows:

1. Loans are costlier and heavy dependence on loans will increase the cost of credit. The cost of credit or the cost of operations of a cooperative is decided by the mobilization of cheaper credit. Loans with higher rate of interest will increase the cost of credit or cost of operations.
2. While borrowing loans, the lender will dictate terms. When a cooperative is unable to repay the loan in time, the lending agency may threaten it with consequences. Sometimes, the name of the cooperative will also be spoiled as being the poor repayer of loan.
3. Lending institution will directly or indirectly interfere in the affairs of the cooperatives. The democratic freedom of the cooperative will be affected. Sometimes, the lending agencies stipulate conditions even to use the loans for various purposes.
4. Once a cooperative start borrowing loan form outside agencies, they many not be in a position to raise funds from owned funds. So the concentration to raise owned funds will be affected by borrowed funds.

Self-learning Activity

Try to answer the following questions on your own.

1. What are the components of owned funds?
2. Explain borrowings and its sources?
3. What are the types of deposits in cooperatives?

Summary

- Cooperatives work with owned funds and borrowed funds. Owned funds are raised through share capital and reserve funds.
- Share capital is collected from members. Cooperatives fix a ceiling for an individual's share holding. Unlike the corporate sector, cooperatives do not allow an individual to take huge number of shares.
- Share capital can be increased in a cooperative by means of increasing the membership year after year. Share capital can also be increased by means of increasing the value of shares. This can be undertaken by means of amending the bylaw of the cooperative.
- Reserve funds are appropriated from the net profit of the cooperative every year. The proportion of reserve funds to be appropriated is mentioned in the bylaws of each cooperative.
- Borrowed funds form the major part of the funds of cooperatives. But a cooperative must try to mobilize more owned funds to attain self reliance in resources.

- Borrowed funds consist of deposits and borrowings from other agencies. Though deposits are coming under borrowed funds, for all practical purposes it is considered to be a fund for self reliance of a cooperative.
- Cooperatives raise deposits in the open market from members and non-members. In many cooperatives non-member deposits exceed the proportion of deposits mobilized from members. Cooperatives have to provide higher rate of interest and attractive customer service to mobilize deposits.
- Cooperatives borrow from their higher level agencies and from government, NGOs and commercial banks.
- Borrowings from outside agencies are costlier and the freedom of the cooperative is affected. As far as possible, cooperatives must borrow from within the cooperative movement.
- Borrowings from government sometimes help the cooperatives if they are interest free or bears lower rate of interest.
- In countries like Ethiopia, due to the absence of strong cooperative banking structure, cooperatives borrow from commercial banks.

17

Creating Viability

Viability Study

A viability study is an economic analysis of the past and present performance of an enterprise, a department or a special project, of the soundness of its financial structure and economic basis, of its competitiveness, and of the capabilities and efficiency of its management. It is based on the figures obtainable from the accounts of the enterprise and from any supplementary statistics available.

A viability study is important for cooperatives to measure their financial strength and ability to raise owned funds and borrowed funds.

Viability norms and applications may vary from cooperatives to cooperatives. Such variations may be as follows:

A. *Cooperative Banks*—For cooperative banks, agricultural credit cooperatives and cooperatives which are undertaking banking business the viability norms will be based mainly on the banking services undertaken and customer attraction aspects.

B. *Producers' Cooperatives*—For producers' cooperatives like agricultural producers' cooperatives, manufacturing cooperatives, weavers' cooperatives, etc the viability norms can be based on production efficiency, operational efficiency, input-output relations, and cost considerations.

C. *Service Cooperatives*—For service cooperatives like consumer cooperatives, cooperative supermarkets, etc the viability indicators are customer satisfaction, efficient customer service and price considerations.

D. *Marketing Cooperatives*—Marketing cooperatives are one of the prominent cooperative organizations. Their viability can be decided on the basis of their operational efficiency, marketing services undertaken; price provided to producers and input services provided.

E. *Cooperative Training Centers*—For such institutes the viability is decided by factors like number of training programs conducted, quality of training programs, efficiency of training instructors and the managerial abilities inculcated by such institutions.

In general, viability norms for all types of cooperatives can be fixed on the following criteria:

1. ***Organizational Aspects***—The general structure of the society, its organization, activities, volume of business and membership. The society should have adequate membership and it should have enough number of activities to satisfy the needs of the members. Later stage the society can increase its number of activities. Likewise, the volume of transaction is an important aspect. The society should have adequate volume of business to manage the recurring costs of the society. Any society must attain a break-even analysis within three years of its starting.
2. ***The financial structure***—Any cooperative to be viable should be strong in its financial basis. The ultimate objective goal of a cooperative should be to stand on its own leg and to be self-reliant in its resources. The other financial aspects are as follows:
   (*a*) ***The solvency and stability of the society***—This denotes that a cooperative should be able to raise its own resources and it should keep its credibility in the eyes of the members, depositors, creditors, government and the public.
   (*b*) ***The self-sufficiency in finance***—This is considered to be one of the most important criteria for the viability of a cooperative. As far as possible, a cooperative should mobilize resources by way of owned funds (consisting of share capital and reserves). When this source is not successful, the cooperative can resort to raising of resources by way of accepting deposits from the members and non-members. Borrowings will lead to dependency on other agencies and a cooperative may have to sacrifice its own financial freedom thereby inviting the interference of such creditors.
   (*c*) ***The capital intensity,*** i.e. the relationship of fixed assets to total assets – This factor denotes that a cooperative, in the long run must be able to build strong assets in order to face any financial and business challenges. This will also facilitate the cooperative to face competition in the open market.
3. ***The Financial Viability***—A cooperative can attain financial viability by mobilizing its own funds. In addition to such self-reliance in resources a cooperative can attain the financial viability through the following measures:

(*a*) ***Administrative Cost***—As far as possible a cooperative must try to check the administrative cost to the total cost of operations. Another way of keeping the administrative cost under control is by way of increasing the operational efficiency, volume of business and services by having the same staff structure.

(*b*) ***Recovery of Loans***—This is one of the significant viability norm for cooperative banking institutions or cooperatives engaged in lending operations. The loans must be recovered in time. Any overdue loan will increase the financial commitment of the cooperative. It will lead to unnecessary locking of capital and the cost will increase by means of paying additional interest for overdue loans. So, an efficient loan recovery measure is a strong indicator for a viable society.

(*c*) ***Length of Operations***—This denotes the loaning and other service operations of a cooperative is short term or long term in nature. Depending on the length of operations, a cooperative must raise its resources properly. Short term resources should not be employed for long term ventures. Prior planning is necessary in raising resources and deploying the funds.

(*d*) ***Investment of Funds***—As cooperatives are coming under the purview of the central bank of a country (National Bank of Ethiopia), in investing their funds the cooperative has to follow the guidelines given by the central bank of the country. Within the purview of such regulations, a cooperative must invest its funds productively and remuneratively in the form of loans, investments and related aspects.

(*e*) ***Growth and Diversification of Activities***—A cooperative, in order to attain viability must grow year after year as well as it must diversify its operations, having the main objective of fulfilling the basic needs of members. Diversification of functions will ensure a cooperative to distribute the financial and business risks equitably.

(*f*) ***Sources and Costs of Funds***—As discussed earlier, a cooperative must be self-reliant in its resources. While raising the resources it must see that the cost should be cheaper and the overhead charges should be minimum. For example, while raising deposits, a cooperative can concentrate on current deposits and savings deposits, which are cheaper than on completely relying on fixed deposits.

4. ***The performance of the society***—Finally, the performance of a cooperative in terms of its profitability, productivity and earning power will decide its viability.

(*a*) ***The profitability***—An enterprise is basically profitable if the income of the period under consideration meets the current expenditure. For the purpose of comparison this relationship can be expressed as:

Income/Expenditure

Absolute profitability is assured if the result is more than 1.0. Relative profitability is indicated by the figures after the decimal point. In the case of co-operative enterprise the relative profitability will normally remain well below 2.0.

The maximum profitability of enterprise is reached if it can achieve the highest revenue with the lowest costs. As co-operatives are restricted in their revenue by the principle of 'service at cost', a society can reach its maximum profitability by putting the main emphasis on reaching an optimal cost structure.

(*b*) ***The productivity***—Productivity is measured by an input-output analysis. As the correlating of the output or results of the society to the individual factors of production, i.e. labour, capital and organization, is extremely difficult, if not impossible, productivity is usually measured as one-factor-productivity (I-III below) or as overall-productivity (IV). The measurement can be based on quantity or value, though it is only feasible to measure the out put in quantity if it has a degree of uniformity. Possible relationships are:

I. Turnover or output/W.H. (working hours) or labour costs

II. Turnover or output/Interest on the average capital Invested in the business.

OR

$$\frac{\text{Turnover or output}}{\text{Average capital invested in the business}}$$

III.

$$\frac{\text{Turnover or output}}{\text{Cost of management (salaries + expenses)}}$$

IV.

$$\frac{\text{Turnover or output}}{\text{Total operation cost}}$$

A co-operative society has reached its maximum productivity if it can realize a maximum of service to the members at minimum cost.

(*c*) ***The earning power***—This is an indicator of success comparing profit with invested capital. The earning power of a co-operative society can be established in two ways:

I the earning power of the capital owned:

$$\frac{\text{(patronage refunds and similar payments + interest paid on share-capital + allocations to the reserve fund + estimated additional benefits to members in the form of price advantages compared to the market)} \times 100}{\text{average capital owned i.e. equity capital, during the period considered}}$$

II the overall earning power:

$$\frac{\text{(as under I + interest paid on capital borrowed)} \times 100}{\text{average total capital invested in the society during the period considered.}}$$

The desirable rate of earning power depends, in the case of the individual society, on the degree of risk involved in its activities, though the invested capital should at least earn the current commercial rate of interest on capital borrowed.

Self-learning Activity

Try to answer the following questions on your own.

1. What are viability norms for a cooperative bank?
2. How can you compute productivity in cooperatives?

Summary

- To have strong financial base, cooperatives must undertake viability studies. Viability studies cover organisational aspects, financial structure, and financial viability.

18 Sources of Funds
Need for Organizing Cooperative Banks

Cooperative Banker as a Social Banker

Co-operative Banks are acting as social bankers. To be a social banker a banker must have 'service motive and not profit motive'. His lending activities must have social relevance and justify the national causes. The people who are served by a social banker must also be the masses who are unable to get a banking facilities and financial arrangements from other sources. A social banker must not hesitate to operate in places which are economically backward and whose populations are illiterate or economically backward and whose population are illiterate or economically weaker. His cost of service and lending rates must also necessarily be reasonable or helpful to the weaker sections of the community. Now we can see how does a co-operative banker become a social banker.

Firstly, the motive of a co-operative banker is put up in a different ideological plane. Exploitation should be eliminated by a co-operative banker. In that sense he has to charge reasonable rate of interest to his credit and reasonable commission to render other banking services. All co-operative banks satisfy this aspect. On the other hand, private banks whose motive is to maximize profits charge higher rates of interest and higher commission for other banking services. When commercial banks are vying with each other to earn profit naturally competition is created and to thrive in that competition they spend huge money for publicity etc., which again is collected from the customers by way of increased interest or charges. The approach to problems is different by a co-operative banker.

He avoids competition and avoids profit motive. Whatever surplus a co-operative banker gets is surplus and not profit in the sense of the terms. Even this surplus is distributed according to specific rules, under which allocations are made for creating and strengthening various kinds of reserves, dividend to members on the basis of equitable distribution, creation of common good fund, funds for educational purposes, shows that a co-operative banker is not working for a profit and even if he earns a surplus the surplus is distributed for the social cause of the members. By this process, a co-operative banker acts as a social banker of the members.

Secondly, the lending activities of a co-operative banker have social relevance and justify the national cause. Our country is dominated by rural masses and their main occupation or for that matter the major employer of our country is agriculture. The agriculturists in our country are traditionally exploited by moneylenders and it is the duty of the national financing institutions like banks to focus their attention towards the field of agriculture. Priority sectors of our economy like agriculture, small-scale industries and export trade are in need of financial help from organized banking sector. The very organization of the co-operative movement in our country took its root in the field of agricultural credit and their purpose was to liquidate rural indebtedness and to drive the moneylenders out of agricultural financing scene. When the agricultural financing had been considered as a riskier proposition and unprofitable avenue of lending, it was the co-operative banker who took the risk of lending agricultural financing by commercial banks is of recent origin. Not only the sectors that are helped by the co-operative banker are weaker but the sections of the beneficiaries in the priority sections themselves have low social and economic status. It was the co-operative banker who first came forward to lend the small farmers, tenant farmers, village artisans, weavers and such depressed sections of the community. To a smaller extent urban weaker sections are financed by urban co-operative banks. Though they are not universally organized, wherever they are organized, they are doing yeoman service to the urban weaker sections. As for the encouragement of various sections in the economy, co-operative banks are helping the needed sectors like agriculture and small-scale industries.

Thirdly, a social banker must help such people who are unable to get help from organized sources. As has been pointed out earlier, the credit goes to the co-operative banker in initiating the financial assistance to all sections of the farming community. When commercial banks locked up their doors for agriculturists the co-operative banker went ahead with the program me of agricultural lending. Not only that he invented new methods of financing, the security concept which was tied down to the agricultural finance was ultimately given up since the introduction of the crop loan system. Tenant farmers, who were denied credit for a long time due to their inability to provide landed security, are getting short-term credit from the co-operative banker. Organizationally, majority of the co-operative banks are set up in rural areas to provide needed financial assistance and banking facilities. Till recently rural areas were shunned by commercial banks. Because opening of branches in rural areas by the commercial banks may not help them to attract enough deposits and make the branches economically viable to earn sufficient profit. Great leap forward was undertaken by the central co-operative banks which are opening section of the population served by co-operative banks have low social and economic status. Majority of them are illiterate and they do not know the intricacies of banking activities and the co-operative banking habits, to such people. The advantageous aspect is that a co-operative bank is organized and managed by themselves and the members whether economically weak or strong feel the sense of belonging to the co-operative banks. In the case of other banking institutions the users like farmers or weavers are outsiders to the institution. Personal contact, proximity and looseness between the lender and borrower are lacking in other banking institutions. Co-operative banks are closer to their members and they know the problems of their members.

Functions of Co-operative Banks

1. In addition to the business of banking a co-operative bank may engage in any one or more of the following forms of business namely:

   (*a*) The borrowing, raising or taking up of money, the lending or advancing of money either upon or without security; the drawing, making, accepting discounting, buying, selling, collecting and dealing in bills of exchanges, promissory notes, coupons, drafts, bills of lading, railway receipts, warrants, debentures, certificates, scrips and other instruments and securities whether transferable or negotiable or not; the granting and issuing of letters of credit, travellers cheques and circular notes; the buying and selling of foreign exchange, the buying, selling and dealing in bullion and specie, including foreign bank notes, the acquiring, holding, issuing on commission, under writing and dealing the stock, funds, shares, debentures, debenture stock, bonds, obligations; securities and investments of all kinds, the purchasing and selling of bonds, scrips or other forms of securities on behalf of constituents or others, the negotiating of loans and advances, the receiving of all kinds of bonds, scrips or valuables on deposit or for safe custody or other wise. The providing of safe deposit vaults; the collecting and transmitting of money and securities;

   (*b*) Acting as agents for any government or local authority or any other person or persons; the carrying on of agency business of any descriptions including the clearing and forwarding of goods, giving of receipts and discharges and otherwise acting as an attorney on behalf of customers;

   (*c*) Contracting for public and private loans and negotiating and issuing the same;

(*d*) The effecting, insuring, guaranteeing, underwriting participating in managing and carrying out of any issue, public or private of state, municipal or other loans or of shares, stock, debentures or debenture stock of any company, co-operative society. Corporation or association and the lending of money for the purpose of any such issue;

(*e*) Carrying on and transacting every kind of guarantee and indemnity business;

(*f*) Managing, selling and realizing any property which may come into the possession of the co-operative bank in satisfaction or part satisfaction of its claims;

(*g*) Acquiring and holding and generally dealing with any property or any right, title or interest in any such property which may form the security or part of the security for any loans or advances or which may be connected with any such security;

(*h*) Undertaking and executing trust;

(*i*) Undertaking the administration of estates as executor, trustee or otherwise;

(*j*) Establishing and supporting or aiding in the establishment and support of associations, institutions, funds, trusts and conveniences calculated to benefit employees or ex-employees of the co-operative bank or the dependents or connections of such persons; granting pensions and allowances and making payments towards insurance; subscribing to or guaranteeing moneys for charitable or benevolent objects or for any exhibition or for any public, general or useful object;

(*k*) The acquisition, construction, maintenance and alteration of any building or works necessary or convenient for the purposes of the co-operative bank;

(*l*) Selling, improving, managing, developing, exchanging, leasing, mortgaging, disposing of or turning into account or otherwise dealing with all or any part of the property and rights of the co-operative bank;

(*m*) Doing all such other things as are incidental or conducive to the promotion or advancement of the business of the co-operative bank;

(*n*) Any other form of business, which the central government may, by notification in the official gazette, specify as a form of business in which it is lawful for a co-operative bank to engage.

Need to Organize Cooperative Banks

At present in Ethiopia, a useful step has been taken to organize cooperative banks at regional level and primary cooperatives in the form of savings and credit cooperatives (SACCOs). But to the emerging needs of the population and the cooperative movement, the present growth of cooperative banks is not sufficient. So, energetic measures must be taken to organize cooperative banks at primary level, regional level, and national level in Ethiopia. Following are the reasons to organize a strong cooperative banking basis in Ethiopia:

1. ***To mobilize rural savings***—In a vast country like Ethiopia, rural population is spread out to remote places. They are unable to get banking services by the established banking organizations like the commercial banks. Year after year, the income of the rural population is increasing and they need to have a safe modern banking structure. Cooperative banks can provide banking facilities and can mobilize the savings of the rural population.
2. ***To inculcate banking habits***—At the rural areas, people are mainly uneducated and they do not have formal education to read and write. But at the same time, such people would like to know the banking habits of opening a bank account, depositing money, and withdrawing money. A commercial bank cannot come to the lower level of such poor people and can extend banking services. On the other hand, a cooperative banker can extend the banking services to the uneducated rural population. In many developing countries, the cooperative banks, credit unions, and micro-finance institutions have been providing banking habits to the rural population.
3. ***To mobilize resources for the expansion of cooperatives***—Various cooperatives like agricultural cooperatives, producers cooperatives, industrial cooperatives, housing cooperatives, etc are expanding fast. But their major problem is lack of finance to meet their investment opportunities and business activities. So, the cooperative movement must raise resources within the movement by means of organizing cooperative banks at various stages like the primary level, regional level, and national level.
4. ***To attain self-reliance in resources***—One of the preconditions for the operational efficiency and the successful working of cooperatives is to be self-reliant in the financial resources. For this purpose, a cooperative must raise resources by way of owned funds and by deposits. Cooperative banks are the best agencies to mobilize deposits from various sources and deploy them to other cooperatives that are in need of working capital and long-term capital.

5. ***To create new investments***—Existing cooperatives add more businesses, which are cost intensive. A primary cooperative can first provide agricultural credit to the farmers. Later, it can undertake marketing activities, processing activities, hiring of machineries, construction of godowns, etc. For such new investments, the cooperative need heavy finance, which could be provided by the cooperative banks.
6. ***To create new assets***—By means of new investments, new assets could be created to the cooperatives. For example, cooperative processing units like cooperative sugar factories add new units like liquor units, paper units, etc, which could create new asset and income generating capacity to the cooperatives.
7. ***New employment opportunities***—One of the objectives of cooperatives is to provide employment opportunity to the members and the people around them. New employment opportunities could be created by means of new investments mentioned above. For this purpose, the needed investment must come from the cooperative banks.
8. ***Balancing center function***—Balancing center function means, re-distributing the surplus funds from one cooperative to the other cooperatives. Such balancing center activity can be undertaken by regional level cooperative banks and national level cooperative banks for their lower level cooperative unions. Through this balancing function, the shortage of funds in one cooperative could be managed by drawing the surplus funds from the other cooperative banks.
9. ***Branch banking***—Cooperatives banks have to go a long way in developing their activities by means of opening branches. Branch banking alone can expand the financial operations and business activities of cooperatives. Rural banking can also be undertaken by branch banking.
10. ***To develop processing and marketing cooperatives***—Marketing and processing cooperatives are very essential to change the income and the destiny of the farmers. Only these cooperatives can provide value-addition to their commodities and increase their income. These cooperatives can also release the farmers from the exploitation of middlemen and traders. Such cooperatives need heavy finance, which could be provided by cooperative banks.
11. ***To create link with international cooperative banks***—Cooperative banks in various countries have created national cooperative banks and such national cooperative banks have created international cooperative banking federation named as "International Cooperative Bank Association (ICBA)". This unit is working under the auspicious of Internal Cooperative Alliance. In future, in Ethiopia, if a national cooperative bank is created, this could be affiliated to the ICBA and lot of resources could be drawn from such international cooperative banks.

12. *Reduce the dependence on commercial banks*—At present, in Ethiopia and in several developing countries, cooperative are depending on commercial banks for their financial resources. This is bad ethics and cooperatives must depend on cooperative banks for their resources. This presupposes to create a strong cooperative banking structure starting from the primary level to the national level.

Regional Cooperative Banks in Ethiopia

Recently, steps have been taken in Ethiopia to organize cooperative banks at various regional levels. The first regional cooperative bank has been opened in Oromia region. Though this bank has been registered as a share company, it has all the characteristics of a cooperative bank.

One of the initiatives to establish Cooperative Bank of Oromia (S.C.) is originated from the demand supply gap observed in the financial markets among cooperative business operators. The high need to finance agricultural inputs and other cooperative businesses like purchase of farm implements, financing agro-processing, out put marketing and the need for banking services greatly initiated cooperatives to pioneer their own bank.

The Project Office of Cooperative Bank of Oromia was instituted in June 2002 and begun its duties slightly after two months in August 2002. The office executed sales of shares and finalized the operational policies and legal procedures required to register Cooperative Bank of Oromia (S.C.). The bank was registered commercially on October 29, 2004 in accordance with Article 304 of the Commercial Code of Ethiopia and licensed by National Bank of Ethiopia as per Licensing and Supervision of Banking Business Proclamation No. 84/1994 with license No LBB/008/2004.

The main objective of the bank is to stimulate the economic and social development of Oromia by mobilizing financial resources for cooperatives investments, private businesses and public institutions. Specifically, CBO has the following objectives:

1. Mobilize deposit and promote the culture of saving whereby guarantees the supply of funds;
2. Create access to loans and advances and similar banking services for broad portions of population, and of course;
3. The commercial objective of the bank is to earn a profit.

CBO will perform banking activities of the following nature:

- Accept demand, saving and time deposits and money transfer;
- Granting loans and advances;
- Issue letters of credit;

- Buy, sell, hold and otherwise deal in foreign exchange;
- Encouraging income generating projects;
- Providing financial counseling services;
- Administer managed funds;
- Draw, accept, discount, buy and sell bills of exchange, drafts, and promissory notes payable within or outside Ethiopia;
- Issue cheques and traveler cheques, and generally deal in cheques;
- Negotiate, underwrite and manage the issue of shares, bonds and debentures;
- Purchase shares in the name of and for the account of the Bank in productive and service enterprises and sell such shares;
- Act as agent for the Bank's customers and in this capacity, engage in the purchase and sale of money and securities;
- Enter into contracts of suretyship on guarantee with or without security;
- Acquire, maintain and sell residential and business premises as deemed necessary for conducting the company business;
- Borrow money for the purpose of conducting the company's business, pledge, hypothecate or assign the company's assets as security for money borrowed; and
- Engage in all other banking business transactions.

The apex body of CBO is the General body of shareholders/owners of the bank who have the basic right to decide the objectives and the bank's existence and operations. They elected their representatives, the Board of Directors, to whom all the powers to run the bank are bestowed upon. Board of Directors hired the General Manager of the bank who is entrusted to perform the functions relating to the policy matters, implementation and supervision. Functional departments at head office level and Branches are in charge of the implementation of decisions. The authorized capital of CBO is three million shares worth of birr 300 million. Over 120,000 shares valued birr 120 million are subscribed by the founders out of which nearly birr 110 million is currently paid up capital. Shareholders of CBO are cooperatives, development organizations, individuals/residents and Pvt. Ltd. companies. Cooperatives paid up (75.8%), development organizations hold (17.7%) and individuals/residents and Pvt. Ltd. Shares (6.5%) of the total paid up capital of the bank.

Cooperative banks, including Oromia cooperative bank, are expected to finance primarily the cooperatives. For the cooperatives to be self reliant in their resources they have to depend on cooperative banks. Their dependence on commercial banks and other agencies must be reduced in due course.

Self-learning Activity

Try to answer the following questions on your own.

1. Why should we organize cooperative banks?

Summary

- Cooperative banks are one of the important segments of cooperatives. Cooperative banks undertake all types of banking activities like a commercial banker.
- Cooperative banks act as a social banker. A social banker has to work for service motive and not for profit motive. To fulfill this objective cooperative banks go to rural areas and do service for the villagers. Their lending operation is also relating to the poorer sections of the community.
- Ethiopia needs to create a strong cooperative banking structure, from the primary level to the national level. At present the SACCOs are undertaking the role of primary cooperatives.
- In Ethiopia, regional cooperative banks are coming up, with the beginning made by Oromia Cooperative Bank during 2002. In other regions, cooperative banks are expected to come soon.

19 Borrowing from Other Agencies

Cooperatives raise resources by way of owned funds and borrowed funds. Owned funds are raised in the form of share capital and reserve funds. Borrowings consist of mobilization of deposits and borrowings from other agencies. Cooperatives borrow from the higher-level cooperative institutions or cooperative banks. In the absence of cooperative banks, they borrow from agencies like government, commercial banks, and NGOs.

Borrowings from Government—In many developing countries, the government has sponsored cooperatives. It has become the duty of the government to encourage the cooperatives to promote agriculture, food security and employment opportunity. Cooperatives are the suitable agencies for the government to promote agriculture, small-scale industries, etc. So it is natural that governments help the cooperatives by way of providing finance to them. Various forms of government finance to cooperative are noted below:

(*a*) ***Share capital contribution***—In many developing countries, governments take the shares of cooperatives in order to increase the share capital base and funds position of the cooperatives. Governments make it a point to withdraw the share capital after certain years, once the cooperatives are able to mobilize their own resources. While taking the shares in the cooperatives, government is also represented in the board and in several cases the government nominee in the board is given exceptional powers.

(*b*) ***Funds for procurement operations***—Governments use to provide funds in the form of short-term working capital for the cooperatives like the primary cooperatives, cooperative unions, and marketing cooperatives to procure agricultural commodities. For such loans, governments charge a lower rate of interest or sometimes loans are given free of interest. In Ethiopia many regional governments provide interest-free loans for the primary cooperatives and the cooperative unions to engage in grain marketing operations and input purchasing operations.

(*c*) ***Investing in bonds and debentures of cooperatives***—In many countries, cooperatives raise long-term resources by floating bonds and debentures for specified periods like 10 years, 15 years, 20 years, and beyond that. Governments and government-owned public sector organizations subscribe such bonds and debentures. In certain cases, the central bank of the country insist banking institutions of the country to invest their surplus funds in the bonds and debentures of the cooperatives.

(*d*) ***Subsidies***—Governments are also providing subsidies to the cooperatives in their investment ventures. For example, cooperatives like sugar cooperatives get 20-25 per cent as subsidy from government on the investments they make on machineries and equipments. In many developing countries, governments provide subsidies for the construction of buildings, purchase of equipments, etc.

Commercial banks—In countries like Ethiopia, cooperatives borrow liberally from the commercial banks. Borrowings from commercial bank are not a good ethics for cooperatives because commercial banks are competitive agencies for the cooperative banks. But in the absence of cooperative banks, cooperative are compelled to borrow from commercial banks. Merits of borrowings from commercial banks:

(*e*) Needed amount of finance will be available from the commercial banks.

(*f*) Flexibility is introduced in the borrowings from commercial banks.

(*g*) Repayment of the loans will be made on scientific basis

(*h*) Various types of short-term loans and working capital are available from commercial banks

Demerits of borrowings from commercial banks:

(*a*) The rate of interest for the borrowings from the commercial bank will be high.

(*b*) Due to high rate of interest the cost of operations of the cooperatives will increase.

(*c*) Commercial banks put lot of conditions to borrow loans.

(*d*) Commercial banks are security oriented and they demand tangible securities for the borrowings.

Due to the absence of strong cooperative banking structure, Ethiopian cooperatives since their organization in 1960, have been borrowing from commercial banks. Commercial banks in Ethiopia had the history of nationalization as well as privatization. At present the primary cooperatives and the cooperative unions borrow heavily from the Commercial Bank of Ethiopia to manage their financial needs. Such borrowings may have to continue for a long time, till a strong cooperative banking structure is created. The need to have an exclusive cooperative banking structure in Ethiopia has been dealt elaborately in section 1 of this unit.

The first privately owned bank, Addis Ababa Bank share company, was established on Ethiopians initiative and started operation in 1964 with a capital of 2 million in association with National and Grindlay Bank, London which had 40 per cent of the total share. In 1968, the original capital of the Bank rose to 5.0 million and until it ceased operation, it had 300 staff at 26 branches.There were other financial institutions operating in the country like the Imperial Savings and Home Ownership public Association (ISHOPA) which specialized in providing loans for the construction of residential houses and to individuals under the guarantee of their savings. There was also the Saving and Mortgage Corporation of Ethiopia whose aims and duties were to accept savings and trust deposits account and provide loans for the construction, repair and improvement of residential houses, commercial and industrial buildings and carry out all activities related to mortgage operations. On the other hand, there was a bank called Agricultural Bank that provides loan for the agricultural and other relevant projects established in 1945. But in 1951 the Investment Bank of Ethiopia replaced it. In 1965, the name of the bank once again hanged to Ethiopian Investment Corporation Share Company and the capital raised to Eth. Birr 20 million, which was fully paid up. However, proclamation No.55 of 1970 established the Agricultural and Industrial Development Bank Share Company by taking over the asset and liability of the former Development Bank and Investment Corporation of Ethiopia.

Following the declaration of socialism in 1974 the government extended its control over the whole economy and nationalized all large corporations. Organizational setups were taken in order to create stronger institutions by merging those that perform similar functions. Accordingly, the three private owned banks, Addis Ababa Bank, Banco di Roma and Banco di Napoli Merged in 1976 to form the second largest Bank in Ethiopia called Addis Bank with a capital of Eth. Birr 20 million and had a staff of 480 and 34 branches. Before the merger, the foreign participation of these banks was first nationalized in early 1975. Then Addis Bank and Commercial Bank of Ethiopia were merged by proclamation No.184 of August 2, 1980 to form the sole commercial bank in the country till the establishment of private commercial banks in 1994. The Commercial Bank of Ethiopia commenced its operation with a capital of Birr 65 million, 128 branches and 3,633 employees. The Savings and Mortgage Corporation. and Imperial Saving and Home Ownership Public Association were also merged to form the Housing and Saving Bank with working capital of Birr 6.0 million and all rights, privileges, assets and liabilities were transferred by proclamation No. 60, 1975 to the new bank.

Proclamation No. 99 of 1976 brought into existence the Agricultural and Industrial Bank, which was formed in 1970 as a 100 per cent state ownership, was brought under the umbrella of the National Bank of Ethiopia. Then it was reestablished by proclamation No. 158 of 1979 as a public finance agency possessing judicial personality and named Agricultural and Industrial Development Bank (AIDB). It was entrusted with the financing of the economic development of the agricultural, industrial and other sectors of the national economy extending credits of medium and long-tem nature as well as short-tem agricultural production loans. The financial sector that the socialist oriented government left behind constituted only 3 banks and each enjoying monopoly in its respective market. The following was the structure of the sector at the end of the era.

- The National Bank of Ethiopia (NBE)
- The Commercial Bank of Ethiopia (CBE)
- Agricultural and Industrial Development Bank (AIDB)

Following the change in the economic policy, financial sector reform also took place. Monetary and Banking Proclamation of 1994 established the National Bank of Ethiopia as a judicial entity, separated from the government and outlined its main functions.

Monetary and Banking proclamation No. 83/1994 and the Licensing and Supervision of Banking No. 84/1994 laid down the legal basis for investment in the banking sector. Consequently shortly after the proclamation the first private bank, Awash International Bank was established in 1994 by 486 shareholders and by 1998 the authorized capital of the Bank reached Birr 50.0 million. Dashen Bank was established on September 20,1995 as a share company with an authorized and subscribed capital of Birr 50.0 million. Bank of Abysinia, another private bank was founded by 131 shareholders with subscribed and authorized capital of 25.0 million and 50 million, respectively. Wegagen Bank with an authorized capital of Birr 60.0 million started operation in 1997. The fifth private bank, United Bank was established on 10th September 11998 by 335 shareholders and now has four branches. The last bank to be established to date is Nib International Bank that started operation on May 26, 1999 with an authorized capital of Birr 150.0 million.

On the other hand, modern forms of insurance service, which were introduced in Ethiopia by Europeans, trace their origin as far back as 1905 when the Bank of Abysinia began tlo transact fire and marine insurance as an agent of a foreign insurance company. According to a survey made in 1954, there were 9 insurance companies that were providing insurance service in the country. Except Imperial Insurance company that was established in 1951, the rest of the insurance companies were branches or agents of foreign companies. The number of insurance companies increased significantly and reached 33 in 1960. At that time insurance business like any business undertaking was classified as trade and was administered by the provisions of the commercial code. This was the only legislation in force in respect of insurance except the maritime code of Ethiopia that was issued to govern the operations of maritime business and the related marine insurance. The minimum paid-up capital required to establish an insurance company was as little as 12,500 Ethiopian Birr as stipulated in the commercial code. There was no restriction on foreign insurance The first remarkable event that the Ethiopian insurance market witnessed was the promulgation of proclamation No. 281/1970. This proclamation was issued to provide for the control and regulation of insurance business in Ethiopia. It is peculiar in that it created an Insurance Council and an Insurance Controller's Office.The controller of insurance licensed 15 domestic insurance companies, 36 agents, 7 brokers, 3 actuaries and 11 assessors in accordance with the provisions of the proclamation immediately in the year after the issuance of the law. The law required an insurer to be a domestic company whose share capital (fully subscribed) to be not loess than Ethiopian dollars 400,000 for a general insurance business and Ethiopian dollars 600,000 in the case of long-term insurance business and Ethiopian dollars 1,000,000 to do both long-term and general insurance business. Non-Ethiopian nationals were not barred from participating in insurance business. However, the proclamation defined 'domestic company' as a share company having its head office in Ethiopia and in the case of a company transacting a general insurance business at least 51 per cent and in the case of a company transacting life insurance business, at least 30 per cent of the paid-up capital must be held by Ethiopian nationals or national companies.

Four years after the enactment of the proclamation, the military government that came to power in 1974 put an end to all private entreprenurship. Then all insurance companies operating were nationalized and from January 1, 1975 onwards the government took over the ownership and control of these companies and merged them into a single unit called Ethiopian Insurance Corporation. In the years following nationalization, Ethiopian Insurance Corporation became the sole operator. Following are the changes of the political environment in 1991, the proclamation for the licensing and supervision of insurance business heralded the beginning of a new era. Immediately after the enactment of the proclamation private insurance companies began to flourish. Presently there are 9 private insurance companies in operation. National Bank of Ethiopia has authorized 11 insurance broking firms, 510 insurance agents and 7 loss assessors until July 2000.

Formation and Progress of Commercial Bank of Ethiopia

1943-1963: After the victory over Fascist Italy, the State Bank of Ethiopia was established by a proclamation issued in august 1942 Although the intention was to establish it as a full-fledged commercial bank, a year later, in 1943, it was given additional central banking duties and became fully operational. Hence, the year is marked as the birth date of today's Commercial Bank of Ethiopia (CBE). Thus the state Bank of Ethiopia provided central banking and commercial banking functions until 1963. With the issuance of the Monetary Proclamation in 1963, the National Bank of Ethiopia and the CBE were established to handle commercial banking and national banking functions, respectively.

1963-1993: In 1963 CBE was legally established as a share company to take over the commercial banking activities of the State Bank of Ethiopia and to carry on all types of banking business and operations. Following the advent of a Socialist regime in the country in 1974, the Commercial Bank of Ethiopia was merged with Addis Ababa Bank, which was a private bank, and nationalized in line with the Socialistic reform. This had an added strength to CBE, through the general policy environment had not been supportive of commercial banking operations. During the command system that lasted for about 17 years, CBE had been the sole commercial bank in Ethiopia and a mere instrument of the central planning and Socialist ownership policy of the government.

1994-1998: The period was characterized by the country's shift from a command economy to market-oriented economy due ton a policy redirection. A new Banking Proclamation enacted in 1994 created several new opportunities for the private sector to be involved in the banking sector. This enabled CBE to relinquish its monopoly position in the country's banking industry. During this period, CBE had to go through several changes to cope with the environmental turbulence created by the country's policy redirection. According, the Bank undertook a major organizational restructuring and redefined its Vision, Mission an Values.

1998-2000: As the business environment continued to become increasingly competitive due to the establishment of private banks, CBE commissioned a Comprehensive Audit Program (CAP) with the renowned expatriate consulting firm, Ernst and Young. The purpose of the CAP was to assess the Bank's operational and Managerial strength and weaknesses with a view to enhancing its capacity to render banking services of improved standard. The consulting firm reviewed the then status of the Bank and its problems and recommended a 'Target Model' that would help the Bank attain the improved services.

2000-onwards: An effort was made to move towards the target model as recommended in the CAP. To this effect, an attempt was made to hand over the management of the Bank to a reputed expatriate bank. Based on the international bid conducted, the State Bank of India had won the bid and a successive negotiation had been undertaken towards handing over the Bank's management. However, the State of India (SBI) failed to honour its commitment to reach an agreement on the liability and attrition clauses of the contract.

The Bank has since opted for another alternative, i.e., management consultancy. Accordingly, the Bank has already commissioned a financial audit with an audit firm, KPMG, East Africa LTD, as a prerequisite to the management consultancy programme. The Bank actually concluded a management consultancy contract with the Bank of Scotland (Ireland) on April 16, 2003. Currently the Commercial Bank Of Ethiopia is the leading bank in the country. The Bank's leading position is expressed by virtue of its:

- Market share;
- Volume of business;
- Wide customer base;
- Wide branch network; and
- Capital base.

The CBE has continued to grow in its overall asset and capital level. It has managed to record a total amount of birr 23.1 billion assets and birr 1.3 billion capital at the end of June 2001. Such reliable capital base has enabled CBE even to exceed the international requirement stipulated in the Basel Agreement (8% of risk-weighted assets).

- Moreover, having a loan-to-deposit ratio of 58 per cent, the Bank is in a very comfortable liquidity position.
- The reserve account kept at the Central Bank was more than 11 per cent, whereas the legal reserve requirement is only 5 per cent.
- The CBE currently has a correspondent account relationship with 69 renowned foreign banks.
- The CBE also maintains SWIFT bilateral arrangement with more then 368 foreign banks.
- With a view to assuming technological leadership, wide ranges of studies have been conducted in the area of electronic banking services. ATM is one of the outcomes of these studies. And the bank has successfully launched the service a few years ago for which CBE is a pioneer in the nation.

Having Entered into an agreement with the Western Union in 1994, the CBE is a pioneer in giving nationals incoming money transfer worldwide through the Western Union Money Transfer.

Types of Credit Facilities

Currently, the Commercial Bank of Ethiopia (CBE) offers the following credit products:

- Term Loan
  - Short-term loan
  - Medium-and long-term loans (Project Loan)
- Overdraft
- Merchandise loan
- Agricultural loan.

Term Loan

- A term loan is a loan granted to customers to be repaid with interest within a specific period of time.
- The loan can be repaid in periodic installments or in a lump sum on the due date of the loan as the case may be.
- This loan is granted in three forms, i.e., short-term and long-term loan.

Short-term Loan

Definition

A short-term loan is a loan that has a maturity period of one year or twelve months from the date the loan contract is signed.

Purpose of the Loan

The loan is extended to finance the working capital needs and/or to meet other short-term financial constraints of customers.

Eligibility

Applicants can be individuals and business entities engaged in any type of business that can meet the following conditions:

- The client must have been in the business for which the loan is requested or in related business for at least one year with a permanent address.
- The applicant needs to have opened an account at the branch where the loan is requested.
- The applicant has to present the necessary documents required by the Bank.

- The applicant must not have any record of default and misuse of his checking account in the banking system.

Collateral

The security offered must be able to cover both the principal and the interest of the loan.

Repayment of the Loan

- The loan can be repaid monthly, quarterly, semi-annually or annually in a lump sum upon maturity, depending on the nature of the business and cash-flow statement.
- The periodic repayment amount incorporates both principal and interest.

Medium-and Long-term Loan (Project Loan)

Definition

- A medium-term loan is a loan which has a maturity period exceeding one year but less than or equal to five years from the date the loan contract is signed.
- A long-term loan is a loan that has a maturity period of five to fifteen years.

Purpose of the Loan

The purpose of the loan is to finance new projects, support the expansion of existing projects, investments and meet working capital needs.

Eligibility

Applicants can be either new or existing customers. To be eligible for the loan, customers must present the following:

- For new projects
  - — A feasibility study
  - — Lease agreement and certificate, land holding-certificate and bill of quantity and specification (if the project involves construction)
  - — A business licence from authorized government bodies
  - — Memorandum and Articles of Association
  - — Proforma invoice (not exceeding two months)
  - — Equity contribution by the cusomer
  - — Curriculum vitae of the management group.
- For existing projects
  - — A feasibility study

- Audited financial statements
- A list of fixed assets which include their book value and market value
- A list of the market value of fixed assets to be purchased
- Projected financial statements
  - ❖ Without project expansion
  - ❖ With project expansion

- For enterprises to be purchased from the Privatization Agency
  - Bid documents
  - Sales contract
  - Bill of quantity and specification (if the project involves construction)
  - The curriculum vitae of the management group.

Collateral

In addition to the acceptable securities, customers have to offer the entire asset of the project as additional collateral.

Repayment of the Loan

- Based on the nature of the project and projected cash-flow statement, then loan will be repaid quarterly, semi-annually and annually.
- The Bank may provide a grace period for the commencement of repayments.

Overdraft

Definition

An overdraft (O/D) is a credit facility by which a customer can withdraw in excess of her/his/its current account balance up to the limit approved by the Bank.

Purpose of the Loan

The loan is intended to finance the day-to-day operational needs of a viable business.

Utilization of the O/D facility

- Applicants have to open a current account to utilize and overdraft facility.
- The O/D account should not be overdrawn.
- An O/D facility is approved only for a period of six months and, in some cases, for a year. Therefore, it has to be renewed every six months or year.

- The request for renewal must be presented to the Bank two months before the expiry date of the facility.
- Approval of request for renewal of overdraft is subject to fulfilling the Bank's requirements,

  Such as:

  — Sound financial conditions

  — Good operational results evidenced by acceptable financial statements

  — Satisfactory utilization of the O/D

  — Stability of the collateral value

  — In addition, during renewal request, the O/D account has to show the credit balance.

Eligibility

Overdrafts can be considered for manufacturing, trading and service-giving enterprises. To be eligible for the facility, customers should meet the following conditions:

- The business must be in operation for at least two years.
- Applicants should have a record of satisfactory utilization of current accounts for at least the year preceding their application for overdraft facility.
- Applicants must have settled at least one term loan with a good repayment record.
- O/D requests will not be considered for businesses with non-performing credit status and/or currently blacklisted by the CBE or any other bank.
- Customers' seasonal or temporary financial needs will not be entertained by an overdraft.
- Customers' O/D accounts may be cancelled or converted to a term loan (partially or fully) if they fail to properly utilize the facility.

Collateral

An O/D facility can be approved against any collateral acceptable by the Bank, except motor vehicles and machinery.

Loan Repayment

- In case of an O/D facility, interest is calculated on the amount used by the customers.
- Customers have to pay the accrued interest regularly so that the facility will not be overdrawn.

- By the time of the request for renewal, the O/S overdraft balances have to be fully settled.
- The Bank can claim the outstanding balance of the O/D facility at any time.

Merchandise Loan

Definition

Merchandise loan is a credit facility provided by the Bank against which the merchandise is held as collateral for the loan.

Purpose of the Loan

The purpose of the loan is to overcome the cash-flow problem of customers when money is tied up in merchandise.

The loan is approved for a period of three months (90 days) or it may be approved on a renewal basis.

Self-learning Activity

Try to answer the following questions on your own.

1. What are the sources of borrowings?
2. Discuss the importance of collateral?
3. Describe project loan?

Summary

- Cooperatives do borrow from other agencies like government and commercial banks.
- Government used to provide interest free loans to the cooperatives to undertake marketing operations and other activities.
- Government also takes shares in the cooperatives and it subscribes to the bonds and debentures floated by the cooperatives.
- Borrowings from commercial banks are not a good ethics, because commercial banks are competitors to the cooperatives. But in the absence of cooperative banks, cooperatives are compelled to borrow from commercial banks.
- Ultimately, the cooperative movement must develop its own cooperative banking structure and must reduce their borrowings from government and commercial banks.

20 Need for Organizing Federal (National Level) Cooperatives

One of the special characteristics of the cooperative movement is the organization of federal cooperatives having various tier systems. The Danish cooperative movement had shown the way in organizing cooperative federations consisting of primary cooperatives, secondary cooperatives, and national level cooperatives. Regional and national level cooperatives are usually called as cooperative federations. Cooperative federations are called by various tier systems namely, two-tier systems, three-tier systems and four-tier systems.

1. *Two-tier system*—Under two-tier system at the national level, there will be primary cooperatives and a national level cooperative federation. The national level cooperative federation is organized by the primary cooperatives under this system. The national level federation will undertake the organizational and business activities needed for the primary cooperatives.
2. *Three-tier system*—under three-tier systems at the lower level, primary cooperatives are organized, these primary cooperative organize regional level cooperatives and various regional level cooperative organize national level cooperative federation. The higher-level cooperative units are organized by the lower level units and it is the duty of the higher-level cooperative units to help and coordinate the activities of lower level cooperatives.
3. *Four-tier system*—Under the four-tier system, primary cooperatives are organized at village/city level, they organize woreda level or zonal level cooperatives, woreda level or zonal level cooperatives organize regional cooperatives and the regional cooperatives organize a national federation.

Need to Organize Cooperative Federations

1. *To guide the lower-level cooperatives*—Under the cooperative tier system or cooperatives federated system, the lower level cooperatives are

guided and helped by the higher-level cooperatives. In fact, the immediate higher-level cooperatives are formed by the lower level cooperatives and the higher-level cooperative has to work for the success and welfare of the primary cooperatives located in its area of operation.

2. ***To create cooperation among cooperatives***—By means of organizing various levels of cooperatives under federal structure, the bond between one cooperative and the other level of cooperative is strengthened. This paves the way to create cooperation among cooperatives at various levels of the tier system.

3. ***To make spokesman among the cooperatives***—Under the federal cooperative structure, the higher-level units at woreda level, zonal level, regional level, and national level will become the spokesman for the particular type of cooperative. They represent the problems of the member cooperatives to woreda level, zonal level, regional level and national level governments and administration.

4. ***To create contact with international cooperative bodies***—The national level cooperative federations can become the spokesman of the particular cooperatives like cooperative banking, marketing cooperatives, dairy cooperatives, etc. Such national level federations can become members of the International Cooperative Alliance and get its benefits. Like-wise, national level federations can contact ILO, FAO, and similar internal bodies that are working for the promotion of cooperatives.

5. ***To create contact with other countries' cooperatives***—In many countries, the cooperative movement has separate national level federations. Such national level federations help other countries' cooperatives through the respective national level federations. For such mutual help and to draw the help of developed countries' cooperatives, we should create national level cooperative federations of various cooperatives.

6. ***Liaison with government***—In developing countries, government is extending lot of help to the cooperatives. At the national level, we need only one agency in the form of national cooperative federation to move with the government.

7. ***To implement the principle, concern for community***—The seventh principle of cooperation is 'concern for community'. This implies that cooperatives should not limit their service to members but also extend their service to the non-members and to the community where they are located. To implement this principle, we need cooperative federal structure.

8. ***To become third sector of the economy***—In majority of the countries, cooperatives have become the third sector of the economy next to the

private sector and public sector. To make the cooperative a third sector in countries like Ethiopia, the movement is to be strengthened on a broad-base scheme.

9. *To face competition*—Cooperatives have to face the private sector under the policy of economic liberalization. In many developing countries, governments are withdrawing the help extended to the cooperatives slowly. The cooperatives must make themselves ready to face the open market. The leadership to face competition can be provided by the cooperative federal structure.

10. *To mobilize all cooperatives*—Within regions and at the national level, various types of cooperatives must be mobilized to unite their activities. Only through such process the members can get the benefits of combined effort and the cooperative effort. For this purpose, strong federal cooperative structure is needed.

11. *To remove regional imbalances*—Cooperatives are not developed uniformly in all regions in many countries. In some regions, they are well developed and in some regions, they are not well developed. Through federal structure, the underdeveloped regions can be developed cooperatively.

12. *To make the cooperative movement strong and viable* – To make the cooperative movement strong and viable, an organized and strong cooperative federal structure is needed. Only cooperative federal structures at regional level and national level can provide leadership to the lower level cooperatives and can mobilize resources to them.

Legal Aspects of Forming Cooperative Federations

According to Hagen Henry, the cooperative laws must take into the following considerations in organizing cooperative federations:

The freedom of association includes the right of cooperative organizations to form apex organizations, unions, federations or confederations. The state should refrain from any intervention except monitoring these organizations' compliance with their duty to represent their members.

The cooperative law must consequently define:

The legal form of the different levels of this cooperative pyramid, specifying the activities which each level can exercise.

The rights and obligations of the organizations of second and third degree in terms of:

- representation of their members at national, regional and international level;

- promotion, education and training;
- advice;
- financial and insurance services;
- economic services (marketing, supplies, exports, imports, etc.), at regional, national and international level;
- development of inter-cooperative relations;
- research and development;
- arbitration between the member organizations;
- control, audit, etc.;
- popularization of the cooperative law.

Functions of Federal Cooperative Structure

1. To provide a forum for the lower level cooperatives, federal structures can be of great use to the cooperatives.
2. The federal structures at the national level can provide a good forum to discuss the problems of separate units, like credit, marketing, etc.
3. The federal structure can represent the problems of the cooperatives to the government and the concerned bodies.
4. The higher-level cooperatives in the federal structure can act as balancing center for the resources and transfer them to the lower-level cooperatives who lack funds to manage their affairs.
5. For the purpose of expanding branches and opening new offices, federal structure is very much needed.
6. Greater amount of financial help can be provided to the lower-level units.
7. Technical guidance and business guidance can also be given by the higher-level units to the lower-level units.

Problems Relating to the Federal Structure

1. Having weak primary units, federal structure cannot be run successfully.
2. Having weak higher-level units, federal structure cannot be run successfully.
3. There must be felt need among the lower-level units to organize higher-level units.
4. Adequate resources must be mobilized by all units in the structure.

5. Government interference must be stopped to make the federal system successful.
6. The cooperative legal system must be helpful to the successful running of federal system of cooperatives.

Self-learning Activity

Try to answer the following questions on your own.

1. Why to organize Federal Cooperatives?
2. Discuss the legal aspects of organizing federal cooperatives?
3. What are the functions of federal cooperatives?

Summary

- For the growth and development of cooperatives federal structure in the cooperatives must be introduced. Federal structures can have two-tiers, three-tiers and four-tiers.
- National federations can become spokesmen for the particular sectoral cooperatives like marketing cooperatives, credit cooperatives, consumer cooperatives, housing cooperatives, etc.
- Ethiopia needs to create national level federations of cooperatives in order to become a member of the ICA and get financial and promotional benefits from ICA.
- Interaction with other countries cooperatives can also be created only by means of organizing national level cooperative federations.

21 Need for Organizing Special Types of Cooperatives

Need for Creating New Cooperatives in Ethiopia

Cooperatives in Ethiopia have been organized on a broad base, from the very beginning in the field of agriculture. Previously service cooperatives and producers cooperatives formed the major part of agricultural cooperatives. At present, primary cooperatives and cooperative unions are widely organized. There is need to strengthen certain cooperatives like dairy cooperatives and there is need to create new types of cooperatives like sugar cooperatives. Such new cooperatives are needed to increase employment opportunity in the country, to provide better price and benefits to the farmers, to avoid the exploitation of consumers by the merchants, etc. The following types of cooperatives either need to be strengthened or need to be organized afresh.

A. Sugar Cooperatives

1. The country has good fertile soil and climate for the cultivation of sugarcane.
2. Good rainfall is a positive factor.
3. There is good demand for sugar within the country.
4. An export opportunity for sugar is also bright.
5. Government support can also be expected for licensing, capital formation, etc.
6. Foreign private capital or cooperative capital can be invited to meet the financial needs of sugar cooperatives in Ethiopia.

B. Dairy Cooperatives

Introduction—Dairy Economy of Ethiopia

Ethiopia is an agricultural country and has the largest cattle population in Africa comprising 26 million cattle, 24 million sheep, 17 million goats, 7

million equines, 1 million camels, and 52 million poultry (FAO, 1981). In 1984 there were about 8.33 million cows and heifers older than two years, of which 65 per cent were yielding milk. Milk production in Ethiopia grew by 1.7 per cent between 1965 and 1976 and by 1.1 per cent per year from 1976 to 1985. During 1981 milk produced in Ethiopia was 27 kg/per person. But it dropped to 17 kg/person during 1985. But it is still higher than the Sub-Saharan African average of 15.7 kg/person. By 1983 local cows produced 400 to 680 kg of milk per lactation period of less than 7 months.

Milk Production

Sour milk or yoghurt is produced in the traditional system by leaving the fresh milk to sour for few days. Soured milk keeps longer than raw milk, so this process is useful for storing milk during the days of Wednesday and Friday where Coptic Christians are forbidden to consume animal products. Sour milk not consumed at home is usually is sold to neighbours.

Sour milk can also be churned to make butter. The byproduct butter milk is rarely sold and it is fed to calves, consumed at home, or further processed. Ethiopian farmers prefer butter manufacturing and indigenous methods are followed.

Production Systems

Milk production system in Ethiopia is followed on the following pattern:

1. ***Pastoralism***—Pastoralists are livestock owners who maintain natural grasslands in arid areas (lowlands) with their herds of camel, sheep, goat, and cattle. Pastoralists move from one place to another place searching for fresh grazing areas. Milk is the main source of food for pastoralists.
2. ***Agro pastoralists***—They are the farmers who cultivate food crops for food and for sale. Their livestock are fed on grazing land and crop land after harvest. Livestock are used for draught, milk production, and savings.
3. ***Mixed Farming***—Food or cash crop cultivation is the main activity. The farm size will be very small ranging from one to five hectares. Livestock are kept for draught, milk, and meat.
4. ***Intensive Dairy Farming***—These farmers do dairy farming intensively and cultivate fodder crops exclusively. The dairy animals are not used for draught but manure is used for growing fodder. Milk is a major source of farm income. Labour intensity is high in this system.
5. ***Peri-urban Milk Production***—This system is developed around cities that have high demand for milk. Milk is traded directly to the consumers of the city and is the major source of income to the farmers.

Measures to Improve Milk Production in Ethiopia

1. ***Reduced mortality of stock***—Efforts must be taken to protect cattle against the major diseases such as East Coast fever and tick-borne diseases.
2. ***Lower calving intervals***—These are necessary to increase the number of calves born and to reduce the period when cows are not producing milk.
3. ***Improved calve rearing***—This is necessary to ensure that a greater proportion of pure bred and cross bred are born and reared to reduce mortality.
4. ***Upgrading indigenous stock***—In the short run it will be beneficial to the farmers to improve the productivity of indigenous stock through cross-breeding and better management.
5. ***Adequate levels of feeding***—Efforts should be taken to reduce dry season shortage of feed. Such crops as maize, sorghum, and elephant grass must be used as feeding stuff.
6. ***Commercial dairying***—Commercial dairying through cooperatives with production and market orientation must be encouraged to make the dairy farming a successful venture.

Dairy Cooperatives in Ethiopia

There are two types of dairy cooperatives organized in Ethiopia. One by the producer cooperatives and the other by the service cooperatives. There are about 98 producer and service dairy cooperatives in Ethiopia. Exclusive dairy cooperatives were not organized in Ethiopia. Dairy Development Enterprise (DDE), a government enterprise, was having 14 dairy state farms under its control. These dairy farms supplied milk to Addis Ababa city.

Scope for Organizing Dairy Cooperatives in Ethiopia

The scope for organizing dairy cooperatives in Ethiopia is very high. The following factors favour the speedy organization of dairy cooperatives in Ethiopia.

1. The high cattle population and dairy animals favour an atmosphere for increased production of milk and milk products through dairy cooperatives.
2. The farmers are traditionally experienced in managing dairy farming and they can improve their conditions by organizing dairy cooperatives.
3. With the economy moving fast, the income of the population is increasing, which may result in higher consumption of milk.

4. Milk being an essential food for children, the scope is very high to increase milk production through dairy cooperatives.
5. Enormous scope is there to have an export market. By means of setting processing units by dairy cooperatives, milk products can be exported to other countries.
6. The atmosphere with the government is favourable for the organization of dairy cooperatives in Ethiopia.
7. International help through NGOs can be available to organize diary cooperatives and dairy industries.

C. Fisheries Cooperatives

Present Fishing Conditions in Ethiopia

1. Ethiopia is landlocked country and hence, the fishing outlet is limited to lakes.
2. Lakes form the major part of inland fishing in Ethiopia.
3. River fishing is not popular in Ethiopia.
4. Unlike other countries, the population is not divided as fishermen in Ethiopia.
5. Fisheries cooperatives are practically non-existent in Ethiopia.
6. There is no institutional protection in the form of bank financing, government subsidy, etc given to the fishery industry in Ethiopia.

Scope for Organizing Fisheries Cooperatives in Ethiopia

1. The scope for organizing fisheries cooperatives in Ethiopia is limited to the lake areas.
2. As the size of population depending on fishing is negligible in Ethiopia, the number of fisheries cooperatives that could be organized is limited.
3. Fisheries cooperatives in the lake areas can be organized as an outlet of employment for the unemployed youth.
4. Several NGOs have experimented in organizing fisheries cooperatives in lake areas and they are running successfully.
5. As the priority for the government is on food security, government has greater concentration on the promotion of agricultural and marketing cooperatives. Hence, the focus is not on fisheries cooperatives.
6. The hold of the private traders is strong over fish catching and marketing, any organization of fisheries cooperatives has to face stiff resistance from the private traders.

7. The government has to help in a big way for the organization of fisheries cooperatives in the form of providing long term capital, technical help, processing facilities, and marketing facilities. Without government initiatives, fisheries cooperatives on a popular scale cannot be organized in Ethiopia.

D. Forest Cooperatives

1. Forest cooperatives have greater relevance to the highland people of Ethiopia;
2. Through the organization of forest cooperatives, employment opportunities can be created to population;
3. Afforestation measures can be undertaken through forest cooperatives;
4. Soil erosion which is a major problem for Ethiopia can be handled properly by the forest cooperatives;
5. Minor forest produces can be encouraged through forest cooperatives;
6. Forest cooperative can also wider scope to export forest goods.

E. Industrial Cooperatives

1. Ethiopia has an ancient civilization and the handicraft industry is very old and scope is high for organizing handicraft cooperatives.
2. Industrial cooperatives can create employment opportunities for the educated and unemployed youth.
3. Locally available agricultural raw materials provide enormous scope for the organization of industrial cooperatives.
4. Handloom weaving is a popular industry in Ethiopia and industrial cooperatives can be organized in this sector.
5. Sugar industry is a fast growing industry and sugar cooperatives can be organized on the model of India.
6. International NGOs are helping to create self-employment for rural population in Ethiopia. Such ventures can be organized through industrial cooperatives.
7. The federal government and regional governments are favourable to promote cooperatives in Ethiopia.

F. Labour Cooperatives

1. Ethiopia has a growing population of unemployed farmers, who can be absorbed by labour cooperatives.
2. By forming labour cooperatives, government contracts could be executed by labour cooperatives.

3. Ethiopia has sizeable population of handicrafts workers, weavers and artisans who can be brought under the fold of labour cooperatives.
4. In Ethiopia, construction industry is getting importance in urban areas, and the urban workers can be brought under labour cooperatives to improve their livelihood.

G. Irrigation Cooperatives

Ethiopia is a land locked country and irrigation cooperatives have been organized in lake areas. The purpose of forming such cooperatives is to distribute lands in lake areas for the unemployed youths and to provide sources of irrigation by erecting pump sets. In Ethiopia, irrigation cooperatives are not engaged in the construction of small dams, filter points, etc., like other countries. There is enormous scope for the organization of irrigation cooperatives in Ethiopia because the country has continuous rainfall for four months, which could be saved by irrigation cooperatives and can make the farmers to grow more than two crops a year. At present, irrigation cooperatives cover only lake areas. On the other hand, highland areas, river basins and low land areas have also immense scope for the organization of irrigation cooperatives. It is to be noted that in Ethiopia only 5 per cent of the agricultural lands are getting assured irrigation facilities. By encouraging the irrigation cooperatives this percentage could be increased and food production and agricultural production can be increased tremendously.

Problems of Irrigation Cooperatives

1. Irrigation cooperatives need heavy investment, which is a major problem.
2. Poor management led to the dormancy of many irrigation cooperatives. The initial enthusiasm of organizing the cooperatives fades away after few years.
3. Land scarcity is a problem to organize irrigation cooperatives.
4. Government help is very much needed in the form of constructing minor irrigation projects.
5. Failure of monsoon, drought, etc., affect the working of irrigation cooperatives.

H. Cooperatives exclusively for women

Certain cooperatives like SACCOs, dairy cooperatives, artisan cooperatives, etc., can be organized exclusively for women in Ethiopia. Such exclusive women cooperatives are necessary due to the following factors:

1. Empowerment of women;
2. To create employment opportunities;

3. To enhance their leadership in cooperatives;
4. To provide opportunity to participate in the management of other cooperatives.

I. Rural Electricity Cooperatives

Rural electricity cooperatives are popular in countries like USA and India. Rural population need electricity supply to get irrigation facilities and to do their agricultural operations successfully. As rural areas are vast and spread out, the commitment of the government to provide electricity to such rural areas may take long time. So, farmers in Ethiopia can organize rural electricity cooperatives.

Self-learning Activity

Try to answer the following questions on your own.

1. Why to organize cooperatives of existing type?
2. Discuss the need for organizing new types of cooperatives?

Summary

- Ethiopia has certain types of cooperatives like agricultural cooperatives, dairy cooperatives and irrigation cooperatives.
- Cooperative movement in Ethiopia is strong only in the field of agriculture, which is subscribed by primary cooperatives and cooperative unions.
- Ethiopia needs to create special types of cooperatives like labour cooperatives, forest cooperatives, women cooperatives, housing cooperatives, etc.
- Ethiopia needs to strengthen the existing cooperatives like dairy cooperatives, irrigation cooperatives, etc.

22 Linkage Concepts, Merits and Limitations

Forward Linking and Backward Linking in Cooperatives

Linking the activities of cooperatives is an integral part of the functioning of cooperatives. Such integration takes place from one society to another society, between one region's cooperative and the other region's cooperative and between one country's cooperative and other country's cooperatives.

Forward linking denotes the increasing of one particular economic activity of a cooperative year after year and period after period. Such linking can be created by means of organizing federal structures in the cooperatives.

Forward linking is also called as *vertical integration* of cooperatives. Franz Helm has observed the advantages of vertical integration, as "Vertical integration has been one of the important factors influencing the growth of the cooperative movement, especially in a competitive economy, as many primary cooperatives would have been unable to success or would have been greatly restricted in their rate of development without the support of federative organization".

Backward linking denotes the adding of more and more economic, business, and service activities of a cooperative. For example, a credit cooperative in due course can undertake the adding of marketing functions, processing function, consumer function, etc. Backward linking is also called as *horizontal integration* of cooperatives. The ICA Third Principles Commission has pointed out the advantage of horizontal integration as "Cooperative serve their members most effectively and strengthen the cooperative movement by working through local, national, regional, and international structures".

Advantages of Forward and Backward Linking

Cooperatives get the following advantages out of forward and backward linking:

1. *Viability*—A primary cooperative or a central cooperative society gets strengthened by means of these two linkages. Viability denotes in creased business opportunities and a good financial standing.
2. *Increased business*—By means of forward and backward linking, cooperatives get increased volume of business. When agricultural operations and production are seasonal, in the absence of one activity another activity could be undertaken and the total business operations can be increased. A primary cooperative society can increase its business operations by means of undertaking various multi-purpose activities like credit, marketing, processing, dairying, consumer activities, etc.
3. *Interdependence*—The process of forward and backward linking strengthens the bond between one type of cooperative and another type of cooperative. Mutual dependence of cooperatives helps to increase their loyalty and bond of good relationship.
4. *Self-reliance*—Cooperatives can stand on their own legs by means of such forward and backward linkages. A credit cooperative can depend on marketing cooperative for its output marketing. Likewise, various types of cooperatives can have self-reliance in their operations.
5. *Strong financial base*—One of the drawbacks of cooperatives is lack of finance. Mutual dependence through forward and backward linkage can strengthen the financial base of cooperatives. For example, cooperative banks can help processing, marketing, and consumer cooperatives in their financial needs.
6. *Efficient business*—New business techniques in the fields of procurement of inputs, selling output, etc could be arranged by cooperatives under such linkages. Inputs could be purchased lump sum by national or regional marketing federations and consumer federations and such commodities can be sold for a lower price to the lower level cooperatives and members at a price lower than the market. In the selling of commodities, higher-level cooperatives can purchase from primary societies and can sell them in the wholesale market for a higher price. National level marketing federations can engage in import and export of commodities.
7. *Managerial excellence*—Through forward and backward linkages, representation for different types of cooperative can be given in the board. For example, in a regional marketing federation, a consumer cooperative director can be given representation in the board. Such representation helps to share the managerial excellence and business techniques of various cooperatives.

8. ***Common cadres***—Under the federal cooperative structure, employees can be selected on a national basis and they can be trained and inducted to various primary cooperatives. Through common cadres, employees can get transfers, promotions, and monetary benefits.
9. ***Training and development***—Common training and development schemes for the members, cooperative leaders and employees could be arranged by the national and regional federations through forward and backward integration.
10. ***Applying the principles of 'cooperation among cooperatives'***—The principle of cooperation among cooperative denotes the mutual business and managerial cooperation between one type of cooperative and another type of cooperatives. This is one of the major principles of cooperative recommended by the Second Principles Commission and Third Principles Commission.
11. ***More service to members***—Members like the farmers and consumers get price advantage and marketing facilities from such integration.
12. ***Facing competition***—Through forward and backward linking, the primary cooperative, which are working at the lower level can face the competition posed by private agencies. With the background help of higher-level cooperatives, the primary cooperatives can face any competition.
13. ***Sustainability***—Sustainability denotes the continued growth, development and survival of a cooperative without any stoppage. Through linkages, all types of cooperative from the primary level to the national level get the sustainability.
14. ***All service at one point***—Primary members could get all types of goods and services like credit, marketing, processing, consumer, etc at one focal point, namely the primary cooperative.
15. ***Business experience for members***—Integrated cooperative can provide new experiences and benefits to the members in the fields of management, business activities, and broad exposures. Through this process, cooperative members and leaders are able to get exposure to the outside happenings and competitions that are taking place in their day-to-day operations.
16. ***Concern for community***—This is the Seventh principle of cooperation introduced by the ICA's Third Principles Commission. This principle pre-supposes that cooperatives in addition to helping the members go beyond the member's service and extend their service to the non-members and the community. They have to undertake the community

services like educational service, road construction, drinking water facilities, health and hygienic activities, and taking care of the welfare of the village community.

The Process of Forward Linking

The forward linking takes place by means of a primary cooperative undertaking increased business year after year. To help the primaries, regional level and national level cooperatives on the same business are created. The purpose of forward linking is to increase the particular business and strengthen the various cooperatives forming that tier of federal system. The process of forward linking takes place through the following ways with the advantages:

1. *More membership*—To have the process of forward linking successful, a cooperative must increase the membership year after year. Within the particular area of operation, all families must made as members of the cooperative. Only through increase membership, increase in share capital and increase in business volumes will take place.
2. *New practices*—Within a particular business activity, new practices must be introduced by the cooperative. For example, a credit cooperative to undertake the recovery of loans can introduce new practices like joint loans to recover the loans quickly without difficulty.
3. *New markets*—Cooperatives like the marketing cooperatives can explore new markets to sell their produces. Depending on conventional markets, a cooperative cannot provide services and face competition. The time has come for the cooperatives even to undertake export markets.
4. *Competition strategy*—When forward linking is taking place on one particular business activity, the cooperatives have to work out a clear marketing strategy to win the members and customers. Without working a competitive strategy, the viability and the survival of the cooperative will become difficult.
5. *Customer service*—Customers are the kings for the cooperatives. To sustain the continued loyalty of the members, attractive services and increased market benefits must be given to the customers. The survival of consumer cooperatives depends on selling pure goods at a lower price.
6. *Employee motivation*—The employees are the pillars for the success of cooperatives. They should be motivated continuously by means of paying good salary and better service conditions. The employee turnover is on the increasing scale on the cooperatives due to lack of motivation and better salary and service conditions.

7. *Prompt recovery of loans*—Many credit cooperatives and cooperative banks are facing the challenge of non-recovery of loans. The loan provided by the cooperatives should be recovered in time; otherwise, the liquidity of the cooperative will be eroded. The cooperative cannot give next loans in time due to the failure of recovering previous loans.

8. *Reducing the cost of borrowing*—While raising the resources, the cooperatives like cooperative banks must look after the less costly resources. They must try to raise owned funds, which are cheaper and must go fully to collect the deposits in the open market. Wherever government loans are available at a cheaper rate and subsidies are given, such resources must be exploited fully.

9. *Reducing overheard charges*—The cooperatives should not employ excessive staff and must prune unnecessary costs relating to their daily operations. Honorary service must be encouraged, so that expenses could be reduced. But in the name of reducing overhead charges, employees should not be underpaid or discouraged in terms of their monetary benefits.

10. *Tie up with similar cooperatives*—While going for marketing of joint ventures, in the absence of federal cooperatives, few cooperatives can join together and engage in purchasing and selling operations on a high volume basis.

11. *Training*—The employees and the board members and leaders must be given adequate training in the business operations and management. Training should be a continuous process and all employees and members must be given training.

12. *Exposure visits*—Employees, members and leaders must be taken to exposure visits to the neighboring cooperatives, other region's cooperatives and if possible to other countries where similar cooperatives have made success.

Backward Linkage—Process and Advantage

Backward linkage implies the increasing of business operations by a cooperative from one business and service to other businesses and services at every stage. Ultimately, a primary cooperative should become a multi-purpose cooperative and it must have membership with other central cooperative of various types. The process and advantage of backward linkage are as follows:

1. *New products*—In handling or servicing, a cooperative must add new products. For example, a marketing cooperative can handle food grains marketing, vegetable marketing, commercial crop marketing, etc. As

agricultural commodities have various seasons for harvest, adding new products can give business operations to a cooperative continuously throughout the year.

2. *New services*—Cooperative like the cooperative banks can introduce new services. They can provide various types of credit like short-term credit, medium term credit, and long-term credit. They can introduce modern banking systems like teller system, credit card system, etc.
3. *New markets*—In addition to the existing markets, new markets within the country and export market must be explored by the cooperatives through regional and national federations organized by them.
4. *More capital*—When cooperative are undertaking backward linkage, they need more and more capital to undertake new businesses. They must explore the possibilities of raising capital at a lower rate of interest; otherwise, costlier loan will increase the cost of their operations.
5. *Technical feasibilities*—While undertaking new business, technical feasibilities in the form of the process of production, technology, etc must be weighed properly. This is quite applicable for the cooperative like the dairy cooperative, which have to undertake processing activities.
6. *Market survey*—Before undertaking a new business or service, a cooperative must undertake marketing survey to explore the possibilities of success for such new business activities.
7. *Business plan*—The existing cooperatives must undertake business plan for every frequent period, say three to five years. Only through business plans, a cooperative can benchmark its activities progressively.
8. *Tie up with other cooperatives*—Backward linkage preconditions the coordination with other cooperatives. Cooperation between primary cooperatives of various cooperatives and cooperation among various federal level cooperatives are needed to make the backward linkage successful.
9. *Efficient staff*—The manager and the staff members must be efficient to run the cooperative. They must be given enough training and exposure visits. They must be paid adequate salary to work for the success.
10. *Profit distribution*—While distributing the profit, less amount of dividend can be given during the initial years. Money saved by such dividend can be ploughed back for the coming years businesses. Sugar cooperatives in India have not distributed high dividend for a long time, they saved the money through such process and constructed colleges, educational institutions, health centers, etc around their area.

Situation for Forward and Backward Linkage

Forward Linkage

The situations for forward linkage are as follows:

1. ***Federal system***—Federal system means organization of cooperatives from the primary level to the national level. Primary cooperatives at village level and city level can organize central or regional level cooperatives and regional level cooperatives can organize national federations. Only such federal system can make the cooperative programme success.
2. ***Benefits***—The benefits accrued by the process of forward linkage can be exploited fully to benefit more members. Within the area of operation, all non-members must be made members of the cooperative.

Backward Linkage

The situation for backward linkage is as follows:

1. ***Multi-purpose activities***—A primary cooperative should not stop with a single activity to make the process backward linkage successful. It must undertake more than one activity and at one stage number of activities must be added. Such multi-purpose activity will benefit the members and make the cooperative viable and strong.
2. ***Linking of credit with marketing***—Linking of credit with marketing denotes the linking of a primary cooperative and the nearest marketing cooperative in their credit and marketing operations. When the primary society provides credit, it can be recovered from the produce of the members by means of selling the produce through the marketing cooperative. Linking of credit with marketing can make the process of recovery of loans easier.
3. ***Linking of marketing with processing***—Marketing cooperatives and processing cooperatives can create a linkage. The raw materials needed by a processing cooperative can be supplied by the marketing cooperative. Through this process, a processing cooperative can get regular supply of raw materials and the marketing society can get assured business.
4. ***Linking of marketing, processing, and consumer activities***—A marketing cooperative, a processing cooperative, and consumer cooperative can create linkages. A marketing cooperative can supply raw material to the processing cooperative and the processed item of the processing cooperative can be sold through the consumer cooperative.
5. ***Linking of other cooperatives with dairy cooperatives***—Dairy cooperatives could be linked with marketing cooperatives and consumer cooperatives. The end products of dairy cooperatives like butter, cheese, etc could be sold through the marketing cooperatives.

Cooperation Among Cooperatives

This is one of the important principles of cooperation insisted by the Second Principles Commission and followed by the Third Principles Commission. This principle of cooperation is stated in the ICA rules as follows. "All cooperative organizations in order to best serve the interests of their members and their communities, shall actively cooperate in every practical way with other cooperatives at local, national, and international levels, having as their aim the achievement of unity of action by cooperation throughout the world".

Explaining the need and background of inter-cooperative relationship, Professor D.G. Karve, the chairman of the Second Principles Commission observed that "the process of concentration and common action is gathering momentum in other forms of organization. The need and opportunity of wholehearted, progressive and joint action among cooperators was never so great as the present moment. A new industrial revolution of unprecedented magnitude and potentiality is sweeping over the world. National, regional, and world bodies are being set up by private business as well as by governments. If cooperatives do not act without loss of time in support of their cause, singly and in combination, they may soon be swamped by the new forces of giant units in public and private sector. Cooperation among cooperatives, almost an instinctive and compelling action, must hence forthwith be treated as an essential and indispensable course of action on the part of each cooperative."

Need for Cooperation Among Cooperatives

The time has come among various types of cooperatives within a country and among cooperatives of one country with other countries, to create integration between them. The threat has come from the private sector and multi-national corporations to strengthen bond of the cooperatives. The following are certain needs to have cooperation among cooperatives.

1. *To stabilize financial conditions of various cooperatives*—Cooperatives are having various sectors like credit, marketing, processing, consumer activities, etc. Not all the cooperatives are having strong financial resources. If a cooperative banking system is strong, it can help other types of cooperatives in their financial resources. Cooperatives are in need of various types of finances like short term long, medium term loans, and long term loans.
2. *To create viability from primary level to national level*—In many countries, we could see the establishment of cooperatives of a particular business, from the primary level (village level) to the national level. Village level cooperatives organize regional cooperatives and regional

cooperatives organize national level federations. In the federal structure, the higher-level unit is taking care of the lower level units and the viability of primary cooperatives can be taken care by the higher-level federal units.

3. *Exchange of information*—In the fields of agricultural credit, marketing, processing, etc, lot of developments are taking place. To compete in the open market, cooperatives have to change their business strategies and must introduce customer attraction methods. For this purpose, they need lot of information from various sources and the marketing information system must be strengthened by the higher-level cooperative institutions. Such information must be passed on to the lower level institutions to update their member services. Exchange of information will facilitate the cooperation among cooperatives.
4. *To create interdependence on finance and business*—Certain activities in cooperatives are inter-related like the credit, marketing, processing, and consumer activities. Naturally, this will make one type of cooperative to depend on other types of cooperatives. A processing cooperative can take the help of consumer cooperatives to distribute its products. Likewise, a marketing cooperative can take the help of processing cooperatives to sell their products.
5. *Mutual increase in business*—Cooperation among cooperatives helps each unit of the cooperative to increase their business volumes. Mutual dependence helps them to increase their business operations by means of handling more commodities and adding new businesses and new services. In the absence of cooperation among cooperatives, there is possibility of weaker cooperatives to face business losses and ultimately it may become a sick unit.
6. *For better practice of cooperative principles*—Cooperatives all over the world are expected to practice the seven principles of cooperation proclaimed by the Third Principles Commission declared during the year 1995. Among those principles, the important one are, cooperation among cooperatives and concern for community. To practice these two principles and other remaining five principles, the application of cooperation among cooperatives is very much needed among various types of cooperatives.
7. *To face competition*—Cooperative are facing continuous threat from the private sector and the public sector organizations. We could see in Europe and other developed countries, many multi-national corporations are collapsing due to competition. But we come across rare examples of failure in the case of established cooperatives. Still applying the principle of cooperation among cooperatives, cooperatives can stabilize themselves and face any future challenges from the private sector.

8. *Reduce cost of operations*—Through joint efforts and consulting their business efforts, cooperatives can reduce cost of operations. This is possible by means of operating the principle economies of large-scale operation. This can be undertaken in the field of joint purchasing, selling, housekeeping, etc.
9. *Employment opportunity*—Cooperatives can create more employment opportunity by means of opening more branches and offices through integrating their activities from the primary level to the national level.
10. *Branch banking*—Branch banking and branch office operations can be developed effectively by means of following the principle cooperation among cooperatives.
11. *Import and Export Trade*—Import and export trade among the cooperatives between countries can be realized through this principle.

Levels of Cooperation among Cooperatives

The levels of cooperation among cooperatives can be created as follows:

1. *At the local level*—At the village level or at a small city level, various types of cooperatives can integrate their activities. For example, at the village level a primary cooperative can integrate its activities with the nearest marketing cooperative, dairy cooperative, processing cooperative, and consumer cooperatives. Likewise, at a small city level, credit cooperatives/cooperative banks, housing cooperatives, consumer cooperatives, etc can create integration among themselves.
2. *At divisional/regional level*—At the regional level, various types of cooperatives can create integration with their activities. Supplies needed for regional marketing cooperatives can be provided by other types of cooperatives. The regional level consumer cooperatives can procure their commodities through the regional marketing cooperatives or regional processing cooperatives.
3. *At national level*—It is very much important to create integration of various cooperatives at national level. For this purpose, various types of national cooperative federations like banking, marketing, housing, dairying, fisheries, etc could be formed. All these national federations can form a Cooperative League, which can integrate the activities of various types of national level federations. In Ethiopia, a provision has been created in the cooperative proclamation and cooperative policy, to create a cooperative league consisting of the federations of various cooperatives.

Areas where cooperation among Cooperative can be created

1. *Resources*—This is one of the basic areas where cooperation among cooperative can created. At present, among all countries, one of the

major problems faced by cooperatives is the lack of resources. Mutual dependence of various cooperatives can help to raise the resources and such resources can be pooled among various cooperatives. For example, to raise long-term resources, a cooperative bank can issue bonds or debentures. Such instruments can be subscribed by other types of cooperatives. Cooperatives can mutually subscribe to the shares of other cooperatives, so that their capital base could be increased.

2. *Cooperative education*—Various members of cooperatives and cooperative leaders must be given cooperative education by the movement. Separate national level, regional level, and local level cooperative structure can be created exclusively to provide cooperative education for the members and leaders. The service of such cooperative towards cooperative education can be used by various types of cooperatives to their members.
3. ***Training***—Training is one of the important areas of cooperation. The employees of cooperatives must be given continuous training and all types of employees must be given training. To give training to the cooperative employees, one separate cooperative training structure can be formed by various cooperatives and they can share the service of such cooperative training center or cooperative training college. Such college must run training programmes for specific areas like credit, marketing, processing, etc.
4. ***Exchange of information***—Sharing of information is one areas where cooperation among cooperatives can be created. Information that are available with one cooperative may be useful to other types of cooperatives also. By means of pooling all information through a management information center of cooperatives, information can flow to the needed cooperatives, which should be very much beneficial to the cooperative to face competition. Information relating to price movements, market behavior, government policies, taxation policies, etc can be shared by all cooperatives.
5. ***Trade and development***—Mutual dependence of cooperatives can increase the volume of trade within the country and outside the country. One country's cooperative can import or export products to other countries' cooperatives. For example the coffee producers' cooperatives of Ethiopia can export coffee to the KF of Sweden or CWS of England. Likewise, Danish cooperatives and Irish cooperatives can export their dairy products to countries like Ethiopia through the National Federation of Cooperatives.
6. ***To make the principle, cooperation among cooperatives, viable*** – This being a vital principle, cooperatives must give continuity to this principle.

To make this principle a success, cooperatives at each country's level and international level must provide viability and sustainability to their business.

7. ***Import and export through cooperatives*** – As mentioned earlier, cooperative can import and export commodities needed to their members taking into the help of other countries' cooperatives.
8. ***Joint collaborations*** – Like the multi-national corporations and private sector, cooperative can enter into collaboration with other countries' cooperatives. The best example has been shown by Indian Farmers' Fertilizer Cooperatives, which has established fertilizer units in the cooperative sector in Senegal. Such example can be followed in the fields of dairying, fruit processing, meat processing, etc.
9. ***Consultancy*** – Cooperatives can create common consultancy forums to solve various problems of particular businesses. Such consultancy service can be used by all types of cooperatives and all tiers of cooperatives.
10. ***Feasibility studies and Business Plans*** – A common forum can be created comprising experts from various fields of activities to conduct feasibility studies for cooperatives. Such a team can prepare business plans needed by various types of cooperatives.
11. ***Organising new cooperatives and reviving old cooperatives*** – In many developing countries new cooperatives are facing the problem of sickness and such sickness could be solved by higher level cooperatives. To organize new cooperatives higher level cooperatives can make arrangements.
12. ***Cooperative Extension*** – This is one important area where a joint effort could be made by various types of cooperatives and the benefits of cooperative extension can be extended to the needed cooperatives.

Self-learning Activity

Try to answer the following questions on your own.

1. Write short notes on forward linkage?
2. Discuss the advantages of backward linkage?

Summary

- Linkage is a concept that is very often applied to the cooperatives, expressing their integration of activities at various levels.
- Forward linkage denotes the increasing of business activities of a cooperative in a particular business. Such business may be agricultural credit, marketing, processing or consumer activities.

- To have forward linkage, vertical integration is needed. Vertical integration denotes the organization of particular type of cooperatives from primary level to regional level and from regional level to national level.
- To have backward linkage, horizontal integration is needed. Horizontal integration implies the increasing of more and more business activities by a cooperative. A multipurpose cooperative can come under this category of horizontal integration.
- The situation for forward linkage takes place through the three-tier or two-tier cooperative systems.
- The situation for backward linkage takes place in the form of linking of credit with marketing, linking of marketing with processing and linking of processing with consumer activities.
- The linkage concept has close relevance to the principle, "Cooperation among Cooperatives", which was recommended by the second principles commission and reemphasized by the third principles commission.
- Cooperation among cooperatives can stabilize the cooperative movement from the primary level to the national level.
- Various types of cooperatives like credit cooperatives, marketing cooperatives, consumer cooperatives, etc., get stabilized out of creating cooperation among cooperatives.
- To have competitive power and to face the private sector cooperation among cooperatives is needed.
- Cooperatives can go beyond the territory of a nation and can create, contact with other countries' cooperatives. Through this process import and export trade between countries could be undertaken by cooperatives.

References

Abbott, J.C. (1987). Agricultural Marketing Enterprises for the Developing World with Case Studies of Indigenous Private, Transnational, Co-operative and Parastatal Enterprises. Cambridge: Cambridge University Press.

ALRO (1991). A Study Report on Agricultural Land Reform Cooperative Development. Bangkok: Kasetsart University.

Anschel, Kurt R., Russell H. Brannon and Eldon D. Smith (1969). Agricultural Cooperatives and Markets in Developing Countries. New York: Praeger Press.

Brake, J. et al. (1972), "The National Agricultural Cooperatives Federation: An Appraisal", Korean Agricultural Sector Study (KASS), Special Report 1, Mechigan State University, East Lansing.

CAD (1991). Annual Report on Financial Statistics: Agricultural Land Reform Cooperatives. Bangkok: Ministry of Agriculture and Cooperatives.

Chowdhury, PK.; Huq, MA.; Rahman, SA. (1987). Cooperatives as Institutions for Development of the Rural Poor. Kotbari: Academy for Rural Development.

CLT (1993). The Second Conference Proceedings: Chuan 1 with Cooperative Development 24- 25 Feb. 1993. Bangkok: Cooperative League of Thailand.

CPD (1989). A Study on the Growth of Agricultural Cooperatives in Thailand 1978-1987. Bangkok: the Cooperative Promotion Department.

Datta, AK.(1984). Landlessness in Bangladesh: The Processes and Mechanisms; a Survey of Research. 1984, 1 Bangladesh; Community Development Library.

DiMarcello, Carol. "ICA: Building Community Jobs by Replicating Model Worker Co-ops." Online. World Wide Web. Available at http://www.wisc.edu/uwcc/info/ica.htm. *Article gives a Brief Description of how ICA helps out the Worker Cooperatives. It includes a Five Phase Plan that it follows.*

Duelfer, Eberhard (1994) and Jahani Laurinkari [Eds]. The International Handbook of Cooperative Organizations. Goettingen: Vandenhoeck und Ruprecht, 961 pages.

Ergstrom, Lee (1994). Make No Small Plans: A Cooperative Revival for Rural America. Rochester, Minnesota: Lone Oak Press Ltd., p. 294.

FAO (1986). Profile of Agricultural Cooperatives in Selected Asian Countries. Bangkok: FAO Regional Office for Asia and Pacific.

Gehres, Donald J. (1968). Report on Cooperatives in Guatemala. A Report Prepared for US-AID, Guatemala, May.

Gumpert, David E. "How to Really Create a Successful Business Plan." Boston: Inc. Magazine Publishing, 1994. McLaughlin, Harold J., "Building Your Business Plan." New York: John Wiley & Sons, 1985. Osgood, William R. "Basic of Successful Business Planning." American Management Association, 1980.

Hazell, Peter B.R. and Sidney Hoos (1962), "Cooperative Enterprise and Organization Theory", Journal of Farm Econoics, 44, pp. 275-290.

Henehan, Brian, Bruce L. Anderson, Timothy P. Pezzolesi, and Robert L. Campbell. "Putting Cooperation to Work: A Guidebook for Educators, Advisors, Consultants and Rural Economic Developers." pp. 65-76. *Gives Potential Pitfalls, New Cooperative Tendencies, and Various Guidelines Concerning Management.*

Holmen, H.(1987). "The Impact of Egypt's Agricultural Cooperatives on Rural Development". Social-Change. 17: 2, pp. 26-34.

"How to Start a Cooperative." pp. 13-14. Author Unknown. *Gives Twelve Detailed Steps of How to Start a Cooperative.*

ILO (1964). Housing Cooperatives. Geneva: International Labour Office, pp. 154.

International Cooperative Alliance (1979). Recent Changes, Trends and Developments of the Cooperative Movement in South-East Asia. New Delhi : The Model Press Private Ltd.

Kausar, MMB.(1987). What Eludes Rural Prosperity. Pakistan Agriculture. 9: 10, pp. 38-42.

King, R. (1973). Land Reform: The Italian Experience. London: Butterworth & Co (Publishers) Ltd.

Klatt,W. (1976). 'Land and Labour in Asian', in J.R. Brown and S.Lin (ed.) Land Reform in Developing Countries, pp. 56-98. Hartford: The University of Hartford.

Korovkin,T.(1988). The Politics of Agricultural Cooperativism: Peru, Dissertation Abstracts International, A Humanities and Social Sciences. 48: 12, p. 3188; Diss., York University, Canada, 1986.

Kulkarni, R. and Krishna Rao (1956). Agricultural Marketing in India, with Special Reference to Coopertive Marketings of Agricultural Produce in India. Bombay: Cooperators Book.

Larson, Adlowe (1969). "Universalities of Cooperation" in Anschel et al. [eds], Agricultural Cooperatives and Markets in Developing Countries. New York: Praeger.

Lawless, Greg. University of Wisconsin Center for Cooperatives. "Four Phases of Cooperative Development". *The four phases include pre-development, feasibility study, business plan, and business start-up.*

Mathur,K.(1979)'Administrative Institutions, Political Capacity and India's Strategy for Rural Development', in Inayatullah (Approaches to Rural Development in Asia: Some Asian Experiences, p. 5. Kuala Lumpur: APDAC.

Mellor, John W. (1971). Performance of Private Trade and Cooperatives. Cornell University Occasional Paper No. 87.

Michigan Alliance of Cooperatives, Cooperative Action, Summer 1997 pp. 6-7. *Gives strategy that the Michigan Alliance and Various Others Practice for Cooperative Development.*

National Cooperative Bank. "How to Organize a Cooperative." *A Brief Pamphlet Explaining what a Cooperative is, Types of Cooperatives, Getting Started, and Financing.*

NCDC (n.d.) All India Conference on Co-operative Rice Milling Industry. New Delhi: National Co-operative Development Corporation.

Otu, MF.(1988). Cooperative Extension: The Missing Ingredient in Nigeria's Cooperative Development. Land Reform, Land Settlement and Cooperatives. 1988, No. 1/2, pp. 69-77.

Patrie, Bill. "Critical Organization Steps-Cooperative Development." *Gives Four Major Steps in Cooperative Development.* Phases of Co-op Development." Author Unknown. *Gives the Four Phases as Organizing, Start-up, Growth, and Consolidation.*

Patwardhan, V.S. (1969). "Distribution of Consumer Goods by Co-operatives in Rural Areas". *Economic and Political Weekly*, 4, pp. 361-370.

Pope, Jeffrey L. "Practical Marketing Research." American Management Association. 1993. Siegel, Eric S., et al., "The Ernst & Young Business Plan Guide." New York: John Wiley & Sons, 1987.

Roy, Ewell Paul (1964). Cooperatives: Today and Tomorrow. Danville: The Interstate Printers and Publishers.

Sando, RA. (1986). Implications of Development Policies for Agriculture in Taiwan. Practicing Development Anthropology [edited by Green,E. C.]. 195-210. Boulder, Colorado: Westview Press.

Singh, Mohinder (1970). Co-operatives in Asia. New York: Praeger.

Svsrdsrum, K.F. (1969). Agricultural Marketing for Co-operators. Bombay: Allied Publishers.

Texier,J.M.(1978). The Promotion of Cooperatives in Traditional Rural Societies. In Policy and Practice in Rural Development (Edited by Guy Hunter, A. Hugh Bunting, Anthony Bottrall), p. 215. London:Croom Helm Ltd.

Thompson, David (n.d.). Weavers of Dreams. [Authors address for copies: David Thompson, 516 Rutgers Drive, Davis CA 95616, USA]

Umeki,T. (1989). Marketing of Processed Farm Products of Agricultural Cooperatives. Marketing Farm Products in Asia and the Pacific. pp.149-159, Tokyo: Asian Productivity Organization.

University of Wisconsin Center for Cooperatives. "Steps in Forming a Cooperative." Online. World Wide Web. Available at http:// www.uwcc.wisc.edu/info/startc.htm. *The Article gives Seven Steps Informing a Cooperative. The Steps include Establishing a Steering Qommittee, Conducting a Feasibility Study, Draft Articles of Incorporation and Bylaws, Prepare a Business Plan, Secure Financing, Recruit Members, and Recruit Personnel.*

USDA, Rural Business and Cooperative Development Service, Understanding Cooperatives: How to Start a Cooperative, Cooperative Information Report 45, Section 14. *Gives Fourteen Steps in Organizing a Cooperative. Steps include Such Things as Determining Economic Need to Important Factors for Success.*

USDA, Rural Business/Cooperative Service, "How to Start a Cooperative," Cooperative Information Report 7. *A Detailed Booklet Explaining what a Cooperative is, Organizing Steps, Investment, Membership, and General Rules for Success.*

Won, HS.(1989). The Agricultural Co-operative Movement in Korea. Review of International Co-operation. 82: 4, pp.65-74.

Young, Kun Shim (1989). Korea Republic. Marketing Farm Products in Asia and the Pacific. pp. 257-271; Tokyo:Asian Productivity Organization.

Youngjohns,B.J.(1978). Cooperative Organization. In Policy and Practice in Rural Development (Edited by Guy Hunter, A. Hugh Bunting, Anthony Bottrall) pp. 236-238. London:Croom Helm Ltd.).

Yun,KH.(1987). Agricultural Cooperative in Korea. Seoul: National Agricultural Cooperative Federation.

Zimbelman, Karen. "How to Start a Marketing Co-op." Second Draft. June 29, 1995. An Informational Booklet on How to Start a Marketing Coop. *It Includes Sections on "Making Your Co-op Successful, Steps to Starting a Marketing Coop, and Tips and Hints for Success.*

Index

P

R

S